The School Practitioner's Concise Companion to Preventing Violence and Conflict

The School Practitioner's Concise Companion to Preventing Violence and Conflict

Edited by

Cynthia Franklin
Mary Beth Harris
Paula Allen-Meares

UNIVERSITY PRESS

2008

Oxford University Press, Inc., publishes works that further
Oxford University's objective of excellence
in research, scholarship, and education.

Oxford New York
Auckland Cape Town Dar es Salaam Hong Kong Karachi
Kuala Lumpur Madrid Melbourne Mexico City Nairobi
New Delhi Shanghai Taipei Toronto

With offices in
Argentina Austria Brazil Chile Czech Republic France Greece
Guatemala Hungary Italy Japan Poland Portugal Singapore
South Korea Switzerland Thailand Turkey Ukraine Vietnam

Copyright © 2008 by Oxford University Press, Inc.

Published by Oxford University Press, Inc.
198 Madison Avenue, New York, New York 10016

www.oup.com

Oxford is a registered trademark of Oxford University Press

Library of Congress Cataloging-in-Publication Data

The school practitioner's concise companion to preventing violence and conflict / edited by
Cynthia Franklin, Mary Beth Harris, and Paula Allen-Meares.
p. cm.
Includes bibliographical references and index.
ISBN 978-0-19-537070-6
1. School violence—United States—Prevention.   2. Conflict management—United States.
3. School social work—United States. I. Title: Concise companion to preventing violence and conflict.
II. Franklin, Cynthia. III. Harris, Mary Beth. IV. Allen-Meares, Paula, 1948-
LB3013.32.S346 2008
371.5'8—dc22   2008018232

9 8 7 6 5 4 3 2 1

Printed in the United States of America
on acid-free paper

Preface

School-based practitioners are frequently called upon to address violent and conflicted relationships in school settings. School violence exists in a social context and involves aggressive acts that are perpetuated against other students or staff members within a school. Perhaps, nothing provokes more fear and angst among both professionals and parents than the threat of school shootings, and other murderous acts that have been widely publicized in today's society. Neither can any issue provoke more controversy than some of the school policies that have been enacted to curtail violent actions (e.g. no tolerance policies, metal detectors and search dogs). We currently live in a society where interpersonal conflicts are constantly brewing and school-based professionals are too often confronted with an assortment of violent actions. Potentially violent situations may emerge on a school campus at any moment and range from verbal threats to acts of bullying, to sexual assault, and the use of weapons to assault or murder someone. Effective practices are especially needed to assist vulnerable and high-risk populations of students that may be predisposed to violent behavior. Practitioners are asking what the nuts and bolts of researched-based, information for addressing violence and interpersonal conflict are. The School Practitioner's Concise Companion to Preventing Violence and Conflict is a book designed to provide knowledge for timely issues and practices for assisting students with violence and interpersonal conflict.

Contents of this Book

The School Practitioner's Concise Companion to Preventing Violence and Conflict was developed with the practicing school professional in mind. This companion book offers targeted content on how to address the violence and interpersonal conflict of students through identifying promising programs and practices. Contents of this book provide easy-to-read practice information, including case studies and practice guidelines to use when intervening with students, families, and school systems. This book covers several issues concerning violence and interpersonal conflicts between individuals and groups. Content includes best violence prevention strategies, behavioral strategies for developing a violence-free school culture, and guidelines to assess the risk of violence. The book also covers specific types of violence such as bullying, how to manage students who want to harm others, peer-based conflict, classroom conflict and sexual harassment, date rape, and domestic violence. In addition, strategies on how to use family and staff alliances to prevent violence and on how to work with gangs in order to prevent violence are discussed. To add to the usefulness of the content of this book each chapter follows a practice friendly outline that includes the headings: *Getting started; What We Know; What We Can Do; Tools and Practice Examples; and Points to Remember*—thus, providing a quick reference guide to the violence prevention information.

The School Practitioner's Concise Companion to Preventing Violence and Conflict is one of four companion books that were created to equip school professionals to effectively take action on social and health issues, and mental health problems that are confronting schools. All four books in this series offer a quick and easy guide to information and solutions for today's pressing school problems. Content for the companion books was developed using chapters from Oxford's popular resource volume, *The School Services Sourcebook*. In contrast to the exhaustive and comprehensive *Sourcebook*, the briefer companion books were designed to provide succinct information for those who want to address a particular topic.

Objectives of the Companion Books

When planning the concise companion books we had three main objectives in mind. First, our objective was to provide a series of affordable books whose content covered important and timely topics for school-based practitioners. We wanted the companion books to be like a search command on a computer where a quick search using a key word or phrase can selectively lead you to the information you need. Each companion book contains updated knowledge, tools, and resources that can help practitioners to quickly access information to address a specific problem area or concern. The second objective was for this book to communicate evidenced-based, knowledge from research to practice but to do so in a way that practitioners could easily consume this knowledge. As editors, we wanted each chapter to be applied, providing practice examples and tools that can be used in day-to-day practice within a school.

A third objective was to create a practical book that school practitioners could use daily to guide their practices, prepare their presentations, and to answer questions asked to them by teachers, parents and administrators. For this reason, each chapter in this concise companion book on violence prevention and interpersonal conflict resolution is replete with quick reference tables, outlines, and practice examples, and Internet resources to consult.

How the Topics Were Selected

There are many important concerns facing today's schools and you may be wondering why we chose to address these particular issues for violence prevention instead of a dozen other related problem areas? School professionals who helped us create the timely topics addressed in this companion book provided selected topics. The original chapter topics in this book were identified through feedback from school social workers in six regions of the country. Social workers in California, Georgia, Michigan, New Mexico, Oregon, and Texas communicated with us through an email questionnaire, individual interviews, and focus groups. We asked about the overall challenges of working in a school setting. We asked for the most urgent and frequent problems school social workers and other practitioners encounter with students and families. School practitioners told us, for example, that their practice requires knowledge and skills for a variety of mental health and behavioral problems. A primary aspect of their work is direct services to individuals (school staff as well as students), to groups, and to families. Practitioners further told us that they need information on how to work with school professionals to interpret educational policies and design effective interventions for violence prevention.

Acknowledgments

First and foremost we want to thank the Oxford University Press for supporting this work. Our deepest gratitude goes to Joan H. Bossert and Maura Roessner for their help and guidance in developing the companion books. In addition, we are thankful to Dr. Albert Roberts who gave us inspiration and support to develop resource books for practitioners. We would further like to thank all of the team of professionals that worked on *The School Services Sourcebook*, Melissa Wiersema, Tricia Cody, Katy Shepard, and Wes Baker and our editorial board. Finally, we give credit to all the school social workers and school mental health professionals who participated in our survey and all those who informally gave us feedback on what topics to cover.

Cynthia Franklin, PhD
The University of Texas at Austin
Mary Beth Harris, PhD
Central Florida University
Paula Allen-Meares, PhD
The University of Michigan

Contents

Contents

Contributors

Ron Avi Astor, PhD
Professor
School of Social Work and School
of Education
University of Southern California

Rami Benbenishty
Professor
School of Social Work
Herbrew University Jerusalem

Beverly M. Black, PhD
Associate Professor
School of Social Work
Wayne State University

Gary L. Bowen, PhD, ACSW
Kenan Distinguished Professor
School of Social Work
University of North Carolina, Chapel Hill

Erin A. Casey
School of Social Work
University of Washington

Timothea M. Elizalde, MSW, LMSW
Adjunct Professor
New Mexico Highlands University
School Social Worker
Highland High School
Albuquerque, New Mexico

Elayne Haymes, PhD
Associate Professor
School of Social Work
Southern Connecticut State University

Esther Howe
Southern Connecticut State
Department of Social Work

Roxana Marachi, PhD
Assistant Professor
Department of Child & Adolescent
Development
California State University,
Northridge

Martha J. Markward, PhD
Associate Professor
School of Social Work
University of Missouri, Columbia

Mark A. Mattaini, DSW
Associate Professor
Jane Addams College of
Social Work
University of Illinois, Chicago

James K. Nash, PhD, MSW
Associate Professor
Graduate School of Social Work
Portland State University

Jacqueline A. Norris, EdD
Assistant Professor
Department of Education
Administration
The College of New Jersey

Paula S. Nurius, PhD
Professor
School of Social Work
University of Washington

Ronald O. Pitner, PhD
Assistant Professor
George Warren Brown School
of Social Work
Washington University

Gilbert A. Ramírez, MSW, LMSW
School Social Worker
Highland High School
Albuquerque, New Mexico, and
Adjunct Professor
School of Social Work
New Mexico Highlands University

Michelle Rosemond
Department of Psychology
University of Southern California

Tanya Tenor
Waterbury School District

Arlene N. Weisz, PhD
School of Social Work
Wayne State University

Debra J. Woody, PhD
Associate Professor
School of Social Work
University of Texas, Arlington

The School Practitioner's Concise Companion
to Preventing Violence and Conflict

Evidence-Based Violence Prevention Programs and Best Implementation Practices

Ron Avi Astor
Michelle Rosemond
Ronald O. Pitner
Roxana Marachi
Rami Benbenishty

Getting Started

Social work as a profession has contributed to the national and international dialogue concerning violence prevention programs in schools. School social workers play an increasingly important role in shaping and implementing policy, interventions, and procedures that make U.S. schools safer. The chapters in this book provide a comprehensive guide to best practices in nearly all aspects of school conflict and violence, from organizational and procedural modifications (see especially chapters 2 and 3), to diminishing interpersonal conflict between individuals and groups on school grounds and in the classroom. The dynamics of such serious problems as bullying, physical aggressiveness, date rape, sexual harassment, and physical violence among adolescent couples are explained in tandem with full and detailed guidance to practice responses and interventions.

In order to use resources to the best advantage and to maximize program effectiveness, it is helpful for school mental health professionals to not only know the dynamics and best approaches for assessing and intervening in school violence but also be familiar with available model programs already studied and found to be effective. As an overview leading into this section of the manual, this chapter will review several examples of effective violence prevention programs as well as model school safety programs.

One great weakness in establishing evidence-based violence prevention programs is that they are often introduced to schools with a "top-down" approach, ignoring variations in local school contexts. Even model programs that have been demonstrated to be effective in large-scale research studies have a better chance for success at any given school if the program matches the needs and values of the community, the school, and the school staff. To assist readers in achieving such a match, we offer monitoring and mapping approaches as a guide to develop a bottom-up program and in tracking program interventions.

What We Know

In this section of the chapter we present examples of the most researched model school safety programs available to schools and practitioners. Table 1.1 includes the names of the programs, Web sites where the programs can be explored, program components, outcome measures, and results from studies. We also include a more extensive list of Web sites and resources for each program at the end of the chapter. The programs listed in Table 1.1 have been rated as "effective" by multiple national organizations. Our designation of effective is a composite of ratings from 11 independent scientific organizations that evaluated the most popular school violence prevention programs. Criteria considered in designating a program as effective include (1) evidence of effectiveness based on rigorous evaluations with experimental or quasi-experimental designs; (2) the clarity of the program's goals and rationale; (3) the fit between the program content and the characteristics of the intended population and setting; (4) the integration of the program into schools' educational mission; (5) the availability of necessary information and guidance for replication in other settings; and (6) the incorporation of post- treatment and follow-up data collection as part of the program. We describe in detail four of the five programs listed in Table 1.1.

Table 1.1 Model Violence Prevention Programs and Evaluation Sources

Program (Authors): Bullying Prevention Program
(Olweus, 1993)
www.clemson.edu/olweus

Grade: 4th–7th grades

Participants: 2,500 students in 42 primary and secondary schools in Norway. (The program is now international and is being applied in 15 countries. The materials are translated into more than 12 languages.)

Program Components: Core components of the program are implemented at the school level, the class level, and the individual level.
Including:

- Distribution of anonymous student questionnaire assessing the nature and prevalence of bullying
- Development of positive and negative consequences for students' behavior
- Establishment of a supervisory system
- Reinforcement of schoolwide rules against bullying
- Classroom workshops with video and discussions to increase knowledge and empathy
- Interventions with perpetrators and victims of bullying
- Discussions with parents

(continued)

Table 1.1 *(Continued)*

Outcome Measures: Student self-report measures collected at introduction of the program, 4 months after introduction, 1-year follow-up, and 2-year follow-up.
- Reports of incidents of bullying and victimization
- Scale of general youth antisocial behavior
- Assessment of school climate—order and discipline
- Measure of social relationships and attitude toward school

Results: The results show a 33%–64% reduction in the levels of bully incidents. The author found a 30%–70% reduction in aggregated peer rating variables. In addition there was no displacement of bullying to before or after school. There was also a significant reduction in antisocial behavior such as fighting, theft, and truancy. The school climate showed marked improvement, with students reporting an increased satisfaction with school in general, positive social relationships and positive attitude toward schoolwork and school.

Rated effective—1, 2, 3, 4, 6, 7, 8, 9

Program (Authors): Child Development Project
(Battistich, Schaps, Watson, & Solomon, 1996)
www.devstu.org/

Grade: 3rd–6th grades

Participants: 4,500 students in 24 elementary schools from 6 diverse districts throughout the United States.

Program Components: This is a comprehensive model focused on creating a cooperative and supportive school environment.
Classroom components include:
- staff training in cooperative learning
- implementation of a model that fosters cross-grade "buddying" activities
- a developmental approach to discipline that fosters self-control
- a model to engage students in classroom norm setting and decision making

Schoolwide community-building activities are used to promote school bonding and parent involvement activities such as interactive homework assignments that reinforce the family–school partnership.

Outcome Measures: Data were collected after 1 year and 2 years of intervention. Teachers were assessed through four 90-minute observations and annual teacher questionnaires.
Student assessments were self-report surveys of drug use and delinquent behavior.

Results: Results showed that students experienced a stronger sense of community and more motivation to be helpful, better conflict-resolution skills, greater acceptance of people who are different, higher self-esteem, stronger feelings of social competence, less loneliness in school, and fewer delinquent acts.

(continued)

Table 1.1 *(Continued)*

Statistically significant decreases were found for marijuana use, vehicle theft, and weapons. By the second year of the program, students in schools showed significantly lower rates of skipping school, carrying weapons, and stealing vehicles ($ps<.01$).
Rated effective—3, 4, 5, 6, 7, 9

Program (Authors): FAST Track–Families and Schools Together
(Conduct Problems Prevention Research Group, 2002)
www.fasttrackproject.org

Grade: Three cohorts of students, grades 1–10 (still ongoing)

Participants: At-risk kindergartners identified based on combined teacher and parent ratings of behavior (CBCL). Highest 10% recruited for study.
N=445 intervention children
N=446 control group children

Program Components: Long-term program.
Weekly enrichment program for high-risk children and their parents
Students placed in "friendship groups" of 5–6 students each. Discussions, modeling stories and films, role plays
Sessions focus on reviewing and practicing skills in emotionalunderstanding and communication, friendshipbuilding, self-control, and social problem solving
Parents meet in groups led by family coordinators to discuss parenting strategies, then 30-minute parent-child cooperative activity time; biweekly home visits
Academic tutoring provided by trained tutors in 30-minute sessions 3X/week

Outcome Measures: Externalizing Scale of CBCL—oppositional, aggressive, and delinquent behaviors.

- Parent Daily Report: degree to which child engaged in aggressive and oppositional behaviors during previous 24 hrs (given 3x)
- Child behavior change
- Teacher assessment of acting-out behaviors in school (Teacher Report Form, Achenbach)
- Scale from the TOCA-R (Teacher Observation of Classroom Adaptation-Revised)
- Authority Acceptance Scale
- Peer rating of aggressive and hyperactive-disruptive behaviors.

Results: Intervention group had higher scores on emotion recognition, emotion coping, and social problem solving compared to control group. It also had lower rates of aggressive retaliation compared to control group.
Direct observation results:

- Intervention group spent more time in positive peer interaction than did the control group.
- Intervention group received higher peer social preference scores than control group.
- Intervention group had higher language arts grades than control group.

Rated effective—2, 3, 6, 8, 9, 11

(continued)

Table 1.1 *(Continued)*

Program (Authors): PATHS curriculum (Component of FAST Track)

Grade: 1st–5th grades over three cohorts
(Results from grade 1 findings only are reviewed here)

Participants: 198 intervention classrooms
180 control classrooms matched by school size, achievement levels, poverty, and ethnic diversity
7,560 total students
845 students were in high-risk intervention or control conditions
(6,715 students non-high-risk children)

Program Components: PATHS (Promoting Alternative Thinking Strategies) administered to classrooms, 57 lessons (half-hour sessions, 2–3X/week)

- Skills related to understanding and communicating emotions
- Skills related to increase of positive social behavior
- Self-control and social problem solving

Presented through direct instruction, discussion, modeling stories, or video
Teachers attended 2.5 day training and received weekly consultation from FAST Track staff
Quality of implementation was assessed by teacher's observer ratings

- Skill in teaching PATHS concepts
- Management of the classroom
- Modeling and generalizing PATHS throughout day
- Openness to consultation

Outcome Measures:
1) Teachers were interviewed about behavior of each child in class (fall/spring of first grade)
2) Sociometric assessments (peer nominations made by students) collected to assess
    - Peer aggression
    - Peer hyperactivity/disruptiveness
    - Peer social status
3) Quality of classroom atmosphere was assessed by observer ratings assessing the following:
    - Level of disruption
    - Ability to handle transitions
    - Ability to follow rules
    - Level of cooperation
    - Use of problem-solving skills
    - Ability to express feelings
    - Ability to stay focused on task
    - Criticism vs. supportiveness

(continued)

Table 1.1 *(Continued)*

Results: Hierarchical Linear Modeling
(Accounting for gender, site, cohort, and intervention)
Intervention classrooms had lower ratings of hyperactivity/disruptive behavior and aggression and more favorable observer ratings of classroom atmosphere. Three cohorts of intervention, so teachers administered curriculum, 1, 2, or 3 times. When teacher experiencewas included in analyses, teachers who taught more cohorts had higher classroom atmosphere ratings (by neutral observer). Teacher skill in program implementation was also related to positive outcomes. Rated effective—2, 3, 6, 8, 9, 11

Evaluating sources:

1. American Youth Policy Forum. See R. A. Mendel (2000), *Less hype, more help: Reducing juvenile crime, what works and what doesn't.* Washington, DC: American Youth Policy Forum. Programs are categorized as *Effective* (refer to www.aypf.org).
2. Blueprints for Violence Prevention. Programs are divided into *Model* and *Promising* (refer to www.colorado.edu/cspv/blueprints).
3. Center for Mental Health Services, U.S. Department of Health and Human Services, Prevention Research Center for the Promotion of Human Development. Programs are divided into *Effective* and *Promising* (refer to www.prevention.psu.edu).
4. Center for Substance Abuse Prevention, Substance Abuse and Mental Health Services Administration, Department of Health and Human Services, National Registry of Effective Programs. Programs are divided into *Model, Promising,* and *Effective* (refer to www.modelprograms.samhsa.gov).
5. Department of Education, Safe and Drug Free Schools. Programs are divided into *Exemplary* and *Promising* (refer to www.ed.gov/about/offices/list/osdfs/index.html?src=mr).
6. Communities That Care. See R. Posey, S. Wong, R. Catalano, D. Hawkins, L. Dusenbury, & P. Chappell. (2000). *Communities that care prevention strategies: A research guide to what works.* Programs are categorized as *Effective* (refer to www.preventionscience.com/ctc/CTC.html).
7. Sherman et al. (1998): *Preventing crime: What works, what doesn't, what's promising.* University of Maryland Department of Criminology and Criminal Justice. NCJ 165366. Programs are categorized as *Effective* (refer http://www.ncjrs.org/works/).
8. *Youth violence: A report of the surgeon general.* Programs are divided into *Model* and *Promising: Level 1—Violence Prevention; Level 2—Risk Prevention* (refer to www.surgeon-general.gov/library/youthviolence).
9. Title V (OJJDP). *Effective and promising programs guide.* Washington, DC: Office of Juvenile Justice and Delinquency Prevention, Office of Justice Programs, U.S. Dept. of Justice. Programs are divided into *Exemplary, Effective,* and *Promising* (refer to www.dsgonline.com).
10. Centers for Disease Control: National Center for Injury Prevention and Control—Division of Violence Prevention. *Best practices of youth violence prevention: A sourcebook for community action* 2002. Programs are categorized as *Effective* (refer to www.cdc.gov/ncipc/dvp/bestpractices.htm).
11. Hamilton Fish Institute on School and Community Violence. Programs are divided into *Effective and Noteworthy* (refer to www.hamfish.org/programs/).

What We Can Do

Bullying Prevention Program

The Bullying Prevention Program (BPP) is a comprehensive multicomponent bullying reduction and prevention program designed for students in grades 1–9. It was developed during the 1970s by Dan Olweus to reduce bully and victim problems in Norwegian schools. Since then, it has been translated into more than 12 languages and successfully established in schools in more than 15 countries. The BPP has been shown to reduce levels of bully and victim incidents by 33%–64% (see Table 1.1). We also refer the reader to Chapter 4 for an in-depth review of bullying as a school problem, as well as comprehensive guidance on program selection and specific examples of evidence-based interventions and tools in a bullying prevention program.

Content

As seen in Table 1.1 under Program Components, the BPP is implemented at three levels of the school environment—the total school, classroom, and the individual student. At the schoolwide level, the BPP establishes antibullying policy in the school system. To raise awareness and quantify the prevalence of bullying in the school, administrators distribute an anonymous 29-item student questionnaire to all students. A school conference day about bullying is established to talk about the results of the assessment and discuss interventions. Additionally, schools create a BPP coordination team in which a representative administrator, teacher, counselor, parent, and student come together to lead the program implementation. In the BPP program, the school adopts rules against bullying and explains to students the negative consequences for bullying behavior. All staff receive training to learn about the harmful consequences of bullying, to increase supervision in areas on campus that are prone to violence, and to provide systematic reinforcement of rules applied to all students.

At the classroom level, students have regular workshops about the harmful consequences of bullying. Students have discussions about bullying and violent behaviors, watch video presentations of bullying situations, write about ways to combat the problem, and engage in role play. Students are encouraged to increase their knowledge and empathy regarding bullying.

The individual student level involves direct consequences for bullying behaviors. There are focused interventions with those identified as bullies and victims, as well as the bystanders. The parents of involved students are given help and support to reinforce nonviolence at home. School mental health workers play an essential role in more serious cases of bullying.

The goal of using interventions through all three levels is to ensure that students are given a consistent, coordinated, and strong message that bullying will not be tolerated. The BPP teaches students that everyone has a responsibility to prevent bullying, either by refusing to support bullying behavior or by alerting an adult to the problem.

Theoretical Rationale and Conceptual Framework

The BPP program is based on a systematic restructuring of the school environment that redirects bullying behavior and provides rewards for more prosocial behavior. The conceptual framework is based on research on the development and modification of aggressive behavior, as well as positive childrearing dimensions (Olweus, Limber, & Mihalic, 1999). The goal is to create a school environment that (1) is characterized by adults who are engaged and caring, (2) has firm limits to unacceptable behavior, (3) has consistent responses of no rewards and negative consequences for violent behavior, and (4) has adults who act as authorities and positive role models (Olweus et al., 1999).

Much of the success of the BPP can be attributed to its being a schoolwide program, so that it becomes an integral part of the school environment. Students and adults participate in most of the universal components of the program. Indeed, teachers, parents, and administrators play an important role in the success of the program. School staff and parents are expected to (1) become aware of the extent of the bullying problem in their school through assessments, (2) gain an understanding of the significance and harmful effects of bullying, and (3) take an active role in enforcing rules against bullying behavior (Olweus et al., 1999).

Evaluation

As seen in Table 1.1, the first and most comprehensive evaluation study of this program was conducted with 2,500 students in Norway (also see Olweus et al., 1999). However, since then, this program has been implemented and positively evaluated in many countries. Evaluation of this program has consistently demonstrated significant reductions in bully/victim reports across many cultures. General antisocial behaviors such as vandalism, fighting, theft, and truancy are reduced. Improvements are also found in classroom culture in that students reported improved order and discipline at school, more positive social relationships, and more positive attitudes toward school and schoolwork.

Child Development Project

The Child Development Project (CDP) is an ecological approach to intervention that collaboratively involves teachers, parents, and students working to influence all aspects of the school community (Developmental Studies Center, 1995). Its main objective is to create a cooperative and supportive school environment for children in grades K–6. Established in 1981, the CDP strives to foster shared commitment to prosocial, democratic values in two specific ways: through adult guidance and through direct participation by children (Developmental Studies

Center, 1995). Throughout this process, children are able to develop a feeling that the school community cares for them, and they, in turn, begin to care about the school community.

Teachers are trained to implement most components of the intervention, and ongoing consultation and support are provided by the Developmental Studies Center. Research indicates that schools should make a minimum of a 3-year commitment to the CDP if it is to be effective (Northwest Regional Educational Laboratory, 1998). The CDP has been established in 165 elementary schools, and it has been shown to be effective in both ethnically and socioeconomically diverse settings (Battistich, Solomon, Watson, & Schaps, 1997; Battistich, Schaps, Watson, & Solomon, 1996; Northwest Regional Educational Laboratory, 1998; Solomon, Watson, Battistich, Schaps, & Delucchi, 1996).

Theoretical Rationale and Conceptual Framework

The Child Development Project's theoretical framework is guided by research on socialization, learning and motivation, and prosocial development (Battistich, Schaps, Watson, Solomon, & Lewis, 2000). Its overall objective is for schools to be transformed into caring and supportive communities in which everyone works collaboratively in the learning process. Such a focus is expected to foster children's intellectual and sociomoral development, self-direction, competence, and belonging (Battistich, Schaps, Watson, Solomon, & Lewis, 2000). And where these qualities are fostered, children become attached to and invested in the school community, which in turn leads them to internalize the school norms. School norms typically promote prosocial activity (e.g., concern for others) and proscribe antisocial activity (e.g., drug use or gang activity). The program is based on the idea that children's internalization of school norms will solidify their commitment to the school's community values.

Content

There are four interrelated goals on which the components of the CDP are based: (1) building warm, stable, supportive relationships; (2) attending to social and ethical dimensions of learning; (3) honoring intrinsic motivations; and (4) teaching in ways that support students' active construction of meaning (Battistich et al., 2000). These goals are interwoven into the five major components of CDP, which are presented in Table 1.2. The five components are literature-based reading and language arts, collaborative classroom learning, developmental discipline, parent involvement, and schoolwide activities.

The first three components are all designed for the classroom. The literature-based readings component is most directly focused on teaching for understanding. Thus, the selection of books is designed to help teachers foster a deeper and more empathic understanding of the readings among the students. The component that involves collaborative learning emphasizes the importance of working with others in a fair and cooperative manner. The final classroom component

Table 1.2 Components of Child Development Project

Components	What Is Done
1. Literature-based reading and language arts	1. *Reading aloud* allows students to have shared experience of hearing stories told aloud. 2. *Partner reads* help students build automaticity through the support of their partner. *In each of these scenarios, the teacher asks open-ended discussion questions about issues evoked by books and gives students an opportunity to discuss these issues with one another.
2. Collaborative classroom	1. *Peer collaboration* involves equal-status peers working in pairs or learning small groups on challenging projects that require collaboration. 2. *Adult guidance* involves the teacher monitoring peer groups. The teacher discusses the specific learning goals and behaviors required for successful cooperation at the beginning of each activity. The teacher also assists students in reflecting on group interaction at the conclusion of each task.

3. Developmental discipline	1. The teacher involves children in
	  a. shaping norms of classroom;
	  b. developing collaborative approaches to resolving conflict;
	  c. practicing skills of nonviolent problem solving;
	  d. helping them to anticipate problems so that they might be avoided;
	  e. determining source of problems, thinking about solutions, and trying its effects on others.
	2. Playground disputes become opportunities for children to engage in many of the above activities.
	3. The teacher avoids extrinsic incentives in order to foster personal commitment to justice.

(continued)

Table 1.2 (Continued)

4. Parent involvement	1. A school "coordinating team" of parents and teachers collectively plans schoolwide activities. 2. Family participation includes "homeside activities" that are designed to connect the home and school life. There are 18 activities per grade level, and each requires interaction between the parent and the student. For example, parents may discuss their culture and heritage with their child. The child then presents this information to the class.
5. Schoolwide activities	1. Buddies Program brings older and younger students together in activities, such as playing a game or going on a field trip. 2. Grandperson's Day draws older family members to the school to discuss their experiences. 3. Family Read-Aloud or Family Film nights bring parents and children together to engage in a learning activity.

Source: Battistich, Schaps, Watson, Solomon, & Lewis, 2000 (with permission of Springer Science and Business Media); Developmental Studies Center, 1998.

involves building care and respect for everyone in the classroom community (Northwest Regional Educational Laboratory, 1998). The two other components' foci go beyond the classroom. Parent involvement is designed to develop meaningful conversations between adults and their children; schoolwide activities are focused on allowing participation by all and avoiding hierarchies and competition (Northwest Regional Education Laboratory, 1998).

Implementation
At least 80% of the school faculty must support their school's adoption of the CDP for it to be established there. Training is conducted by Developmental Studies Center's staff and involves initial consultation and planning to identify needs and goals; a 3-day summer institute to orient teachers on the CDP components and materials; three half-day follow-up workshops conducted during the school year; three on-site sessions, each lasting 2.5 days, which include consultation, in-class demonstrations, co-teaching, planning; and professional development support kits that can be used to train new staff (Developmental Studies Center, 2004).

Evaluation

As seen in Table 1.1, CDP strengthens students' sense of their school as a community, their ethical and social resources (e.g., conflict-resolution skills, social problem-solving skills, commitment to democratic values, concern for others), their academic motivation (e.g., liking for school), and their abstention from drug use and other problem behaviors (e.g., gang-related activity) (Battistich et al., 1996; Battistich et al., 2000; Battistich et al., 1997; Northwest Regional Education Laboratory, 1998). Moreover, positive effects were reported 2 years after students left elementary school with regard to those students' conflict resolution skills, self-esteem, and involvement in extracurricular activity (Developmental Studies Center, 1995).

FAST Track

The FAST Track Project is a long-term comprehensive intervention that encompasses multiple facets of children's social contexts. The intervention is comprehensive in that it has both universal (schoolwide) components and targeted components, which attempt to provide focused assistance to both children at high risk of antisocial behaviors and to their social systems. One of the great strengths of this program is its detailed attention to the intersection of the multiple contexts that contribute to children's developmental outcomes. The FAST Track prevention program aims to improve child competences, parent effectiveness, the school context, and school–home communications with the intention of preventing antisocial behavior across the developmental trajectory.

Theoretical Rationale and Conceptual Framework

The developmental theory guiding this intervention addresses the interaction of multiple influences on the development of antisocial behavior. These various elements include socioeconomic factors, family dynamics, peer influences, school factors, and the child's temperament.

Content

There are four FAST Track sites in the United States, with a total of 891 children (and their families) participating (with near-equal numbers of at-risk children in both intervention and control groups). The initial sample consisted of children identified as "at risk" by a combination of teacher and parent ratings of their behavior. Children in the intervention group were provided with a host of services, including weekly enrichment programs, involvement in "friendship groups," and sessions in which they were taught and had opportunities to practice social skills. The parents of the intervention children were also provided with family coordinators who conducted biweekly home visits in efforts to enhance their parenting behavior management skills, specifically in the areas of praise, time-outs, and self-restraint. Children in the intervention group were also provided with three 30-minute academic tutoring sessions each week.

When the children in the intervention group reached adolescence (grades 6–10), the group-based interventions were de-emphasized. However, the intervention retained its curriculum-based parent and youth group meetings to support children in their transition into middle school (grades 5–7). In continuation of the earlier targeted model, individual support was provided for participants and their families in order to strengthen protective factors and reduce risk factors. The targeted intervention at the adolescent phase focused on academic tutoring, mentoring, home visiting and family problem solving, and supporting positive peer-group involvement. To address the multiple contexts in the adolescents' lives, the school tried to establish relations with the community agencies that served the participants.

FAST Track also included an important universal component for children in the first through the fifth grades in the target schools. This school-based intervention consisted of teacher-led curricula called "PATHS" (Promoting Alternative Thinking Strategies), designed to provide children with strategies in understanding the development of emotional concepts, social understanding, and self-control. Since PATHS has been evaluated separately and shown to have independent positive effects, we will present PATHS separately in the next section. Some schools may choose to adopt only sections of the overall program, such as PATHS.

Evaluation

FAST Track is one of the more rigorously evaluated comprehensive violence prevention programs and has become widely known as one of the leading models of an effective approach to prevention of antisocial behaviors in youth. As shown in Table 1.1, evaluation studies of FAST Track have revealed positive outcomes for program participants. In addition to those differences highlighted in the table, the prevention revealed statistically significant improvements in the targeted children's social-cognitive and academic skills, in addition to reductions in their parents' use of harsh discipline. The intervention children also demonstrated considerable behavioral improvements at home, in the classroom, and on the playground during and following their elementary school years. In addition to these behavioral improvements, the intervention children were at a reduced risk of being placed in special education classes than children in the control conditions. The findings generalized across ethnicity, gender, and a host of child and family characteristics.

Promoting Alternative Thinking Strategies

PATHS is the classroom curriculum component of the FAST Track intervention program. We present it separately because PATHS has been adopted and studied independently of FAST Track. PATHS was designed to promote emotional and social competence and to reduce aggression and other behavior problems in children in grades K–5 (Greenberg, Kusché, Cook, & Quamma, 1995). PATHS focuses on four domains related to school success: (1) prosocial behavior and friendship skills, (2) emotional understanding and self-control, (3) communication and conflict resolution, and (4) problem-solving skills (Conduct Problems Prevention Research Group, 2002). PATHS provides teachers and counselors with training, lesson modules, and ongoing consultation and support. Additionally, parents receive information and activities to complete with their children.

PATHS can be used with all elementary school-age children, and ideally it should be ongoing, beginning in kindergarten and continuing through fifth grade. It has been field-tested and researched in regular education classroom settings and in settings that serve special-needs students such as the deaf, hearing-impaired, learning disabled, emotionally disturbed, mildly mentally delayed, and gifted (see Greenberg et al., 1995; Greenberg & Kusché, 1998).

Theoretical Rationale and Conceptual Framework

PATHS is based on five conceptual models (Greenberg, Kusché, & Mihalic, 1998). First, the ABCD (Affective-Behavioral-Cognitive-Dynamic) model of development promotes skills that are developmentally appropriate. The second model is an eco-behavioral system orientation that focuses on helping the teacher use these skills to build a healthy classroom atmosphere. The third model involves neurobiology and brain organization for cognitive development. The fourth is psychodynamic education that was derived from developmental psychodynamic theory. Finally, the fifth model includes psychological issues related to emotional awareness or emotional intelligence. These conceptual models come together in this curriculum to provide a comprehensive and development-based program that addresses students' cognitive processes, emotions, and behaviors.

Content

The PATHS curriculum (Greenberg et al., 1998) is taught three times a week for a minimum of 20–30 minutes a day. The curriculum contains four units with a total of 119 lessons in each unit. They consist of the following: (1) a "Turtle Unit" focusing on classroom behavior, emotional literacy, and self-control; (2) a "Feeling and Relationship Unit" focusing on building self-esteem and social competence; (3) a "Problem-Solving Unit" with instruction on the 11-step model of social problem solving and positive peer relations; and (4) a "Supplementary Lessons Unit" containing 30 lessons that delve more in depth into PATHS concepts. The lessons are age appropriate, and as we can see in Table 1.3, the lessons for third-grade students match developmental stages and cover the conceptual domains of self-control, emotional understanding, self-esteem, peer relations, and problem solving. (Lesson 93, presented in detail in Table 1.4, covers self-control and problem solving.)

Table 1.3 PATHS Lessons for Grade 3

Lesson Topic	Volume & Lesson #	Conceptual Domains				
		Self-Control	Emotional Understanding	Self-Esteem	Peer Relations	Problem Solving
PATHS Rules	Vol. 1, L 1	X		X	X	X
PATHS Kid/Complimenting/Self-esteem	Vol. 1, L 2	X		X	X	X
Anger Intensity	Vol. 1, L 10		X		X	
Anger Management/Control Signals	Vol. 1, L 11–12	X		X	X	X
Fear Intensity/Sad Intensity	Vol. 1, L 15–17		X		X	
Disgusted, Delighted	Vol. 1, L 21		X		X	
Frustrated, Disappointed/Hopeful, Proud/Ashamed, Guilty, Curious/Interested/Bored, Confused/Worried/Sure, Anxious/Calm, Shy/Lonely	Vol. 2, L 23–32, 37		X		X	
Embarrassed/Humiliated	Vol. 2, L 33–34		X		X	
Intentionality (Accident/Purpose), Manners	Vol. 3, L 38–44		X		X	

(continued)

Table 1.3 (Continued)

Lesson Topic	Volume & Lesson #	Self-Control	Emotional Understanding	Self-Esteem	Peer Relations	Problem Solving
			Conceptual Domains			
Jealous/Content, Greedy/ Selfish/Generous, Malicious/ Kind, Rejected/Included, Excluded, Forgiving/ Resentful	Vol. 3, 48–56		X		X	
Informal Problem Solving	Vol. 5, 90–92	X				X
Self-Control and Problem Prevention	Vol. 5, L 93–94	X				X
Friendship	Vol. 5, L 95–97	X	X	X	X	X
Teasing	Vol. 5, L 98–101	X	X	X	X	X
Apply Problem-Solving Steps	Vol. 4, L 89					X

Table 1.4 PATHS Learning Self-Control, Volume 5, Lesson 93

Introduction	"Today I'm going to tell you a story about a boy who had problems, but he learned a new way to help himself."
Story: "Thomas in Control".	This is a story about a boy who did not like to go to school. Thomas felt very upset about going to school. He wanted to run outside and play with his toys or ride his bike or watch television or play a game. Thomas did not like to sit quietly. It was hard for him to pay attention when the teacher or the other kids were talking in class. Instead, Thomas would tease whoever was sitting beside him, by grabbing their pencils and books, by making faces at them, or by whispering to them. The other kids would get angry at Thomas when he bothered them and would yell at him or would do some of the same things back. Then everyone would get caught and would get into trouble. That's why some of the kids thought that Thomas was troublemaker. Sometimes when they went out to the playground at recess, the other kids would still be mad at Thomas, and they would get into a fight. All of this hate and resentment made Thomas feel very uncomfortable inside. One day when he was feeling his worst, the playground teacher told Thomas that he had to go to the principal's office because he hadn't been following the playground rules. "You know," said the principal in a very calm voice, "you have a very big problem, but I'll share a secret with you. You already have the answer to your problem with you You carry it with you everywhere you go. It's your ability to think. Whenever you feel upset, when you are angry or frustrated, you can use your mind and think. You can stop, take a long, deep breath, and say the problem and how you feel. When you remind yourself to stop and calm down, it's like taking a rest for a minute. You can rest until you feel calm. That is how you can control yourself. And when you can control yourself, then people will say, 'Thomas has good self-control. He thinks before he does something that will cause problems.'" The principal showed Thomas the three steps for calming down. Then the principal reminded Thomas that the next time he felt upset or angry, he could think about the control signals and could calm himself down. Thomas liked the idea and wanted to try it himself. He wanted to do well in school, he wanted his teacher to like him, and he especially wanted to make friends....
On board	Begin drawing on the chalk board Feelings: comfortable and uncomfortable/ Behavior OK and not OK.

(continued)

Table 1.4 *(Continued)*	
Discussion	Ask students to name the different feelings and behavior that Thomas felt and list them under the appropriate categories. Ask them to discuss the relationshipsbetween these feelings and behaviors if they are able to do so. Ask students to name the kinds of things that bug them in the classroom, playground, lunchroom, and so on, and list them in the categories. This will help students become aware of what they do that bothers others. Ask student if using the three steps to calm down would help with any of the things they listed.

Source: Story excerpt reduced for space reasons from Kusche & Greenberg (1995), available for review on www.channing-bete.com

The PATHS curriculum includes comprehensive materials, and the basic PATHS kit (grades 1–5) includes an instructor's manual, five curriculum manuals, feelings photographs, feelings face cards, two wall charts, and four full-color posters. The Turtle Unit (for kindergarten classrooms) includes an instructor's manual, curriculum manual, turtle puppet with pad, turtle stamp, and poster. Teachers receive on-site training and technical assistance to ensure effective implementation of the program.

Evaluation

PATHS was evaluated between 1994 and 2003 in various research studies using randomized control groups and was found to be effective. As seen in Table 1.1, PATHS has been found to be a model or effective program by at least six groups that review violence prevention programs nationwide for effectiveness. An overview of results from all trials reveals a reduction in aggressive behavior, conduct disorder, and violent solutions to social problems. In addition, results found an increase in self-control, vocabulary for emotions, cognitive skills, ability to tolerate frustration, and to effectively use conflict-resolution strategies(SAMHSA Model Programs, 2003). The findings have been consistent across teacher reports, self-reports, and child assessments and interviews.

Tools and Practice Examples

Learning Self-Control, Volume 5—Supplementary
Lesson 93, Grade 3

In the PATHS curriculum, each unit builds on the preceding units. Table 1.4 comprises an excerpt from supplementary lesson 93 and is intended for third graders.

The objective of this lesson is to discuss the idea of self-control as an internalized process. It emphasizes the concept of using thinking to control one's behavior and to distinguish between feelings and behaviors. The teacher reads a story about a boy named Thomas, who had problems with self-control, was angry, and would get into fights with other children. Throughout the story, students learn the three steps for calming down to gain control of their behavior. The lesson is followed by the teacher drawing a hierarchy of feelings and behaviors on the board and asking questions to encourage classroom discussion. Students are encouraged to talk about how they felt when they acted without thinking first, and to say whether things got out of control and how they felt about the outcome. This lesson teaches students anger management and problem-solving skills through a developmentally appropriate story that is easy to relate to and that facilitates discussion.

Monitoring and Evaluating Violence Prevention Programs

A review of the school safety literature strongly suggests that model school safety programs should be developed and implemented in a process that ensures their relevance and applicability to each specific site. These are important assumptions of the programs described in this chapter as well as program interventions described in other chapters of this book:

- Fitting a program to a school involves grassroots participation.
- Students and teachers in the school need to be empowered to deal with the problem.
- Democracy is the core of a good school safety program.
- Schools should demonstrate a proactive vision surrounding the violence problem in their school.

Implementing interventions or components of any model program is likely to be slightly different for every school. An eye toward the overall assumptions and flexibility should enable each school to adapt the program or general principles to its unique demographic, philosophical, and organizational needs.

Data and Program Evaluation

An important element of successful school safety programs is the ongoing and interactive use of data. This perspective proposes that the continuous and ongoing analysis and interpretation of data is an essential part of the intervention process. Data are used to create awareness, mobilize different school constituencies, assess the extent of the problem, plan and implement interventions, and conduct evaluations. Information is provided on a continuous basis to different groups in each step of the intervention process. Unfortunately, many U.S. schools purchase evidence-based programs but do not collect any data about their own district or school.

The process of building and implementing school safety programs is continual and cyclical, always changing to respond to new circumstances and emerging needs. Hence, the evaluation of the program's progress becomes a reassessment of the situation, leading to a new cycle of awareness building, planning, modifying, and evaluating. A school's failure to gather site-specific and comparative data could be a significant obstacle in (a) assessing whether that specific school has a violence problem, (b) adapting a school safety program, and (c) evaluating the implementation process and outcomes of the program.

Monitoring and school mapping can help create a "whole-school response" and help the school to identify, create, and/or adapt programs to the site. Monitoring is the ongoing process of collecting and using data to shape, fit, match, and evaluate the intervention. The value of monitoring comes from the two levels of information processing involved: description and comparison. The description of the basic frequency of certain behaviors may be quite instructive. For example, it is helpful to know how many weapon-related events or sexual assaults occur at a specific school.

Using Comparisons

In general, comparisons enhance the value of information by putting it in context. Before adopting a program, it is imperative to ascertain (a) which acts are more problematic than others, (b) which grade levels are victimized more, and (c) how violence levels in a specific school compare over time and for different ethnic, age, and gender groups. For example, if bullying is not a major problem in the school, it does not make sense to adopt an antibullying program. Perhaps bullying is a problem only in one grade level within a large school, whereas other forms of violence are problems in other grades. Though these concerns may sound like common sense, very few schools actually collect systemic information to ascertain the extent of the school safety problem. Currently, many districts and schools across the United States are purchasing expensive violence prevention programs targeting a specific form of violence (e.g., sexual harassment, bullying, weapon use) without data about the extent of the problem in their schools. This creates a chain of difficulties through the implementation process and later in the evaluation of the program. If the problem was never established, it is difficult to know if the program ever worked. Hence, it is important to examine levels of violence over time.

Using Mapping as a Monitoring Tool

Mapping is a qualitative tool that can help monitor and generate the kind of comparisons discussed above. Mapping does not require extensive training and can provide valuable information that helps implement, monitor, and assess the ongoing health of a program. This procedure is designed to involve school constituents by revealing how forms of violence within a school building interact with locations, patterns of the school day, and social organizational variables (e.g., teacher–student relationships, teachers' professional roles, and the school's organizational response to violence; for more details see Astor, Benbenishty, & Meyer, 2004; Astor, Meyer, & Behre, 1999; Astor & Meyer, 1999; Astor, Meyer, & Pitner, 2001). An important goal of this procedure is to allow students and teachers to convey their personal theories about why specific locations and times in their schools are more dangerous. This process greatly facilitates the implementation and evaluation of the model programs reviewed in the first sections of this chapter.

Step-by-Step Instructions

Mapping, Interviews, and Interventions   The first step in this assessment procedure is obtaining a map of the school. Ideally, the map should contain all internal school territory, including the areas surrounding the school and playground. In communities where the routes to and from school are dangerous, a simple map of the surrounding neighborhood may be added to the assessment process. The focus groups should begin with the facilitator distributing two sets of identical school maps to each individual.

Map A and B: Two photocopied maps of the school are needed for each student and teacher. One map should be used to determine where students and teachers think the most events involving violence occur. Participants should also be asked to identify the locations (on the maps) of up to three of the most violent events that have occurred within the past academic year. Next to each marked event on the map, participants should be asked to write the following information: (1) the general time frame of the event (before school, after school, morning period, afternoon period, evening sports event, between classes, etc.); (2) the grade and gender of those involved in the violence; and (3) their knowledge of any organizational response to the event (someone was sent to principal's office, suspended, sent to peer counselor, done nothing to, etc.). On the second map, members should be asked to circle areas or territories that they perceive to be unsafe or potentially dangerous. This second map provides information about areas within the school that participants avoid or fear even though they may not possess knowledge of a particular event.

Discussion of Violent Events and Areas   The first part of the group discussion should center on the specific events and the areas marked as unsafe or dangerous on their personal maps. We have asked questions such as "Are there times when those places you've marked on the maps are less safe?" "Is there a particular group of students that is more likely to get hurt there?" and "Why do you think that area has so many incidents?" The overall purpose of the group interviews is to explore why bullying or victimization occurs at those specific times and in those specific spaces. Consequently, the interviews should also focus on gathering information regarding the organizational response to the event (e.g., "What happened to the two students after the event?" or "Did the hall monitors intervene when they saw what happened?"), procedures (e.g., "What happens when the students are sent to the office after a fight?" or "Did anyone call the parents of the bully or victim?"), follow-up (e.g., "Do the teachers, hall monitors, and/or administrators follow up on any consequences given to the students?" or "Did anyone check on the welfare of the victim?"), and clarity of procedures (e.g., "Does it matter who stops the bullying, be it a volunteer, security guard, teacher, or principal?").

Interviewers should also explore participants' ideas for solutions to the specific violence problems (e.g., "Can you think of ways to avoid bullying or victimization in that place?" or "If you were the principal, what would you do to make that place safer?"). In addition, the interviewer should explore any obstacles that participants foresee with implementation (e.g., "Do you think that type of plan is realistic?" "Has that been tried before? What happened?" or "Do you think that plan would work?"). Such obstacles could range from issues related to roles (e.g., "It's not my job to monitor students during lunch") to discipline policy and issues of personal safety (e.g., "I don't want to intervene because I may get hurt").

In schools that already have started model programs designed to address school violence, specific questions should be asked about the effectiveness of those interventions, why they work or do not work, and what could be done to make the current measures more effective. We recommend that the interviewer ask both subjective questions (e.g., "Do you think the antiviolence program is working? Why do you think it works, or why does it not work?") as well as specific questions related to the reduction of victimization (e.g., "Do you believe the antiviolence program has reduced the number of fights/name calling [or any other type of violence the school is interested in preventing] on the playground? Why or why not?").

Transferring all of the reported events onto one large map of the school enables students and staff to locate specific "hot spots" for violence and dangerous time periods within each individual school. The combined data are presented to all school constituencies, and they are asked to once again discuss and interpret the maps. Teachers and students use the maps and interviews to suggest ways to improve the settings and what aspects of the program are working or not working. For example, in one school, events were clustered by time, age, gender, and location. In the case of older students (11th and 12th graders), events were clustered in the parking lot outside of the auxiliary gym immediately after school, whereas for younger students (9th and 10th graders), events were reported in the lunchroom and hallways during transition periods. For this school, the map suggested that interventions be geared specifically toward older students, directly after school, by the main entrance, and in the school parking lot. Students and teachers agreed that increasing the visible presence of school staff in and around the parking lot for the 20 minutes after school had great potential for reducing the number of violent events. Younger students were experiencing violence mainly before, during, and after lunch, near the cafeteria. Many students expressed feelings of being unsafe between classes in the hallways. This school already had an antibullying program, and it was able to incorporate this specific type of intervention into existing activities designed to stem school violence.

Compiling all the interview suggestions into themes is an important second step in adapting context-relevant interventions. Students, teachers, and administrators may have differing viewpoints regarding the organizational response of the school to a violent incident. Relaying the diversity of responses to students, teachers, and administrators can provide an opportunity for reflection and may generate ways to remedy the violence problem in certain situations. When the data are presented to students, teachers, and administrators, they can center their discussions on why those areas are dangerous and what kinds of interventions could make the location safer. Mapping methods provide data-based approaches to gathering information about bullying/victimization in schools. Moreover, they provide site-specific information, which makes it easier for schools to address these problems.

Identifying specific target groups for interventions is another way data can/ should be used. A school could use this monitoring system to identify particular problem areas in their school. They could then track progress in reducing violence in these locations over time and by different groups.

Key Points to Remember

Based on our review of programs, it appears that successful schoolwide intervention programs have the following core underlying implementation characteristics:

- They are comprehensive, intensive, ecological, and require "buy-in" from school and community.
- They raise the awareness and responsibility of students, teachers, and parents regarding the types of violence in their schools (e.g., sexual harassment, fighting, and weapons use).
- They create clear guidelines and rules for all members of the school community.
- They target the various social systems in the school and clearly communicate to the entire school community what procedures should be followed before, during, and after violent events.
- They focus on getting the school staff, students, and parents involved in the program.

- They often fit easily into the normal flow and mission of the school setting.
- They use faculty, staff, and parents in the school setting to plan, implement, and sustain the program.
- They increase monitoring and supervision in nonclassroom areas.
- They include ongoing monitoring and mapping, which provide information that schools can use to tailor a program to their specific needs and increase its chance of success.

Resources

Web Sites on Model Programs

Bullying Prevention Program: http://www.clemson.edu/olweus/
Child Development Project: http://www.devstu.org
FAST Track: www.fasttrackproject.org
Promoting Alternative Thinking Strategies: http://www.channing-bete.com/positive youth/pages/PATHS/PATHS.html

Web Sites That Evaluate School Violence Prevention Programs

Blueprints for Violence Prevention: www.colorado.edu/cspv/blueprints
Center for Disease Control: National Center for Injury Prevention and Control— Division of Violence Prevention: www.cdc.gov/ncipc/dvp/bestpractices.htm
Department of Education: Safe and Drug Free Schools: www.ed.gov/about/offices/list/osdfs/index.html?src=mr
Hamilton Fish Institute on School and Community Violence: www.hamfish.org/programs/
Substance Abuse and Mental Health Services Administration: www.modelprograms.samhsa.gov
U.S. Department of Health and Human Services Prevention Research Center for the Promotion of Human Development: www.prevention.psu.edu
U.S. Office of Juvenile Justice and Delinquency Prevention & Title V: www.dsgonline.com
Youth Violence: A Report of the Surgeon General: www.surgeongeneral.gov/library/youthviolence

2 Creating a Violence-Free School Climate/Culture

Mark A. Mattaini

Getting Started

In an increasingly globalized world, rates of violence among the young appear to be increasing nearly worldwide (Buvinic & Morrison, 2000). The incidence of most types of violence is much higher in the United States, however, than in most developed countries. And although schools are the safest places for children, most schools are not safe. Fourteen percent of high school students carry weapons to school; a larger number carry them outside of school (Josephson Institute on Ethics, 2001). Rates of harassment, bullying, threat, coercion, humiliation, and intentional exclusion among children and youth are much higher than what adults usually recognize. Nearly a third of children are regularly involved in bullying (as bully, victim, or both), and those who are not directly involved report feeling threatened by the exposure. One third of U.S. high school students do not feel safe at school. Many others find school environments so socially toxic, so emotionally violent and threatening, that they do not wish to be there (Garbarino & deLara, 2002). Adults who are present often are not aware of the extent of these issues; Garbarino and deLara call this the "secret school life of adolescents" (p. 16). Continual exposure to physical and emotional violence produces damaging levels of stress hormones, upsets the neurochemical balance in the brain, and has a profoundly negative impact on social and academic development. The problem is serious, and it is widespread, spanning all socioeconomic groups.

What We Know

A review by the U.S. surgeon general (2001) found that many common violence prevention programs (including peer-led programs like peer counseling and peer mediation) are largely ineffective, and some (like boot camps) can actually be damaging. By contrast, the most effective programs focus on improving the social climate of the school, in conjunction with supporting other protective factors like parental effectiveness and building individual social competencies. A good deal is known about how to construct school cultures that maintain a positive school climate; combining projects targeting school climate with universal life skills training (discussed in other chapters of this book) can be particularly powerful.

A number of existing programs for constructing cultures that discourage violence and threat and support the development of positive alternative practices are listed in Table 2.1. The Good Behavior Game, Bullying Prevention, Effective Behavior Support, and Positive Action are well-established strategies, supported by multiple controlled studies. PeaceBuilders, Community Builders, and PEACE POWER, which are partial replications of one another, are based on strong science and can be viewed as probably efficacious or promising. Decisions about selecting programs draw in part on data, and also on the resources required. For example, Effective Behavior Support and CommunityBuilders as implemented so far require considerable additional staffing resources, and Positive Action and PeaceBuilders are commercial programs that can involve significant financial

Table 2.1 Key Studies Related to Creating Violence-Free School Cultures

Program and Key Reference	Findings
CommunityBuilders (promising; incorporates well-established practices) Metzler, Biglar, Rusby & Sprague (2001)	Levels of positive reinforcement increased, aggressive behavior declined, disciplinary referrals and harassment declined among some groups, reports of verbal and physical attacks decreased (but did at comparison school as well).
Effective Behavior Support (well established) Sprague et al. (2001)	Social skills improved, and office referrals for disciplinary action declined. Students' perceptions of school safety did not improve, however.
Good Behavior Game (well established) Embry (2002)	Antisocial behaviors declined even when evaluated in long-term follow-up. Results are from approximately 20 independent replications of the Good Behavior Game used with different grade levels, different types of students, and in different settings.
PeaceBuilders (probably efficacious) Flannery et al. (2003)	Prosocial behavior increased, aggressive behavior was reduced, and social competence improved. Results are somewhat variable among age groups, but maintain over 2-year period.
PEACE POWER (promising; incorporates well-established practices) Strickland, Erickson & Mattain (n.d.)	Levels of recognition, respect, shared power, and peacemaking increased in three of four schools.
Positive Action (well established) Flay, Allred & Ordway (2001)	Disciplinary referrals decreased by up to 85%, school performance improved, and number of arrests declined.

cost. Of the programs identified, only Bullying Prevention, the Good Behavior Game, and PEACE POWER are currently readily accessible in journal or manual form.

What We Can Do

Our review indicates that cultures that are effective in reducing violence are characterized by high levels of four interlocking cultural practices among multiple groups of actors (staff, students, parents, community members): (a) recognition of contributions and successes, (b) acting with respect, (c) sharing power to build community, and (d) healing (making peace) when conflicts occur (Mattaini, 2001). Each of these core practices has independent scientific support, and together they are consistent with the recommendations reported in multiple reviews. The four practices are summarized here; examples in practice are presented in a later section of this chapter.

- *Recognizing contributions and successes.* Effective programs universally aim to catalyze large increases in the frequency of reinforcement or recognition for prosocial actions, including contributions to the community and personal successes. High levels of affection and recognition increase the availability of serotonin and dopamine in critical regions of the brain and are associated with prosocial behavior and learning.

- *Acting with respect.* Within a culture of respect, individuals and groups have the opportunity to flourish and achieve their full developmental potential. Threat, harassment, violence, and coercion limit that potential. Building alternatives to adversarial and disrespectful actions and acting to interrupt those behaviors when they occur are therefore critical shifts in constructing organizational and community culture.

- *Sharing power to build community.* Simply suppressing violence is not an effective strategy; violence provides social power and protection, and individuals will give it up only if they learn to exercise effective alternative forms of power. In an organizational community of shared power, all have opportunities to contribute from their own gifts and talents, all have a strong voice in shaping the community, and no one is excluded. (Exclusion itself is a serious risk factor for violence against self or others.)

- *Making peace.* Even in the strongest of groups and communities, conflicts will occur. In many cases, such conflicts are never really resolved, and they often are allowed to fester and spread below the surface. A real process of healing—and not just a forced handshake—is required if the overall climate of the school is to be nonviolent and empowering.

A culture of recognition, respect, nonviolent shared power, and healing emerges not from a single heroic effort but is rather a result of literally thousands of small actions occurring over an extended period. The most powerful efforts strive to establish a healthy culture throughout the school, although it is possible to do something meaningful even in a single classroom. Key steps for building an integrated, collective effort are outlined below.

1. *Form a working group.* Culture-building projects usually begin with one key staff person, often a social worker or a principal. Experience suggests that such a project can succeed only with strong buy-in from the top administrator, so unless the principal is the initiator, the key staff person should begin by discussing and examining printed information about the possibilities with the administrator. It can be enormously helpful to also locate one or two other strong staff supporters who can form the core of a working group. Ultimately, the strongest projects involve staff, students (especially in work with older youth), parents, and community members; so an intermediate goal should be to form a working group including representatives of each. Student energy should be harnessed to the greatest extent possible. Students are often the most hopeful of all participants and seriously interested in making a difference in school and community, even in very stressed schools. Forming the group may happen immediately or may occur after initial staff training, but it is important that everyone be made welcome to participate, so the project is not viewed as belonging to a particular subgroup. The working group should make plans to meet regularly, so that the momentum of the project is not lost.

2. *Provide initial staff and student training.* Successfully shifting a school's culture requires the participation of a substantial proportion of staff members. For this reason, effective initial staff training is among the most critical steps. To the extent possible, *all staff*—teaching staff, administrators, maintenance and kitchen workers, security workers, and transportation staff— should be included, even if multiple training sessions are required. It is often useful to bring in an outside trainer to conduct training, but the initial planning group can also do the training themselves so long as the group includes staff who are well respected, knowledgeable about the model to be used, and skilled as trainers. Training should include the scientific underpinnings of the approach, an outline of the strategy including examples of how it has been applied elsewhere, and opportunities for small-group work among staff to consider adaptations of the basic strategy that are likely to be a good fit in terms of community and staff values, cultures, and resources.

   Some of the best projects also hold a kick-off event for students; planning for those events should involve both staff and students, and the event should be both entertaining and challenging. Details depend on the age of students, but such events usually include videos; student role plays; serious discussion of the damage done by violence, harassment, bullying, and coercion; and specific options for making a contribution (even for being a "hero"). When possible, a presentation to parents and community leaders helps to expand the impact of the project.

3. *Provide ongoing planning and training.* Though a powerful beginning is helpful, the energy to continually innovate and maintain project activities usually comes from the working group. New members should be recruited during initial training and throughout the project, and they should be welcomed warmly into the group. Recruiting persons who have a real passion for this work is a priority, since involvement generally goes beyond the requirements of the job. As with any group, some members will need to participate for a limited period, then withdraw; so open membership is usually the best arrangement. Other staff and students should also be encouraged to make their own project contributions even if they do not wish to join the working group.

Once initial training is over, the group should quickly initiate one or two project activities with high visibility; momentum is critical at this stage. Activities can be selected and adapted from the ideas that emerged from staff during initial training, as well as from samples listed below, the available manuals, and the working group's own creative efforts. Local ownership of the project is critically important; responsiveness to ideas emerging from the staff, students, parents, and working group should therefore be a priority. Although there is considerable room for adaptation, preference should be for ideas consistent with the empirical base. Any that are not should be particularly carefully evaluated. The working group should also plan for periodic brief training sessions for the staff; often one additional session for each of the core practices is a useful arrangement. Those sessions should include both didactic material and opportunities for small-group work. The working group should meet regularly throughout the project, since maintaining momentum requires that new activities be initiated regularly, and existing activities continually evaluated for improvement, maintenance, or discontinuation.

Culture is actualized in continual patterns of action; so the core of culture-building projects is a series of action steps that are widely practiced within the school community. The goal is universality—every member of the culture participates in dynamically shaping and maintaining cultural practices; so everyone's effort is needed. This means that most staff (and not just teaching staff) should be actively involved, even if in modest ways, as well as a large percentage of students. Visibility is essential, so project activities should be consistently "branded" with the name of the project ("Oh, another Project Peace activity!"). Table 2.2 lists a number of tools and activities for increasing levels of each of the core practices. This list should be seen as illustrative rather than comprehensive, since there are many possibilities and adaptations that can be useful within a project. The following sections describe a few actual examples of actions to increase each core practice in schools, to give a flavor for the level of variation possible.

4. *Implement activities and tools to build recognition.* The evidence supporting the importance of high levels of genuine recognition and reinforcement is strong; in classrooms with high (4 to 1 or better) ratios of recognition to reprimands, the level of problem behavior is much lower than in classrooms with higher relative levels of reprimands—which the research indicates are more typical. Verbal and nonverbal recognition is certainly useful with many children, but it sometimes is less so with those who struggle with behavior issues. Written Recognition Notes (sometimes called Praise Notes, Put-Ups, etc., in particular programs), often publicly

Table 2.2 Examples of Tools and Activities to Increase Rates of Core Practices

Recognize Contributions and Successes:	*Act with Respect:*
• Recognition Notes and Boards	• Respect (Good Behavior) Game
• Recognition Circles	• Classroom Assignments
• Group Incentives	• Sportsmanship Education
• Home Recognition Notes	• Gender Fishbowl Exercises
• Peer Monitoring	• Pledge Campaigns
• Wall Charts	• Multiethnic Programs
• Celebrations of Successes	• Gay-Straight Alliances
• Community Recognition Efforts	• Poster Contests
Share Power to Build Community:	*Make Peace:*
• Murals, Sculptures, Gardens	• Use of Structured Making Peace Tool
• Video Projects Highlighting Community Strengths	• Healing Circles
• Service Learning	• Victim-Offender Mediation (not peer mediation)
• Community Service Projects	• Family Group Conferencing
• Youth/Adult Partnership in Prevention Projects	• Guided Intergroup Dialogues
• Participation in Governance	• Family Mediation
• Mentoring Projects	• Recognition of Peace Makers
• Community-Building Research	• Police–Youth Dialogues

posted, have demonstrated considerable power even with those young people and are a common program component. (In some cases, private notes are a better fit for a group.) Home recognition notes are a common variation with good empirical and experiential support. Teachers and other staff complete a home recognition note specifically noting positive action or progress by a student, and the school sends that note on to the child's parent or other caretaker. Recognition bulletin boards for staff, often in a lounge or meeting room, are helpful to stimulate active mutual recognition among staff, an important dynamic in its own right and an opportunity for modeling. In some programs, recognition slips, tickets, or notes can be "cashed in" for privileges or are centrally deposited for a random drawing, after which some are announced over the intercom.

Recognition can also be extended into the neighborhood, with students and staff preparing "wanted posters" recognizing contributions that community members and leaders have made to the neighborhood. Recognition projects shift attention away from what is wrong with the school or community, and they speak in ways that are inconsistent with much of what youth may hear about themselves and their communities from other sources. In one school, the working group distributed posters titled "Recognition: The Foundation of Southhnm" that listed examples of the kinds of things that might be recognized widely throughout the school. Tickets were made centrally available for recognizing anyone, which when completed were both publicly posted and entered in a drawing to win small "foundation stones" decorated by an art class.

Face-to-face recognition can also be very powerful. One approach for encouraging such direct communication is the use of Recognition Circles, in which one person at a time is selected for the "hot seat," and the others go around the circle, completing the statement, "<Name>, what I appreciate about you is ___," and briefly explaining their comments. Some teachers do this weekly; in one middle school classroom, for example, every Friday afternoon, the teacher randomly drew two popsicle sticks with one student name on each and conducted a Recognition Circle for those students, followed by an opportunity for general recognition. This can be a very emotional experience for some children who have never heard many positive messages about themselves.

5. *Implement activities and tools to build respect.* While recognition is generally delivered in discrete moments, respect is a state extending through time and can be more complicated to construct. It is important, therefore, that respect be expressed verbally quite regularly. Including explicit attention to respect in classroom assignments is one

important step. This may range from essays in history class titled, say, "Someone I Respect and Why," to emphasis on one specific dimension of sportsmanship each day in physical education. Respect Months, in which multiple activities focused on respect occur in a concentrated way, are another useful approach (an example from one school is discussed below).

A simple approach with wide applicability is the use of Respect Pledges. Many schools have developed their own, in which those in the school make a daily commitment to act with respect, and to actively stop put-downs, threats, and harassment. The language of such pledges should, of course, be targeted to the developmental level of the students, as well as to the local situation. Schoolwide efforts to have everyone (staff and student) sign locally developed respect pledges in an organized campaign are another option.

The Good Behavior Game is a well-established approach to preventing problem behavior in its own right, and it can also be incorporated into larger projects. The game (which we often call the Respect Game in our projects) is a robust intervention that can be and has been effectively adapted to various age groups and levels of developmental maturity. The general principles of the game are quite straightforward. The teacher first leads a discussion about the way people like to see people act in the classroom, then indicates that they are going to play a game to try to make the classroom more like that. The class identifies list of "fouls" that interfere with a pleasant classroom, which are posted. Students are distributed among two or three teams, which can be changed periodically. During the week, usually for one period on each of 2–5 days, the teacher announces at some point that they are now going to play the Respect Game (ideally varying subjects and days). The teacher sets a timer for a brief interval, perhaps 5 minutes in the beginning but later stretching gradually to the whole period. If a foul occurs during that interval, the teacher immediately and without discussion makes a small check mark on the scoreboard and moves on. When the timer rings, every team with no fouls for that interval gets a point, which is posted on the scoreboard. At the end of the period, the team or teams with the highest scores are proclaimed the winners (and may receive some very small privilege). Used consistently for some months, the Good Behavior Game has produced powerful lasting effects on levels of prosocial behavior in natural settings, even over periods of years.

Corrections are required when disrespect occurs in a classroom; there is good evidence that low-level aggression tends to escalate if not addressed. Very consistent but modest negative consequences, coupled with opportunities to practice acting more appropriately ("new way replays"), are usually the best place to start. See also resources listed at the end of the chapter for additional behavior management materials.

6. *Implement activities and tools to increase the sharing of power to build community.* Building an inclusive school community characterized by recognition and respect, in which everyone is encouraged and supported to contribute from her or his own gifts and power, is the ultimate goal of projects related to enhancing school culture. Such efforts entail finding ways to ensure that everyone has a strong voice, feels welcomed in making his or her own unique contributions, and experiences a sense of responsibility to the collective. This means, among other things, honoring different groups within the school, each of which brings its own gifts, while actively giving up disrespect among groups and maintaining openness to enriching intergroup contact.

Constructing culture often requires serious discussion that clarifies the importance of everyone's contribution. Organized dialogues of many kinds are particularly useful for encouraging positive and respectful action with older children. Dialogues between students and staff, for example, in which each participant feels free to honestly describe his or her own experiences while genuinely listening to the experiences of others, can support voices that are often not heard. Those dialogues may focus on envisioning a school that works better for all, identifying and supporting personal and collective strengths, and planning collective action of many kinds. Student dialogues across groups (by gender, race, culture, or sexual orientation, for example), guided by questions that are likely to elicit different perspectives on the school, the community, and the larger world, can be very powerful; small-group activities may be useful in initiating conversation for such dialogues.

One of the best ways to support the realization of multiple gifts is through service learning and community service projects. Young people who are struggling with some areas of academic and social life often blossom when the right opportunity to make a real contribution emerges. The research suggests that meaningful interpersonal contact (like tutoring) or work that makes a clear contribution produce the best results, while assignments experienced as "busy work" (like filing or cleaning) do not. Individual efforts can be life-changing, and collective projects involving collaborative partnerships (including student–staff partnerships) build community spirit. Even if significant service learning and community service is already present, expansion is always possible. (Note that community service used as a consequence of negative behavior, though useful in some cases, involves different dynamics.)

Among such projects are those in which high school youth bring their talents as resources to prevention projects in elementary schools, including those that aim to build empowered nonviolent cultures and to eliminate bullying. Planning and actively engaging in such programs in their own schools or in the neighborhood are other common options. Active work on projects like murals, community gardens and playgrounds, community sculptures, and even school redesign are other opportunities, often calling for partnerships with others outside the school. Research projects, another possibility, can provide positive new experiences; planning and conducting a respect survey in the school or a survey of personal, associational, and institutional resources in a neighborhood are examples.

7. *Implement activities and tools to increase healing of conflicts.* Conflicts will emerge among any group of people who relate to each other closely over a period of time. Learning a standard framework for addressing such conflicts through repeated practice is an important form of social skills training, especially if used as standard practice in a classroom or school. One model that draws on considerable research begins by preparing each participant to listen respectfully, and then guiding those involved through a structured process in which each participant has an opportunity, in turn, to respond to the following questions:

- What happened here?
- How did that affect you? (optionally, if participant is developmentally able, "and others?")
- What could we do now to heal the damage?
- So what is our plan?

The final step is to provide recognition for contributions that participants have made to the healing process. Staff often require structured practice to make this kind of process work, without being sidetracked into refereeing exchanges of blame.

There is also a range of restorative circle and conferencing approaches that are supported by promising outcome data. Among these are healing circles that follow processes much like the outline above, but enlarged to include other members of classroom, school, or even neighborhood communities. Healing circles draw on traditional indigenous processes; for example, most rely on a talking circle format in which each question travels around the circle, and people speak only in their turn (often by passing a talking piece of some kind). One other somewhat similar process with strong support is Family Group Conferencing, a scripted process with Maori roots, often used as an alternative to suspension or court adjudication. Space precludes further discussion here, but extensive information about Family Group Conferencing is available at www.realjustice.org. It is important in using such processes to avoid "cultural appropriation"—acting as if one owns native traditions not one's own. The meaning of sacred practices is organically grounded in an intergenerational, lived cultural and spiritual reality. Professionals can learn and adapt practices from indigenous cultures, but that learning doesn't make them urban shamans or sacred circle-keepers.

8. *Monitor progress and maintain creative enthusiasm.* Projects that do not incorporate some form of simple feedback are likely to fade in the face of competing demands and priorities. For example, although improved school culture will contribute to test scores, this is a gradual process, while legal demands to demonstrate learning (often in very narrow ways) are often immediate. One valuable approach is the "chart on the wall." One or more simple charts can track a small number of variables over time. For example, ratings by staff and students regarding the frequency of each of the core practices can be graphed on a monthly or quarterly basis, as can annual respect surveys conducted among students, and in some cases the incidence of problem categories such as suspensions, disciplinary referrals, and fights. If the latter are used, it is essential that some positive variables also be tracked, since the real power in culture-building projects lies in increasing prosocial, pro-community actions. Successes demonstrated on the chart should be celebrated periodically, giving those involved opportunities to discuss what they have done and how they made it work so well (management research indicates this is a powerful form of recognition). Though some activities may be useful on an open-ended basis, successful projects also find ways to maintain creative energy by establishing processes for continual innovation. Changes should continue to draw from the evidence base. Still, there are an infinite number of possible program activities that can be tried, and so long as a process for evaluating each is in place, even wild creativity should sometimes be encouraged.

Tools and Practice Examples

South High School

South High School is a public school in a small midwestern city that has experienced significant demographic shifts in the past two decades. The school is now quite multiethnic, and it has experienced significant ethnic tensions in addition to problems almost universal in U.S. schools: harassment, peer group exclusion, and emotional and physical violence. A school social worker came up with a project designed to address some of these problems and began with a full staff-training event. As part of its PEACE POWER project, the school established an extensive system of recognition tickets, including public posting, public-address announcements, classroom efforts, and random drawings of tickets that produced awards. The school also conducts an annual Respect Month, which has included a public pledge campaign, the initiation of a Gay–Straight Alliance and a related Day of Silence, a Mix It Up Day, a powerful theatrical production, interethnic events, participation in citywide intergroup organizing, plus a dozen other events and activities that continue or repeat each year. The school is also experimenting with healing circles for certain conflicts and has developed strong youth representation in planning efforts, although the initial planning was conducted primarily by a core group of staff organized by the school social worker.

King High School

By contrast, King High School is an inner-city public school in one of the largest cities in the country. The program at King was also initiated by the school social worker, who first convinced the powerful school principal of the potential of such a project. From the beginning, the core planning group of 20 was a mix of youth and staff. They began their efforts by designing and distributing posters widely in the school to spark curiosity and interest. A recognition system used specially designed postcards that were collected twice a week from teachers and mailed out to students' homes. A system of daily public-address recognition designed by the youth began at about the same time. The group then selected activities to begin with, including a pledge, youth–staff dialogues, and an extensive poster campaign. The planners wrote small grants to initiate several student organizations under the PEACE POWER umbrella, including two specifically to support the powerful dreams and hopes of groups of African American young women. At that point, the entire teaching staff participated in a brief training workshop to bring them onboard. Plans are under way for larger community activities, and there is interest in additional conflict-resolution efforts. The project works to ensure that every youth participating in the effort at King (about 60 at this writing) has a clear and meaningful role.

Hillside Elementary School

The effort at Hillside Elementary School, located in a smaller city, is typical of work with elementary schools, where full staff planning is the ideal. Training workshops for staff included an introduction and one workshop on each of the core practices. Workshops began with presentation of the scientific underpinnings of each practice and a review of evidence-based strategies for each. Staff then discussed what they were already doing in each area, and they brainstormed about ways to go even further. Many of the ideas shared were very creative. For example, one teacher discussed a technique she used for teaching young children the steps in resolving conflicts. She had a large sheet with several sets of footprints facing each other, one pair for each step. As a child completed one step correctly, he or she moved up to the next. This school conducted monthly staff surveys of the frequency of core practices in the school, and the consistent increases clearly contributed to motivation.

Each of these projects is quite different; in fact every effort to shift school culture should be unique. However, efforts that are effective attend to the identified core practices, often in multiple ways. Although there are inevitable challenges (particularly when key staff leave), positive feedback tended to help maintain each of these projects.

Resources

Olweus, D. (1993). *Bullying at school: What we know and what we can do.* Cambridge, MA: Blackwell. Complete manual for bullying prevention.

PeaceBuilders: http://www.peacebuilders.com

Real Justice: http://www.realjustice.org. Inexpensive books and videos related to Family Group Conferencing and other restorative practices available for purchase.

Saving Our Schools. (1999). Two-video set from Heartland Media available at www.at-risk.com

Sidman, M. (2001). *Coercion and its fallout* (2nd ed.). Boston: Authors Cooperative. Available at www.behavior.org

Violent Times (1996). Three-video set from Attainment Co. Available from www.boystown.org

Key Points to Remember

The following summary points provide the basic framework for a successful effort to construct a school culture of nonviolent power and respect:

- A culture of nonviolent empowerment emerges from high levels of four core cultural practices: recognition, respect, shared power, and peacemaking.
- Evidence-based tools and activities should be preferred in action planning.
- The driving force behind an effective program is a small, creative, committed working group with strong administrative support.
- Effective programs must be adapted to fit the values, cultures, resources, and environment of each program through a process of creative shared power among multiple stakeholders, including students and staff.
- Staff must lead the way as models and active participants who, with other stakeholders, are responsible for the school culture.
- Regular, simple monitoring and feedback loops are necessary to ensure that gains achieved are maintained over time.

Assessing and Predicting Risk of Violence

Empirically Based Methods

Gary L. Bowen

Getting Started

On May 7, 2004, in Randallstown, Maryland, a drive-by shooting following a charity basketball game at a local high school left four students critically wounded. One of the two shooters charged the following day was a 17-year-old student who attended the high school. According to the police, the shootings were retaliation for a name-calling incident involving a girl, which had occurred earlier in the day (Associated Press, 2004). The next day, May 8, 2004, in Jonesboro, Arkansas, three empty chairs at high school graduation ceremonies symbolized missing classmates who were killed in a school shooting six years earlier. The two shooters, 11 and 13 at the time of the incident, both remain in a juvenile detention center (Rousseau, 2004).

Not every incident of school violence ends in death; nonetheless, fights, gang violence, rape and sexual assault, bullying, and other forms of physical and verbal harassment are all too common in lives of students—whether they are victims or witnesses. School incident reports (administrative data) and student surveys indicate that rates of school violence vary among schools and, for any one school, across time.

Although even one serious incident of school violence is too much, school violence, like many other problems, has a "tipping point" beyond which it spreads like an epidemic and places students in serious jeopardy of physical and psychological harm. According to Cantor and Wright (2002), 60% of violence occurs in just 4% of schools, and they group schools into four categories: no crime, isolated crime, moderate crime, and violent crime. In schools with high rates of violent crime, learning and academic performance are secondary to safety.

School social workers and other school-based professionals struggle to find methods to decrease the probability of school violence. Interventions to reduce school violence are, in part, efforts to decrease the risk factors associated with its occurrence; as these risk factors decrease, the probability of school violence also decreases. Interventions also strive to increase protective factors, which decrease the probability of violence either directly or by buffering the effects of risk factors.

Intervention success depends on targeting the risk and protective factors that reside both in the ecologies of schools and in the individuals who attend those schools (Fraser, 2004). School social workers need tools to assess and monitor rates of school violence and of risk and protective factors that have probabilistic linkages to its occurrence. In addition, they need a strategy for using this information to develop intervention and prevention strategies.

This chapter addresses strategies for assessing and predicting the risk of school violence. The review is framed by a seven-step planning strategy: results-focused planning (RFP). Working with student, school, and community stakeholder groups in planning strategies to decrease school violence (the performance team), a status quo assessment is the first step in this planning strategy. Four critical status quo data collection tasks are discussed here. A survey of students, the School Success Profile (SSP), is introduced as a tool that supports the status quo assessment for school social workers and other school-based professionals.

What We Know

RFP emerged from early attempts to help federal employees with the transition to the Government Performance Results Acts (P.L. 103-62). It builds on the performance-based and accountability literature that emphasizes intended outcomes, and the associated planning process supports evidence-based school social work practice (Orthner & Bowen, 2004; Raines, 2004). A key assumption of RFP is that intervention success is promoted when planning focuses on achieving defined performance goals. A seven-step process is used to help stakeholder groups move from identifying issues and concerns that hamper the achievement of performance goals to developing strategies to overcome barriers that restrict implementation of intervention and prevention strategies.

Step 1: Conduct a status quo assessment.

Step 2: Define desired results.

Step 3: Identify key partners and allies.

Step 4: Develop an action plan with each partner and ally.

Step 5: Specify the role and responsibilities of the performance team.

Step 6: Develop a monitoring and evaluation plan.

Step 7: Develop plans to overcome potential implementation hurdles.

RFP is also referred to in the literature as Results Management (Orthner & Bowen, 2004). My colleagues and I have used RFP as a strategy for working with community and school groups addressing a variety of issues and concerns, including school violence (Bowen, Bowen, Richman, & Woolley, 2002). In our use of the RFP process in schools, we work with principals to identify a performance team that will spearhead the planning process. In most cases, such a performance team is already in place, such as the school improvement teams that operate in many schools. We request that the performance team include a variety of stakeholders—teachers, parents, community members, and students. Typically, these performance teams have 10 to 12 members.

We have found that the RFP process in schools works most effectively in the context of survey data from students. The SSP is one such survey tool for middle and high school students, which yields information important to the status quo assessment (Bowen, Richman, & Bowen, 2002; Richman, Bowen, & Woolley, 2004). The SSP provides summary information on 22 core profile dimensions of a student's social environment and individual adaptation, including both neighborhood and school safety dimensions. Results from the SSP can be used to assess and monitor levels of school violence at school and factors associated with its occurrence.

What We Can Do

Status Quo Assessment

Effective planning requires good information. The first step in the RFP process involves conducting a status quo assessment, which includes estimating the magnitude of the problem or issue and identifying predictors or correlates that explain variation in the focal issue or concern. At least four types of information are needed to assess and predict the risk of violence and to plan an intervention strategy to combat it: (a) estimates about the current rate or incidence of school violence, (b) information on the risk factors associated with its occurrence, (c) information on protective factors that decrease the likelihood of school violence—assets that may also be used as resources in planning and implementing intervention strategies, and (d) information on the groups whose members are most at risk of being perpetrators, victims, or witnesses of school violence.

Estimating Current Rates

Intervention planning begins with an assessment to determine the current rate or level of the problem, issue, or challenge. Both student-based and survey-based empirical methods may be used to arrive at estimates about the potential incidence of school violence. Both methods depend on a meaningful definition of what constitutes school violence. The definition proposed by Astor, Vargas, Pitner, and Meyer (1999, p. 140) is used for purposes of the present review: "School violence covers a wide range of intentional or reckless behaviors that include physical harm, psychological harm, and property damage."

Actual reports of school violence provide one basis for estimates about school violence. Rates of school violence may vary, depending on whether counts are determined based on perpetrators, victims, or episodes. Such counts represent the number of incidents that have come to the attention of school officials and have been formally documented as meeting the definitional parameters of school violence over a specified period. These data can be aggregated across various levels (e.g., from classroom to school). Typically, these counts represent "floor" effects—low estimates of the actual level of school violence.

Survey-based estimates rely on the administration of surveys, either to the student population or to a probability sample of the student population, which ask students about behavior that meets definitional criteria of school violence. Students may report on themselves as being perpetrators or victims of school violence, or they may provide estimates about the general level of the problem in the student body, including questions about the level of safety they feel at school.

For example, the SSP asks students to report on the extent to which a number of crime- and violence-related behaviors are a problem at school (answers include "not a problem," "a little problem," and "a big problem"). In a nationally representative sample of middle and high school students who were administered the SSP, more than one in four students mentioned the following crime- and violence-related activities as being a "big problem" at school: fights among students (28%), stealing (27%), destruction of school property (27%), and student use of alcohol (28%) or illegal drugs (30%) (Bowen, Bowen, & Richman, 1998). In the context of these findings, it is not surprising that 38% of middle school students and 24% of high school students in the same survey reported that they were "sometimes or often afraid" of being hurt or bothered at school. These counts usually represent "ceiling" effects—upper limit estimates of what may be actually going on at school. (See also Box 3.1 for a discussion on focus groups)

It is interesting to compare the discrepancy between what comes to the attention of school officials (administrative reports) and what students report in surveys—the larger the gap, the greater the likelihood that school resources for addressing the presenting situation are inadequate or ineffective. In general, the number of identified cases of a problem will depend, in part, on the resources to investigate and handle these cases.

Whether estimates are based on administrative reports, survey data, or a combination of both, the level of reported violence reflects the total effect of current intervention and prevention strategies. If schools are unhappy with the level of school violence (i.e., dissatisfied with the status quo), efforts to reduce violence must involve intensifying current strategies, changing strategies, or some combination of continuity and change. Without alterations in the inputs, there is no reason to assume a decrease in negative outcomes. Such efforts are informed by knowledge about risk and protective factors associated with school violence.

Identifying Risk Factors

Risk factors are defined as influences that increase the probability of a negative outcome and decrease the probability of a positive outcome (Nash &

Box 3.1. Use of Focus Groups

Forming focus groups of students and teachers so as to better understand administrative and survey data is an important data collection strategy in the status quo assessment—satisfying the need to give a "voice" to the numbers. Recently, the School Success Profile (SSP) project team administered the SSP in a middle school in which a high proportion of students reported fights to be a "big problem." School staff agreed that fights were a problem, and this finding was documented in the administrative suspension records.

In focus groups with students, the school staff were surprised to learn that fights at school added excitement to what students perceived as boring and routine. Some students were described as fight promoters—they would select two students, who might not even have a problem with each other at the beginning of the day but who would be fighting by the end of the day. Many students reported that they attended school more as "spectators" than as participants. These findings were supported by SSP data showing low levels of student engagement and low participation in extracurricular activities. The combination of SSP data and focus group discussion shifted the focus of intervention from fights to strategies intended to increase student engagement and extracurricular participation.

Bowen, 2002). The social work literature is replete with studies that identify risk factors associated with high rates of school violence. For example, Bowen, Powers, Woolley, and Bowen (2004) identified risk factors associated with school violence in different ecological domains. In addition, Hawkins et al. (1998) have prepared a comprehensive and rigorous review of predictors of youth violence, and Sprague and Walker (2000) summarize major sources of threats to school safety, including school administrative and management practices. The unit of analysis in studies may be individuals, special groups, or the school as a whole.

These studies employ a variety of methodologies to predict the likelihood of violence, including both quantitative and qualitative data collection strategies. For example, examining profiles of either the victims or the perpetrators of school violence who come to the attention of school authorities can help identify risk factors. One such method is the work of the U.S. Secret Service to profile school shooters and to identify the antecedents in such exceptional cases of school violence (Vossekuil, Reddy, Fein, Borum, & Modzeleski, 2000). Risk factors may also be identified using location analysis, in which areas in the school with a high incidence of violence are mapped for intervention planning (Astor, Meyer, & Pitner, 1999) (see Chapter 1 p. 22). Finally, risk factors can be identified through the analysis of student survey data in an attempt to identify factors associated with high rates of school violence at either a student or an aggregate level (Eamon & Altshuler, 2004). Table 3.1 includes five sample school violence assessment and screening resources.

Although the identification of risk factors and their relative importance as correlates of school violence will vary across studies and in relation to the

---

Table 3.1 Sample School Violence Assessment and Screening Resources

Resource: U.S. Secret Service national threat assessment guide

Description: Threat assessment guide and information from the analysis of school shooters, including warning signs that may precede targeted violence.

Source: National Threat Assessment Center
U.S. Secret Service
950 H Street NW, Suite 9100
Washington, DC 20223
202-406-5470
http://www.treas.gov.usss/ntac

Resource: Early warning guide

Description: Publication sponsored by the U.S. Department of Education, Office of Safe and Drug Free Schools, and the U.S. Department of Juvenile Justice and Delinquency Prevention, which includes early warning signs of violent behavior for youth at risk.

Source: Dwyer, K. P., Osher, D., & Warger, W. (1998). Early warning, timely response: A guide to safe schools. Washington, DC: U.S. Department of Education. (ERIC Document Reproduction Service No. ED 418 372.) http://www.naea-reston.org/guide.pdf

---

Resource: Student-level assessment and screening procedures

Description: An excellent journal article that includes a discussion of multiple gating approaches, including a strategy developed by the authors for use with middle school students, to identify students at high risk of committing violent and aggressive acts. The authors offer important cautions about the use of such procedures.

Source: Sprague, J., & Walker, H. (2000). Early identification and intervention for youth with antisocial and violent behavior. Exceptional Children, 66, 367–379.

(continued)

Table 3.1 *(Continued)*

Resource: Mapping violence-prone public spaces

Description: A journal article that outlines procedures for identifying and reclaiming locations at school and surrounding the school where bullying and victimization are most likely to occur.

Source: Astor, R. A., Benbenishty, R., & Meyer, H. A. (2004). Monitoring and mapping student victimization in schools. Theory Into Practice, 43, 39–49.

Resource: School Success Profile (SSP)

Description: An ecologically based survey research tool for middle and high school students that can be used for assessing and monitoring school violence and selected factors associated with its occurrence. Summary information is presented on 22 core profile dimensions, and school staff receive both individual profiles, summarizing the responses for each student, and a group profile, summarizing responses for all students who complete the instrument. Evidence-based practice resources for each profile dimension are available for SSP users.

Source: Bowen, G. L., Richman, J. M., & Bowen, N. K. (2002). The School Success Profile: A results management approach to assessment and intervention planning. In A. R. Roberts & G. J. Greene (Eds.), Social workers' desk reference (pp. 787–793). New York: Oxford University Press. www.schoolsuccessprofile.org

research strategies employed, school social workers possess an evolving body of literature that informs this process. Surveys like the SSP allow school social workers to monitor risk factors associated with school violence; in situations in which risk factors exceed critical threshold points, the likelihood of school violence is increased. Thus, an important task of the performance team is to determine these critical threshold points.

Several conclusions emerge from a review of the literature. First, school violence has no single "cause"—it results from a combination of individual, relational, and situational factors that interact to increase the probability of school violence. Second, although there may be some central factors associated with every form of school violence, there are unique factors associated with each specific form of school violence. Finally, associated risk factors may vary across both population subgroups (gender) and school level (elementary, middle, and high). Consequently, although it is tempting to use risk and early warning checklists to screen either potential perpetrators or victims of school violence, the application of such checklists to individual students may lead to many false positives and negatives and is therefore not recommended (Dwyer, Osher, & Warger, 1998; Sprague & Walker, 2000). In a recent review of school violence prevention and intervention programs, Erickson, Mattaini, and McGuire (2004) conclude that the most successful programs address the culture and social climate of the school, rather than focusing on the deficiencies and problems of students or groups of students.

Identifying Protective Factors

Few situations are either all good or all bad. Most situations include a balance between the presence of risk factors that increase the probability of a negative outcome like school violence and protective factors that decrease the probability of a negative outcome (Nash & Bowen, 2002). Protective factors may simply be the opposite end of the same continuum as risks, or they may comprise factors separate from risks. Protective factors may directly influence the probability of school violence, or they may buffer or moderate the negative effects of risk factors. It is important that the status quo assessment reflect the full picture—both negatives and positives. Interventions to decrease the incidence of school violence are likely to be more effective when they promote protection in addition to addressing risks.

The strategies involved in identifying protective factors are similar to those used to identify risks. As is the case in assessing risk factors, the unit of analysis in studies of protective factors may be individuals, special groups, or the school as a whole. In addition, both quantitative and qualitative data collection strategies may be used. For example, examining the profiles of students who do not become victims or perpetrators of school violence can identify protective factors. In addition, protective factors can be identified through the analysis of student survey data, looking for individual, relational, and situational factors associated with low rates of school violence at either a student level or an aggregate level.

In general, the social work literature on the role of strengths and assets in decreasing school violence is less well developed than the literature on risk factors (Bowen, Powers, et al., 2004). Surveys like the SSP are invaluable in helping school social workers identify and monitor both the student- and the school-level assets and strengths that decrease the probability of school violence. The identification of protective factors requires sensitivity to the different forms of school violence and to how such strengths and assets may vary across population subgroups and across school settings.

Selecting Populations at Risk

Even in schools with high rates of school violence, students' relative risk of becoming either perpetrators or victims may vary. Selecting populations at risk involves identifying the subpopulations of students who are more likely to experience school violence directly, who are more likely to have risk factors associated with school violence, or who are less likely to have protective factors that decrease their vulnerability to violence. Although many interventions may be directed toward the whole school population (i.e., universal interventions), interventions may also be targeted to student groups on the basis on their demographic profile (i.e., selective intervention) or their risk profile (i.e., indicated intervention) (Bowen, Powers, et al., 2004). The targeting of intervention resources may be particularly important if resources are limited.

Next Steps

The six steps that follow the status quo assessment result in a plan of action. Although the performance team coordinates the planning process, the emphasis must be on *planning with* rather than *planning for* people. Students are seen as active participants in this process. An important focus of the RFP process is helping the performance team to value, acquire, and use information and tacit knowledge from students, employees, and other stakeholders to successfully plan, implement, and evaluate strategies to decrease the risk of violence.

Key Points to Remember

The status quo assessment, which includes the process of assessing and predicting school violence, is the cornerstone of the RFP sequence. We prefer to think of the results of this assessment as providing an "image" rather than the "reality" of the presenting situation. In addition to the tasks discussed here, the status quo assessment also involves a discussion of vision. We ask the performance team to develop a vision of a school with a low likelihood of violence. In particular, we ask participants to describe the social organizational processes in such a school, including the nature of interactions among students, between students and teachers, and among school employees. This vision is then compared to the images that result from the status quo assessment, including the use of data from the School Success Profile. The aim of RFP is to develop an action plan for closing the gap between image and vision.

4

Bullying

Best Practices for Prevention and Intervention
in Schools

Esther Howe
Elayne Haymes
Tanya Tenor

Getting Started

Bullying in schools has historically been a persistent problem worldwide. In the
United States, heightened attention to school violence in the past 15 years has
led to a focus on bullying as demanding attention. The realization that many of
the perpetrators of high-profile school shootings were themselves victims of
bullying has added urgency to this matter. In Europe, suicide among youngsters
who could no longer face their tormentors has led to the coining of the term
bullycide. According to a study from the National Institutes of Health, published
in the *Journal of the American Medical Association,* almost one third of all children
in grades 6 to 10 have experienced some form of bullying (Nansel et al., 2001).
Although bullying can and does occur in other environments, the majority of
bullying takes place in and around school buildings (Smith, Ananiadou, & Cowie,
2003).

Bullying is thought to be the most prevalent form of violence suffered by children (Haynie et al., 2001). For our purposes, we use English criminologist David
Farrington's 1993 definition of *bullying:* "Bullying is the repeated oppression, psychological or physical, of a less powerful person by a more powerful person."
In recent years, the Internet has increasingly been used for these activities, thus
leaving the victims vulnerable even at home. Bullying can include saying or writing inappropriate things about a person, deliberately excluding individuals from
activities, threatening or actually hurting them, making a person do things against
his or her own will, and teasing. This chapter will not address sexual harassment,
a specialized form of bullying, as it is discussed in a separate chapter.

Though other forms of violence in schools have either remained constant or
decreased, the reported incidence of bullying has increased (Rigby, 2002). Bullying
seems to peak in middle school and decline in high school. Approximately 7% of
eighth graders miss at least 1 day of school each month because they are afraid

of being bullied (Banks, 1997). Every year more than 160,000 students report missing some school because they are afraid. Both the widespread nature of the problem and the potential gravity of its consequences mandate that school personnel seek and implement sound evidence-based interventions to alleviate the problem.

What We Know

Research on the effectiveness of antibullying programs instituted in schools is neither strong nor definitive. There are, however, common characteristics shared by most of the programs: a whole-school approach to the problem, involvement of the wider community, inclusion of the subject matter in the curriculum, increased monitoring of student behavior, encouragement of students to seek help and subsequent provision of counseling services, and a plan to deal with cases of bullying. According to Rigby (2002), this final component is what varies most. Some programs, such as Olweus's (1993), emphasize "the need for clear rules" and the need "to apply sanctions when rules are broken." Other programs take a problem-solving approach that is focused less on assigning blame than on generating solutions. Two meta-analyses (Rigby, 2002; Smith et al., 2003) suggest that there is not enough evidence to favor one approach over the other.

Both analyses document the importance of a whole-school approach and of full staff support for the antibullying policy. Rigby concludes that "outcomes were closely related to how thoroughly the programs were implemented," *The specifics of the program are not as significant as the thoroughness with which it is carried out.* Thus, staff training is crucial to the success of any school-based antibullying program.

What We Can Do

The following interlocking program components will be discussed in descending ecological order: (1) an approach to involve the entire school staff; (2) life skills training groups in which all students participate; and (3) specific interventions targeted at individual perpetrators and victims. Though other components, such as better staff monitoring of playgrounds, hallways, and school bathrooms, parental involvement, and curriculum inclusion, are important, the focus of this chapter is to give explicit guidelines on how to implement the three components mentioned above.

Get the School Staff on Board

A significant barrier to the success of a bullying prevention program can be lack of understanding or compliance with the program. School social workers need to begin working with school staff as soon as a mandate has been handed down from the state or the school administration. The first step is to have the faculty and staff fill out a questionnaire (for an example, see Rigby's Bullying Pages at http://www.education.unisa.edu.au). Subsequently, the social worker should schedule several professional development meetings with the staff to discuss the findings of the questionnaire and to lay out the goals of the bullying prevention program. Any staff resistance should be dealt with openly, and staff's suggestions and concerns should be listened to. The school administration's policy on bullying should be clarified. Comprehensive guidelines on what is and is not considered bullying should be presented, as well as clear protocols on how to deal with incidents of bullying both in terms of the perpetrators and the victims. Assure the staff that all of you are in this together and that the school administration and your program will support them as the anti-bullying efforts progress. To that end, monthly refresher meetings in which new concerns and opportunities can be voiced should be held.

Prevention Interventions With All Students

Once staff support has been secured, work should begin with programs that affect all students. The school social worker should encourage teachers to incorporate information about the effects of bullying in their curricula, and they should have access to model curricular units and other resources. (See the Resources section for a list of antibullying Web sites.) School assemblies should be called to inform all students of state law regarding bullying and the school's policies and resources for dealing with bullying.

Whatever intervention the school chooses to use, it is essential to remember the importance of simple vigilance and oversight. In some instances, closer supervision of playgrounds, hallways, and bathrooms has led to a 50% decrease in bullying behavior and physical violence (Smith et al., 2003). Coy (2001) suggests the use of student volunteers to expand the "eyes and ears" of a bullying prevention program: "Students should be encouraged to report incidents of bullying by promising the students anonymity." An essential tool for helping students access help is a suggestion box in a discreet location, which enables students to leave anonymous notes about problems they have or observe. All students should know where it is.

Parental involvement is an essential component of an effective program. Parents should be told about the school's antiviolence/antibullying program and given clear descriptions of what is and is not considered bullying behavior, what the consequence are for children who engage in such conduct, and what resources, including staff, parents can avail themselves of if they fear for their children's well-being. A brochure telling parents the behavioral indicators to look out for is a useful tool for enlisting their support. The school social work should offer to speak on this topic at a meeting of the school's parent organization.

Life Skills Groups

An essential component of a whole-school approach is a prevention-focused life skills training group conducted in collaboration with each grade's scheduled health and/or social skills/life skills curriculum. Life skills training concentrates on prosocial decision making regarding anger management, conflict resolution, peer and family relations, and so on. These groups can be run by members of the school mental health team or by specially trained teachers.

All group sessions are designed to foster self-awareness and behavioral change. Topics include, but are not limited to, developing methods of self-discipline, identifying consequences before taking action, recognizing the effect of one's behavior on others, learning alternative ways of getting what one wants, mastering angry and aggressive impulses and thoughts, and learning peaceful methods of resolving conflicts (Coloroso, 2003).

The curriculum in these life skills groups should focus in part on bullying, besides helping children develop sound decision-making skills. (A model lesson of a 4-week curriculum on bullying is included in Section IV.) Life skills groups represent an opportunity to enhance all students' prosocial decision-making skills while increasing their sense of community, strengthening their social network, and thereby improving the social climate of the school as a whole. Students in such a school are less likely to bully, more likely to report bullying if they observe it, and more likely to seek help if they are victims. Some countries have focused on improving school climate as their major effort to reduce bullying behavior (Smith et al., 2003).

Working With Perpetrators and Victims

Even interventions focusing on victims and perpetrators initially use a prevention paradigm. Prevention, as it is understood in primary intervention, is a model for service predicated on the identification of unique behavioral indicators that are associated with the potential for violent behavior toward self and others (Fraser, Richman, & Galinsky, 1999). This aspect of the intervention usually proceeds according to steps outlined below.

Step 1: Identify students who have been the victims of bullying or who have been involved in a range of experiences that are high risk for aggressive acts. This goal can be realized through an annual, whole-school population survey completed at the beginning of each year as part of an assignment in an English, health, or life skills class. (Students should be allowed to refuse to fill out the survey without repercussions.)

The survey is used to assess and prioritize students for early contact and further evaluation by the staff. The survey asks questions pertaining to a range of social and emotional experiences that have been related in the literature to violent/bullying behavior as aggressor or victim (Fraser et al., 1999). Students assessed to have a high number of risk elements or who present a significant self-description indicating potential aggression or victimization behaviors are interviewed by a staff member as quickly as possible. Risk for bullying or victimization can be assessed in greater detail, and a plan can be developed that may include one or more individual and group modalities, using the prevention components described in the previous section. Staff must gain the trust of students identified as potential victims, perpetrators, and witnesses through carefully orchestrated but informal contacts—in the lunchroom, on the playground, in brief meetings, thus weaving a safety net of social support for students (Haymes, Howe, & Peck, 2003).

Step 2: Implement individual and group interventions when bullying has occurred. The intervention component of the program consists of individual and/or group sessions with antibullying staff, perpetrators, and victims. These incidents may be identified by other students, teachers, victims, or parents. Addressing individual acts of bullying after they occur leads to continued contact with school staff and/or referrals to community social service agencies for both the perpetrators and the victims. Parents should be notified and consent obtained for the staff to meet with their child on a regular basis. Parental support and involvement are made easier by negotiating this consent.

It is at this stage that the various antibullying programs diverge, predicated on whether the program supports a "rules and sanctions" approach or a problem-solving one. Currently there is no compelling evidence that one method is more effective than the other. Some schools now favor a mixed approach, basing the intervention chosen on the severity of the bullying and the responsiveness of the perpetrators to problem-solving methods (Rigby, 2002). For a detailed description of the most well documented rules-and-sanctions approach, see the materials on the Olweus Bullying Prevention program at http://www.modelprograms.samhsa.gov/print

For schools adopting a problem-solving approach, peer mediation can be used to address the actions of perpetrators and victims (Cowie & Sharp, 1996). A mental health worker or teacher trained in antibullying work, students involved in the incident, and neutral students trained in peer mediation skills are brought together for one session to hear the facts of the case from those directly involved. When possible, bystanders who saw the incident are also included. Consequences to the perpetrator for not participating in the mediation are outlined by a school administrator prior to the beginning of the meeting. Guidelines for implementing a mediation session can be found below. Research shows the effects of this intervention are strongest for the victims, who report *feeling* less bullied.

Students—victim and perpetrator—develop a behavioral contract to avoid future incidents, and the perpetrator must make symbolic or actual restitution to the victim, depending on the nature of the incident. Where indicated, students will be referred for additional interventions. Parents are informed of the mediation and its outcome, and their consent to therapeutic sessions is obtained. (See Resources to refer to other interventions using the problem-solving approach.) Treatment goals and treatment techniques are developed from evidence-based practice methods for intervening with both the bullies and the bullied.

Working With the Victims of Bullying

Students who are victims of bullying are typically anxious, insecure, and cautious. They tend to have low self-esteem and rarely defend themselves or retaliate when confronted by students who bully them (Banks, 1997). Outcomes for the child who has been bullied can include depression, isolation, poor school attendance, and diminished grades. At the extreme, bullied children can exhibit patterns of irrational retaliation or suicide.

To reduce the social isolation often exhibited by victims of bullying, teachers should implement cooperative learning techniques in their teaching methods. In addition, victims, who often suffer from poor social functioning (Haynie et al., 2001), should be involved in social skills training groups to enhance their understanding of social cues as well as to provide them with better responses to threats of bullying. Also, research by Young and Holdorf (2003) points to the validity of implementing solution-focused brief therapy support groups for victims of bullying.

Working With the Bullies

Bullies generally exhibit poor psychosocial functioning in comparison to nonbullying classmates. In addition, they tend to be unpopular—but more popular than their victims (Haynie et al., 2001). The lack of self-regulation in their behavior and their risk for future involvement in crime and delinquent behavior make focused interventions a vital part of a school's antibullying efforts. Available research suggests interventions with bullies similar to those suggested for their victims: cooperative learning techniques in the classroom and social skills support groups to reduce aggressive behaviors and strengthen positive social interactions. In addition, there must be consistent enforcement of nonpunitive, graduated consequences along with parental involvement to discuss behaviors of concern, consequences for conduct violations, and systems of support.

Underlying all the recommended interventions is the theme of social support. It is a key ingredient for any antibullying effort, helping the victims, the bullies, and the bystanders. The value of a network of social support should not be underestimated.

Family sessions are scheduled as needed to inform parents of serious aggressive behavior problems and incidents of bullying behavior or victimization. Increasing communication with parents enables them to participate more actively in the "school-family partnership" (Bowen, 1999). Parent awareness and participation are a vital component of a bullying-prevention program, essential for the support of children who are at risk of committing or who have committed acts of bullying as well as for the child who has been a victim. Telephone communication, in-school conferences, and home visits are included among valuable outreach efforts.

All aspects of the school's organizational and curricular components should be taken into consideration when adapting the basic elements of a bullying-prevention or intervention program. The various components must be tailored to the culture of the school and the specific characteristics of the community. A coordinator's clear understanding of possible barriers to implementation will enable him or her to develop the necessary relationships within the school and in the community.

Tools and Practice Examples

To reinforce the value we attach to life skills groups in the prevention of and intervention with bullying behavior, we present a comprehensive lesson plan in its entirety. This module is one part of a four-module antibullying unit within a broader life skills curriculum in a middle school. The curriculum includes most components of the evidence-based best practices delineated in this chapter. An anticipated by-product is the strengthening of social ties throughout the school.

Bullying Lesson One: What Is Bullying?

Objective: To introduce bullying and to explore its prevalence

Grades: 6/8

Time: 25–30 minutes

Materials: Board and markers, "Why Children Bully" sheet, Bully Survey

1. Tell the class that you are starting a unit to prevent bullying. Explain that the goal of this unit is to stop bullying in the classroom, hallway, and school bus. You will learn in this lesson the steps that can prevent bullying.
2. Ask the class to define a bully. You can use one of their definitions or this one: someone who hurts or intimidates other people.
3. Pass out the "Why Children Bully" sheet to the class. Go through sheet with class.
4. Under the "Ways students bully" question, give examples for each category. For physical: spitting, tripping, pushing, shoving, destroying another's things, hitting. Social: gossiping, spreading rumors, ethnic or racial slurs, excluding, humiliating. Verbal: name-calling, teasing, mocking, verbal threats of aggression. Intimidation: graffiti, making a public challenge, coercion.
5. Divide the students into groups of three to six. Ask the groups to rate 1–5 which one of the ways outlined in "Why Children Bully" happens the most at school.

6. Ask the groups to rate 1–5 which one of the ways outlined in "Who is a bully?" is the truest. Ask the groups to rate 1–4 which one of the ways outlined in "Ways students bully" happens the most at school. Ask the groups to rate 1–4 which one of the ways outlined in "Whom do bullies most often pick on?" is the truest. Ask reporters to share the group's results.

7. Pass out the Bully Survey. Make sure the students don't put their names on the top of the sheet. Questions 1 and 2 are optional. Explain that answers won't be disclosed.

8. Review what a bully is, and tell the class they will learn effective ways to deal with bullying in this unit. Ask students to hand in their surveys.

Why do students bully?
1. To gain power.
2. To get attention or become popular.
3. To get material things.
4. To act out problems at home.
5. To copy another person they admire.

Who is a bully?
1. A person who doesn't care if bad things happen to other people.
2. A person who doesn't feel bad when he or she hurts others.
3. A person who likes to be in charge and always gets his or her way.
4. A person who believes others deserve to get bullied.
5. A person who is bullied at home by his or her parents, brothers, or sisters.

Ways students bully
1. Physical aggression
2. Social alienation
3. Verbal aggression
4. Intimidation

Whom do bullies most often pick on?
1. Students who are smaller.
2. Students who don't have that many friends.
3. Students who don't stick up for themselves or get help from an adult.
4. Most anybody, if they think they can get away with it.

What can happen to people who get bullied?
1. Feel scared, alone, and sad
2. Don't like school

3. Get headaches and stomachaches
4. Don't feel good about themselves

Bully survey

1. How do you most often feel at school?
   Answer: (a) Very Sad (b) Sad (c) OK (d) Happy (e) Very Happy
2. The adults at my school are:
   (a) not helpful (b) sometimes helpful (c) always helpful
3. How do you feel in these places? (a) Unsafe (b) OK (c) Safe
   In the classroom
   On the playground
   In the lunchroom
   Going to and from school
4. How often do other students hit, kick, or push you?
5. How often do other students say mean things to you?
6. If you have been bullied this year, whom have you told?
7. If you have been bullied this year, who has helped?
8. How often do you hit, kick, or push?
9. How often do you say mean things?
10. How many people do you think are lonely at school?
11. Do you feel lonely at school?
12. List three students you like to do things with:
13. List three students you don't like to be with:
14. List three students who most need friends:

Additional modules deal with how students can help prevent bullying and get help.

Resources

The following sources provide access to relevant research, tools, and materials for school-based practitioners wishing to develop bullying prevention and intervention programs in their settings:

Avoid violence: Try mediation. Provided by Youth in Action, National Youth Network. http://sadonline.com/campaign/mediation.

ERIC/CASS Virtual Library on Bullying in School. ERIC Clearinghouse on Counseling & Students Services. http://ericcass.uncg.edu/virtuallib/bullying

ERIC Digest. Bullying in schools. (1997). http://www.ed.gov/databases/ERIC_Digests

Dr. Rigby's Bullying Pages. http://www.education.unisa.edu.au. This site also leads to comprehensive resources for both educators and school-based mental health practitioners looking for intervention strategies specific to the needs of their school's population.

Olweus Bullying Prevention. http://www.modelprograms.samhsa.gov/print.

Other Suggested Resources

The no-blame approach. This is a nonpunitive approach to dealing with bully/victim problems in schools. Generally considered to be more appropriate for use in primary schools.

Method of shared concern. This is another nonpunitive approach to bullying. Has been used successfully worldwide.

Mindmatters. A service aimed at promoting the mental health of high school students; it includes a program that addresses the issue of bullying and how it can be countered by schools.

A manual for schools and communities. This manual, provided by the California Department of Education, is comprehensive in its coverage of bullying in schools and is highly instructive.

Key Points to Remember

We conclude with the caveat that the research on the effectiveness of antibullying interventions is not strong. Rigby (2002) points out that the interventions *do* work, but not as effectively as one would hope. It is not clear, given that most interventions are multilayered, which component counts most for positive outcome. We have reviewed the most well-researched, evidence-based interventions: involvement of all the stakeholders in a school, prevention through life skills curricula, problem-solving approaches and those that focus on rules and consequences. Two factors emerge with clarity: (1) the exact components of the program do not matter as much as the quality and thoroughness with which the interventions are implemented; and (2) given the potentially severe consequences of bullying, it is a moral imperative to continue to implement such programs and to formulate and revise the programs based on solid evidence.

An Evidence-Based Approach to Management of Students Who Wish to Harm Others

James K. Nash

Getting Started

This chapter describes an evidence-based approach to management of physical aggression in elementary and middle school students. Drawing from a public health prevention framework, the chapter presents strategies for *selective* intervention (also known as early intervention) with this population (Mrazek & Haggerty, 1994). Selective intervention targets students who display elevated levels of aggression relative to the general population of same-age students, but who do not display a level of aggression that calls for intensive treatment. In contrast, universal intervention (or primary prevention) targets all students in a school regardless of risk status, and indicated intervention (treatment) targets students who have a specific problem or diagnosis (e.g., conduct disorder). Other chapters of this book describe universal and indicated intervention, as well as strategies for crisis intervention. It is useful to note that many programs suitable for selective intervention can also be used in primary prevention and treatment.

Evidence-based practice includes a focus on the research base of intervention. However, the term *evidence based* has a broader meaning (Gambrill, 2003). Evidence refers not only to research results regarding the effectiveness of interventions but also to consumer preferences and clinical wisdom. It refers to research-based knowledge of risk and protective factors and of the processes that lead to, and inhibit, a problem such as aggression. Evidence also refers to knowledge of characteristics that are unique to a particular child, family, school, or community, and to information about the influence of cultural differences. In sum, evidence-based practice is a collaborative process between practitioners and consumers in which all of these types of evidence are used to guide practice (Fraser & Galinsky, 2004).

What We Know

Understanding Student Aggression: An Overview
Aggressive behavior by students has serious consequences for individuals and schools. Victims experience physical injury and, potentially, psychological trauma. Student aggression disrupts the learning and social climate of schools and classrooms (Small & Tetrick, 2001). For perpetrators, elevated levels of aggression

in elementary or middle school represent a potent risk factor for future chronic aggressive behavior, academic failure and dropout, delinquency, and substance use (Dodge & Pettit, 2003).

The rate of all aggressive acts (including simple assault) in schools fell slightly during the 1990s, from 48 per 100,000 students in 1992 to 43 per 100,000 in 1998. The reduction in rates has accelerated in this century. Rates in 2000 and 2001 were, respectively, 26 and 28 per 100,000 students. Rates of more serious types of violence (e.g., rape and aggravated assault) remained stable—at about 10 per 100,000 students—during the 1990s, although a reduction occurred by 2000 and 2001 (5 and 6 per 100,000 students, respectively). Students' perceptions of school safety also changed during this period. In 1995, 12% of students reported being afraid at school, compared with 6% in 2001 (DeVoe et al., 2003; Small & Tetrick, 2001).

Reduction in rates of student aggression is good news, to be sure. Nevertheless, ongoing attention to selective intervention is warranted. Urban schools and schools predominantly serving students of color continue to experience higher levels of student aggression compared to majority culture, suburban, and rural schools. A higher percentage of students report being afraid in the former types of schools (DeVoe et al., 2003). Moreover, rates of aggression aimed at teachers remained stable over the past several years. In 1993–1994, 10% of teachers reported being threatened with injury by a student, and 4% reported being physically attacked. Rates in 1999–2000 were 9% for threats and 4% for attacks (DeVoe et al., 2003).

Accessing and Using Evidence

School social workers are well situated to build on the gains of the past decade and to meet ongoing challenges associated with student aggression through evidence-based selective intervention. Although many programs aimed at managing student aggression have not undergone evaluation (Flannery et al., 2003), evidence of the effectiveness of a growing number of programs is available. Web-based resources that describe in detail the available evidence—and how to use evidence critically—appear in Table 5.1. Terms for categorizing programs (e.g., "proven" vs. "model") differ across Web sites, but criteria for assessing the research base of programs are consistent with those identified by Rones and Hoagwood (2000).

A Web site that may be of particular interest to school social workers is that of the Collaborative for Academic, Social, and Emotional Learning (CASEL). The site provides details (e.g., research base, target) of school-based programs that can be used as selective intervention. It also contains a book chapter that provides a rationale for school-based interventions aimed at promoting social and emotional competence in students as a means of increasing academic achievement. The Web site of the Campbell Collaboration (CC) may come to serve as a gold standard for providing evidence of program effectiveness (Gambrill, 2003). The CC includes representatives of social welfare and educational agencies

Table 5.1 Web Resources for Selective Intervention

Site and Sponsor: Collaborative for Academic, Social, and Emotional Learning (CASEL). A collaborative of scholars and others from universities, institutes, and advocacy groups (including Penn State University, University of Illinois at Chicago).

URL: www.casel.org

Content: The site includes conceptual material that develops an argument for the importance of promoting social and emotional learning as a means of promoting academic achievement (i.e., the central mission of schools). It includes information on model and promising programs. *Safe and sound: An education leader's guide to evidence-based social and emotional learning (SEL) Programs* is available at the site. There is an emphasis on comprehensive (e.g., schoolwide) approaches and universal prevention, but many of the reviewed programs are likely to be useful as selective interventions.

Site and Sponsor: The Campbell Collaboration. Domestic and international agencies and universities (e.g., University of Pennsylvania, Swedish Council for Social Research, UK Home Office).

URL: www.campbellcollaboration.org

Content: This site contains systematic reviews of research on educational, social, psychological, and criminological interventions. A number of these are suitable as selective interventions for managing student aggression. Currently, a limited number of reviews are available, and many more are listed as under way but not yet accessible via the Web.

Site and Sponsor: Office of Juvenile Justice and Delinquency Prevention (OJJDP), U.S. Department of Justice

URL: www.ojjdp.ncjrs.org

Content: This Web site includes content on the prevalence of delinquency including aggressive acts, on research into the causes and consequences of delinquency, and on effective prevention strategies. Many OJJDP publications on topics of interest (e.g., school violence, creating safe schools) are available as PDF files for download. The authors of OJJDP publications are often top scholars in a particular field

Site and Sponsor: U.S. surgeon general's report on youth violence. U.S. Department of Health and Human Services (2001).

URL: www.surgeongeneral.gov/library/youthviolence

Content: This report is available in its entirety or in sections as a PDF file. Chapter 5 describes demonstrated and promising programs, some of which can be used as selective interventions in schools. It also identifies programs that do not work.

Site and Sponsor: Identifying and implementing educational practices supported by rigorous evidence: A user friendly guide. U.S. Department of Education (December 2003).

(continued)

Table 5.1 *(Continued)*

URL: www.ed.gov/rschstat/research/pubs/rigorousevid/rigorousevid.pdf

Content: This report provides a definition of evidence-based practice and presents guidelines that practitioners can use to assess the quality of research on program effectiveness. It as available as a PDF file.

Site and Sponsor: Substance Abuse and Mental Health Services Administration (SAMHSA) Model Programs, U.S. Department of Health and Human Services

URL: http://www.modelprograms.samhsa.gov

Content: The SAMHSA Web site provides details (e.g., target, elements, costs, research base) of *model, effective,* and *promising* programs, many of which are suitable for selective intervention. Of note, program descriptions include information on tracking fidelity and on characteristics (e.g., race/ethnicity, urban) of the samples with whom the reviewed programs were developed and tested. Program summaries with details are available to download as PDF files.

Site and Sponsor: Center for the Study and Prevention of Violence. University of Colorado

URL: www.colorado.edu.cspv/blueprints

Content: The "Blueprints" section of this site distinguishes model and promising violence prevention programs and describes the scope (i.e., universal, selective, or indicated), content, outcomes, and costs of programs. It summarizes the types and results of research studies on effectiveness. The site identifies other Web sites on evidence-based practice, as well as the criteria these sites use to evaluate practices.

Site and Sponsor: Promising Practices Network on Children, Families, and Communities. Private foundations and institutes including Annie E. Casey and Packard Foundations, and Rand Corporation

URL: www.promisingpractices.net

Content: The programs described at this site target a wide variety of child and family domains, and many appear to be best suited as universal interventions. Some programs may be useful as selective interventions for managing student aggression.

Site and Sponsor: What Works Clearinghouse, U.S. Department of Education

URL: www.w-w-c.org

Content: This site aims to serve as a central source of information on science-based education programs, some of which target social and emotional competence. The project is, apparently, in development, but it promises to be a useful resource in the future.

and universities in the United States and abroad. Of note, the CC reviews are described as comprehensive and systematic, and they cover published and unpublished studies.

In addition to information on the research base of programs, a number of Web sites in Table 5.1 provide other content needed for evidence-based selective intervention. For example, the site of the Office of Juvenile Justice and Delinquency Prevention (OJJDP) and the report on youth violence by the U.S. surgeon general describe research into the nature, causes, and consequences of student aggression. This information can help practitioners and consumers understand how individual and environmental factors interact over time to influence students' use of aggression. Such knowledge guides selection of a suitable program or set of programs (Fraser & Galinsky, 2004; Fraser, Kirby, & Smokowski, 2004). A Web-accessible report published by the U.S. Department of Education (DOE) describes various research designs and their strengths and limitations. Practitioners can use the DOE report as a guide for assessing critically the quality of research on program effectiveness.

Research-based information about factors that contribute to student aggression and about the effectiveness of interventions is a key component of evidence-based practice. However, other types of information are needed. Fraser and Galinsky (2004) emphasized the importance of integrating research-based information about risk, protection, and intervention programs with knowledge of *local conditions*, such as the student and staff profile of a school or neighborhood characteristics. Additionally, knowledge of how risk and protective factors operate differently across cultural, racial, and gender subgroups is essential when selecting an approach. These issues highlight a need to identify characteristics of the target population and samples (e.g., European American males, Latina girls) that were included in the available research. For example, a proven program aimed at reducing aggression may be unsuitable for rural students if the program was developed and tested only in urban schools. Programs developed and tested solely with European American students may lack effectiveness with, or harm, students of color (Bernal & Scharrón-Del-Río, 2001). The Web site of the Substance Abuse and Mental Health Services Administration (SAMHSA) provides details of the target population and samples of the studies of many of the intervention programs listed on the site.

What We Can Do

Evidence-Based Selective Intervention

Goals of selective intervention with students who display elevated levels of aggression include protecting students and teachers from harm, improving school and classroom culture, preventing inappropriate special education placement, and preventing future aggression. Many selective intervention programs include a focus on increasing students' social and emotional competence, which has been linked to improved academic achievement (Zins, Bloodworth, Weissberg, & Walberg, 2004).

Ecological Focus

Attention to the broad ecology of childhood is likely to result in more successful outcomes for selective intervention with this population (Fraser et al., 2004). For example, referral of a family to community resources is a feasible strategy in many schools. Individual-focused selective intervention programs can also be delivered within a context of comprehensive primary prevention that targets the whole school (Greenberg et al., 2003).

Intervention Steps

Evidence-based selective intervention with students who display elevated levels of aggression requires completing a series of related steps:

- Conducting screening and assessment
- Developing an intervention plan
- Implementing the plan and evaluating the effects of the intervention

There is nothing new about the steps themselves; they are central to social work practice. However, there are specific guidelines for completing the steps in a manner that is consistent with an evidence-based approach (see, e.g., Fraser & Galinsky, 2004)

Conducting Screening and Assessment

Selective intervention begins with *screening* to identify a pool of students who may be displaying problematic levels of aggression. Screening leads to an individualized *assessment* of a particular student and his or her environment to determine whether selective intervention is warranted and to identify salient risk and protective factors that are amenable to change. Assessment should also identify students who are in immediate need of more intensive treatment. Screening and assessment often involve the use of established measures and procedures with demonstrated reliability and validity (see, e.g., Williams, Ayers, Van Dorn, & Arthur, 2004). However, existing procedures that track students' behavior (e.g., behavior referrals) can be valuable sources of information. Assessment should always occur in collaboration with the family and teacher to develop a shared understanding of why, when, and under what circumstances a student becomes aggressive.

Tools and Practice Exa mples

Develop a Plan

Assessment-based knowledge of the child—environment system is linked with knowledge of risk and protective processes and available programs to develop an individualized intervention plan. An intervention plan should begin with a statement of desired short-term outcomes (e.g., reduced exposure to risk, increased availability of protective factors) and long-term outcomes (e.g., reduced use of aggression). The plan should specify the program or programs that have been selected to bring about these outcomes, and it should detail procedures for tracking progress toward targeted outcomes.

The Web sites listed in Table 5.1 are sources for assessing the quality of research-based evidence about risk, protection, and intervention in the area of student aggression. As practitioners, family members, and teachers evaluate the evidence available from these and other sources, they can use the following questions (Fraser & Galinsky, 2004; Fraser et al., 2004) to guide decision making about an intervention plan for a particular student:

- What individual and environmental risk factors are known to increase the likelihood of aggression in students who are similar to this student? Are any of these risk factors present for this student and, if so, which ones? Are the risk factors amenable to change via intervention?
- To what extent is there a shared understanding among the family and the student, the worker, the teacher, and others, that these risk factors are important?
- Is there evidence of protective factors that can modify the effects of risk for students similar to this student? Do these protective factors exist, or can they be developed, for this student?
- Is there evidence that particular intervention strategies or programs are effective in reducing risk or building protection for students who are similar to this student? How strong is the evidence? What are the characteristics of the students (classrooms, communities, families) with whom the program or strategy was developed and tested?
- Is the strategy or program acceptable to the family and the child? Is it feasible given the unique situation of this student at this school? Are there disadvantages to its use (e.g., labeling, cost, disruption of a student's schedule or classroom climate)?
- To what extent is the program or strategy specified? Is a manual or guide available that spells out exactly what to do and how to adapt the program when this is desirable?
- Does the available evidence identify commonly used programs or strategies that do not work or that may be harmful?

Select an Evidence-Based Program

As Table 5.1 clearly shows, there is an abundance of research-based evidence on programs that can be used as selective intervention for student aggression. Recent literature (e.g., Greenberg et al., 2003) has summarized much of the evidence and provided general conclusions to guide the process of using the literature to develop an intervention plan:

- Many effective programs include a focus on skill building (e.g., problem-solving skills, peer interaction skills) as a means of promoting social and emotional competence and reducing aggression in students.
- Detailed manuals or curricula that specify exactly what to do are essential elements of many effective programs.
- Where possible, long-term programs—those continuing over 1 or more academic years—are generally considered more effective than short-term programs.
- Primary prevention programs that target an entire classroom or school, for example, by providing skills training to all students, developing schoolwide rules and contingencies for positive behavior, or strengthening the instructional practices of teachers, produce better outcomes than do programs that focus solely on changing a particular student.
- Some effective school-based programs include a focus on family factors, for example, promoting a positive family atmosphere or building parenting skills.

Warnings: Identifying a particular student as being "at risk" carries with it a potential for labeling, and this can harm the student (Dodge & Pettit, 2003). Thus, screening should not occur in the absence of safeguards against such harm. One such example of a safeguard is to provide consultation to teachers and other school staff. A related concern involves delivering selective intervention to several students who display increased levels of aggression. Interventions to groups consisting solely of aggressive students have been shown to lead to negative rather than positive outcomes (see, e.g., Dishion, McCord, & Poulin, 1999).

Implement the Program

During program implementation, there should be an emphasis on maintaining and tracking treatment fidelity—that is, implementing the program as it is intended—and on tracking progress toward short- and long-term outcomes. Descriptions of model programs at the SAMHSA Web site (see Table 5.1) include a section on fidelity, but this does not typically describe how to track fidelity or a student's level of exposure to the program. Manualized programs may include materials for tracking fidelity. When these are not available, simple forms can be developed to gather this information. Procedures for tracking fidelity can be burdensome, but this is a key element in being able to demonstrate the effectiveness of the program.

Tracking progress toward short- and long-term outcomes is another key process. A single-subject design is suitable for most situations (see, e.g., Abell &

Hudson, 2000). Practitioners, families, students, and teachers should reach a shared decision about which outcomes to track. There should be an emphasis on using established, culturally relevant, and user-friendly measures of risk and protective factors and aggression. Ideally, an evaluation plan will also emphasize outcomes with high ecological validity for which data are already being collected. For example, students who have problems with aggression may receive referrals to the office because of their behavior. Many schools keep track of such referrals. Thus, indicators of progress may be the number of referrals and, relatedly, the amount of time spent outside class because of behavior.

Key Points to Remember

An evidence-based approach to selective intervention with students who display elevated levels of aggression requires using different types of information from a variety of sources to develop and implement a plan that fits the circumstances of a particular school. Research-based information about the processes that lead to aggression and about effective intervention programs is at the heart of an evidence-based approach. Equally important is information about local conditions and cultural differences, clinical wisdom, and collaboration between families and school staff. Finally, recent research clearly indicates that combining a focus on identified students with attention to the broader environment in which these students function is likely to result in more positive outcomes.

6

Peer Conflict

Effective Resolution Strategies

Debra J. Woody

Getting Started

Extreme acts of violence in schools across the country have increased interest in school-based conflict resolution programs over the last 5 years. Fortunately, such horrendous violence as the acts that occurred at Columbine High School are relatively rare. However, these situations have advanced our understanding of the effects that unresolved conflicts can have on students, teachers, and the school environment and have brought to light the more common, chronic, less extreme acts of violence that occur daily at many school campuses. These chronic acts of violence occur in the form of verbal threats, cursing, name calling, insults, racial slurs, pushing, grabbing or shoving, punching or kicking, and fighting (Bastian & Taylor, 1991; Opotow, 1989). School-based conflict resolution programs have been developed to provide students with skills to better handle, manage, and resolve conflict and to teach and promote tolerance and acceptance among students and school personnel.

What We Know

Research reports on the effects of school-based conflict resolution programs have been positive throughout the literature of social work and other mental health professions. Results from these empirical investigations indicate that teaching conflict resolution skills to students increases their knowledge of nonviolent means to conflict resolution (Johnson, Johnson, Dudley, Mitchell, & Fredrickson, 1997; Woody, 2001), promotes the development of a more positive attitude about nonviolent conflict resolution methods (Dudley, Johnson, & Johnson, 1996; Stevahn, Johnson, Johnson, & Laginski, 1996), increases students' ability to apply nonviolent methods (Johnson et al., 1997; Stevahn et al., 1996; Woody, 2001), reduces the frequency of violent confrontations in the schools (DuRant, Treiber, Getts, & McCloud, 1996; Johnson, Johnson, & Dudley, 1992; Stevahn, Johnson, Johnson, Green, & Laginski, 1997), and has a positive effect on the overall school climate (Burrell, Zirbel, & Allen, 2003). Some students have transferred the skills learned in conflict resolution to nonclassroom and nonschool settings (Johnson,

Johnson, Dudley, Ward, & Magnuson, 1995). These outcomes were true regardless of the age group targeted in the conflict resolution program.

School-based conflict resolution programs are also recognized as cost effective (Batton, 2003). In one report, a cost-benefit analysis compared the cost of a statewide conflict resolution program to the cost of school detentions, expulsions, in-school suspensions, Saturday schools, and other types of disciplinary actions. The cost of the conflict resolution program was less than one-fourth the cost of the disciplinary programs.

What We Can Do

In selecting a conflict resolution program, it is helpful to know the characteristics of programs that have been found most effective. Several key ingredients found in successful conflict resolution programs are summarized in Box 6.1 (Dusenbury, Falco, Lake, Brannigan, & Bosworth, 1997).

Other investigators suggest several factors characteristic of ineffective violence prevention programs (Dusenbury et al., 1997). They warn that programs with these characteristics (presented in Box 6.2) may actually increase aggressive behavior.

One last consideration about effective conflict resolution programs is that they are often based on social learning theory, attribution theory, and anger replacement therapy, with specific curriculum content related to these theories included in the program. The essential content areas that should be included are listed in Box 6.3.

In addition to the elements and specific content included in conflict resolution programs, there are several different types of conflict resolution programs identified in the literature. In one approach, for example, conflict resolution material is infused into regular academic teaching materials (see, for example, Stevahn et al., 1997; Stevahn et al., 1996). In another approach, conflict resolution skills are taught to a select group of students who become peer mediators (see for example, Johnson et al., 1995). And in other programs, groups of students identified as "high risk" were targeted to receive conflict resolution training (see, for example, DuRant et al., 1996; Paschall & Flewelling, 1997). However, the more comprehensive the program, the more the aspects of successful programs identified above can be included in the program.

Tools and Practice Example

A Comprehensive Conflict Resolution Model
In this section I will present an example of a comprehensive school-based conflict resolution approach, constructed and used by two social workers in an

Box 6.1. Key Components of Successful Conflict Resolution Programs

1. A comprehensive approach that includes family, peers, media, and the community (including the school community)
2. Programs that begin in kindergarten or first grade and are reinforced across the school years
3. Programs that go beyond violence prevention to include conflict resolution skills
4. Programs appropriate for the developmental level of the students targeted
5. Programs that teach students how to manage conflict instead of how to eliminate all conflict
6. Program content that promotes personal and social competencies
7. Interactive techniques that use group work, cooperative learning, discussion, and role plays or behavioral rehearsal to develop personal and social skills.
8. Program content that includes materials that are culturally sensitive to groups represented in the student body
9. Programs that include teacher training and development
10. Programs designed to promote effective classroom management strategies, including good and effective discipline and positive control in the classroom
11. Programs that include activities that foster norms against violence, aggression, and bullying
12. An approach that teaches all students—not just a select few—how to resolve conflicts

Adapted from Johnson & Johnson (1995), "Why violence prevention programs don't work and what does." Educational Leadership, 52(5), 63–68. Reprinted with permission. The Association for Supervision and Curriculum Development is a worldwide community of educators advocating sound policies and sharing best practices to achieve the success of each learner. To learn more, visit ASCD policies at www.ascd.org. Also adapted from Dusenbury, Falco, Lake, Brannigan, & Bosworth (1997), "Nine critical elements of promising violence prevention programs." Journal of School Health, 76(10), 409–414. With the permission of Blackwell Publishers.

Box 6.2. Six Elements of Ineffective Conflict Resolution Programs

1. Using scare tactics
2. Adding a violence prevention program to a school system that is already overwhelmed
3. Segregating aggressive students into a separate group for any purpose
4. Programs that are too brief and not supported by a positive school environment
5. Programs that focus only on self-esteem enhancement
6. Programs that only provide information

Adapted from Dusenbury, Falco, Lake, Brannigan, & Bosworth (1997, pp. 413–414). With the permission of Blackwell Publishers.

Box 6.3. Successful Content Areas

1. Information about the negative consequences of violence for the perpetrator as well as victims, friends, family members, and others
2. Anger management skills that teach self-control
3. Social perspective taking, which teaches students that others often have a different, equally valid, and less anger-producing perspective on the same situation
4. Decision-making and problem-solving skills
5. Active listening and effective communication skills
6. Courtesy, compassion, caring, and respect for others, with content that focuses on prejudice, sexism, and male–female relationships

alternative high school setting. The identified school is a relatively small high school with an average enrollment of about 350 students. The school provides a nontraditional academic environment to high school students who have performed poorly in a regular high school setting. Most students are referred to the alternative school by counselors at their home school. Although the focus for referral to the alternative school is academics, for most of these students, poor school performance is symptomatic of interpersonal and psychosocial difficulties; many have problems caused by substance abuse, truancy, lack of family support, abuse, homelessness, or poverty. In addition, some of the students are pregnant or have children. After referral, most students attend the school for the remainder of their high school years. A smaller number return to their home campus after they are able to reach their identified grade level. Thus, students enter and exit the school at various points in their academic process. Many support services, including social work services, are available to students at the school.

Before the conflict resolution program was started, conflict between students and acts of violence were typical of that described in the literature. These occurred regularly, ranging from verbal threats to physical confrontation. As is also typical, when friction arose between students prior to the presence of mental health services on the campus, they were told to ignore it or to "just get over it." When social workers were initially added to the school program, most disputes between students were referred to the social workers for resolution. For more severe acts of violence, such as fighting, students were ejected from the school.

The social workers described this type of reactive referral and intervention structure as time consuming and ineffective. They spent a great portion of their day helping students resolve conflicts. This was problematic, given the many other existing psychosocial needs evident in the student body. Although many students were helped in the resolution of conflicts, relatively few students were actually learning how to resolve conflicts on their own; so many repeat referrals were received. This approach did not reduce the number of conflicts occurring in the school. Thus, the social workers developed a more extensive conflict resolution program.

Structure of the Conflict Resolution Program

Unique to the conflict resolution program developed in this high school is the comprehensive approach to program structure. With the support of the principal, the plan was to create a systematic conflict resolution process. The plan included the two aspects of comprehensive programs called for in the literature. First, it was schoolwide: all students, staff, administrators, and faculty were required to receive the conflict resolution training. Second, the training and intervention process continued throughout the school year.

Phase I

The first phase was to provide training to all students currently enrolled. Twenty students were randomly pulled out of selected classes to attend a 4-hour group training session run by the social workers. The sessions continued until all students had received the training.

Phase 2

In the next phase, all school personnel, including administrators, staff members, and teachers, received the same conflict resolution training. They received the training as a group, in a 2-hour, in-service conference. In addition to the conflict resolution skills presented to the students, the school personnel received instruction on how to integrate the conflict resolution process into the school day. Teachers were instructed to remind students to use their skills when they observed a conflict between students. If the teacher needed to intervene in the situation, he or she was to use the conflict resolution model to help the students express their feelings, concerns, and so on, and move toward resolution. If the conflict could not be resolved with the teacher's help, the teachers were instructed to refer students to social work services while the conflict was still in progress. Teachers were also instructed on how to use the conflict resolution and negotiation skills if they had a direct conflict with a student, another teacher, an administrator, and so on.

Phase 3

Phase 3 was the ongoing, follow-up training process. During homeroom, teachers reviewed a particular concept presented in the initial conflict resolution training and guided student discussion on it. For example, during one homeroom period, the definition of "I" messages was reviewed, and students were reminded to use this type of message when expressing feelings. These review sessions continued daily throughout the entire school year.

The following summer (and every summer thereafter), the social workers provided the conflict resolution program to new incoming students as part of a mandated half-day school orientation.

As additional new students enroll during the school year, the conflict resolution training is provided. Similarly, all new staff and faculty members are trained in the conflict resolution model. During the school year, all students receive "boosters" of the conflict resolution skills in homeroom classes. In addition, teachers continue to remind students to use their conflict resolution skills when they observe a conflict between students, and unresolved conflicts are referred to the social work staff for continued mediation and negotiation.

Curriculum Components and Content

The social workers who created this program also developed the curriculum that they used, and there is empirical support for the effectiveness of their curriculum (see Woody, 2001). However, several other established conflict resolution curricula have empirical evidence supporting their effectiveness. Some of these are listed in the Resources section of this chapter. Consistent with other conflict resolution training, the overall focus of the conflict resolution training used by the social workers in this program is enhancing communication and supplying students with a set of conflict resolution skills that they can use to successfully negotiate conflict situations. The specific content used by the social workers includes many of the areas identified in Box 6.3 as critical in effective conflict resolution curriculum. The social workers use a participatory, experiential format, which includes a significant number of role plays, exercises, and work sheets. The emphasis is on self-exploration and skill comprehension.

Phase 1: Styles and Definition of Conflict

Students are asked for a definition of conflict, and using Worksheet 6.1 below, students are instructed to think about a conflict they have had with another student and a conflict they have either observed or participated in with a teacher. Students are encouraged to talk about their answers and experiences. Next, students are asked to complete Worksheet 6.2, and these responses are also read aloud. Throughout the discussions during this phase, the social workers make several points:

1. Conflict is inevitable and is a part of life encounters and relationships.
2. The goal is to manage and negotiate conflict as opposed to avoiding conflict situations.

Worksheet 6.1

Remember a Conflict

Who was involved?

What was it about?

How did you respond?

When have you heard or had a conflict with another student? What was it about?

Teachers and students having conflict: What was it about?

Worksheet 6.2			
Identifying Conflict Styles in Your Family			
	AVOID	*CONFRONT*	*PROBLEM SOLVE*
GRANDFATHER			
GRANDMOTHER			
MOM			
DAD			
BROTHER			
SISTER			
GIRLFRIEND			
BOYFRIEND			
AUNT			
UNCLE			
MYSELF			

3. There are three basic responses to conflict: submission, aggression, and assertiveness.
4. How most individuals respond is directly and indirectly influenced by family and friends.

Phase 2: Personality Differences/Diversity

In phase 2 of the training, discussion of various responses to conflict is continued, including a discussion of how values and personality type influence one's response in a given situation. The True Colors portrayal of personality (available at www.truecolors.org) is used for this discussion. Through various worksheets included in the True Colors package, students learn characteristics related to their personality type, how these personality characteristics are often viewed by others, and how differences in personality and perception not only contribute to conflict but often also influence how individuals often respond to conflict. For example, the students are asked about which personality color is characteristic of most teachers, and which color is characteristic of most high school students. Through this exchange, students are able to see that differences in values associated with personality (structure, rules, and organization versus fun, action, and entertainment) can result in conflict. This process often results in a revelation for many teachers as well.

Also emphasized in the training is that neither perspective is wrong or right, just different. To further illustrate this point, students participate in an exercise in which they are asked to respond to specific statements. For this exercise, signs that read either "strongly agree," "agree," "strongly disagree," or "disagree" are placed around the room. Students are instructed to place themselves in the section of the room underneath the sign that indicates their response to statements that are read aloud. Example statements include, "Females should always pay for themselves on a date," "Males should not cry or express feelings in public," "Condoms should be distributed in schools," and "Females who carry condoms are sluts." Stressed during this part of the process is acceptance and appreciation for diverse opinions and values.

Phase 3: Communication and Negotiation Skills

In the last part of the training, specific communication and negotiation skills are taught and practiced by the students. These include themes around communication blocks, nonverbal communication, active listening, and communicating with "I" messages. Many worksheets and role plays are used to illustrate these concepts. Several examples are described below.

Example I: Zip Your Zap The two social workers involve themselves in a dialogue in front of the participants. The students are instructed to call out guesses identifying what the social workers are talking about. The social workers continue to talk together, but they occasionally throw out candy to a student who makes a guess. This continues until someone correctly guesses that they are throwing candy to the third person who speaks, or until the set time limit is completed.

With this example, the students are able to describe their frustration and confusion as a result of not understanding what is occurring. These feelings are used by the social workers to discuss feelings about ineffective communication and times they are in an exchange with someone when the communication and intent are not clear. Also the point is made that individuals often end up in situations that they are confused about because they are unaware of or misread the communication exchange.

Example 2 Students are paired. One participant speaks while the other listens. Participants are required to stand during this exercise and are positioned in a way that those who speak have their backs to the social workers; only the listeners can clearly see the adults. Once the dialogue begins between the student pairs, the social workers hold up a series of signs with instructions for the listening partner to follow. One sign instructs the partner to continually interrupt while the other student is talking. Another sign instructs the listener to ignore the speaker.

At the conclusion of the exercise, the social workers announce that they were holding up signs for the listeners to follow and ask the speaking partners to guess what the listeners were instructed to do. They are then asked how they felt during the exchange. The social workers iterate the irritation, dissatisfaction, disappointment, and so on, that the students experienced when their partners presented poor listening skills.

The social workers use this exercise as a lead-in to describing in detail a pyramid of effective communication skills (advice giving, reassuring, asking open-ended questions, summarizing and clarifying) with advice giving at the bottom of the pyramid and empathy and reflective listening at the top. Students are then provided with the opportunity to take turns practicing these skills while the other partner articulates a concern. Students are encouraged to use empathy and reflective listening as much as possible. The participants then discuss what it was like to receive empathy and reflective listening and what it was like to offer support.

Example 3: Misfire   One volunteer from the group of students acts as the source of conflict and is placed in a chair in the middle of the room. The other students are usually already seated in a circle, so that they surround the volunteer. The social workers create a scenario relevant to high school students. They might say, for example, that the student in the middle borrowed another student's car and returned it wrecked. Students are asked to consider what they would really say to this person if the car had belonged to them. Each student is allowed to throw a crumpled piece of paper at the student in the middle of the circle and say what he or she would say to another in this type of conflict situation. After everyone has had a turn, the students are taught the skill of using "I" messages in communication. Students are then given Worksheet 6.3.

Participants are asked again to respond to the scenario created under example 3, but this time to express their feelings and thoughts by completing the sentences provided in Worksheet 6.3. After students have had an opportunity to complete the sentences in writing, each participant reads his or her response to the group. Usually, some participants have difficulty with this assignment and continue to use "you" statements. The social work facilitators point out the difficulty with making the transition from "you"-type blaming statements to "I" messages, and students who have difficulty with the assignment are encouraged to try again, sometimes with advice from other participants. The student volunteer is asked how each set of responses felt to him or her in an attempt to identify that the "I" messages were more tolerable than the blaming statements. Usually the student volunteer is also able to articulate that through the "I want or need" section of the sentence, they felt a resolution was possible.

A review of the concepts discussed during the training is used to wrap up the training session. Students are encouraged to use the "I"-message sentence to communicate effectively and to negotiate conflict situations.

Worksheet 6.3

Using "I" Messages
Try not to use the word "You"

I feel_____

When_____

Because_____

I need or want_____

Resources

Education World: www.education-world.com/a_curr/curr/71.shtm
National Service Learning Clearing House: www.servicelearning.org/wg-php/library/
index.php?library-id=2655
PBS Teacher Resources: www.pbs.org/teachersource/whats_new/health/arr01.
shtm
PeaceBuilders: www.peacebuilders.com/
Practitioner Assessment of Conflict Resolution Programs: www.ericdigest.
org/2001–4/conflict.html
Teaching Students to Be Peacemakers: www.edubooks.com/Teaching_Students_
to_be_Peacemakers_0939603225.html. D. Johnson and R. Johnson (1991),
Teaching students to be peacemakers. Edna, MN: Interaction. www.gigglepotz.
com/peace.htm
Violence Prevention: https://secure.edc.org/publications/prodview.asp?656.
D. Prothrow-Stith (1987), *Violence prevention curriculum for adolescents*. Newton,
MA: Education Development Center.

Key Points to Remember

The conflict resolution program presented in this chapter continues to be effective for several reasons:

- The program is a comprehensive, schoolwide program. All students, faculty, and other school personnel receive the same conflict resolution training.

- The training continues throughout the school year.
- The conflict resolution model is used systematically throughout the school setting. When a conflict between students is observed, teachers and other school personnel prompt the students to use their conflict resolution skills.
- Teachers and administrators serve as role models to the students in that they use the conflict resolution skills in interactions with each other and with the students.
- Unresolved conflicts are referred to the social workers for continued mediation and negotiation.
- Students learn that conflict is inevitable but can be resolved.
- The conflict resolution training requires active, interactive participation by the participants.
- The content of the resolution training includes effective communication and empathy skills and appreciation for diversity.

The conflict resolution program described in this chapter was developed and implemented by two school social workers, Connie Grossman and Gary Grossman at Venture High School in Arlington, Texas. For further information about the program, write to cgrossma@aisd.net and ggrossma@aisd.net.

Using Social and Emotional Learning to Address Conflicts in the Classroom

Jacqueline A. Norris

Getting Started

At one time, classrooms in the United States had desks arranged in straight rows. The furniture was bolted to the floor, and the teacher's desk was on a raised platform in front of the room. Within this classroom, the teacher lectured and the students spoke when they were spoken to, and when a student misbehaved, the consequences were often swift and severe (Ryan & Cooper, 2000).

It may seem as though this classroom was more fiction than reality, but it did exist. To many veteran teachers across the country, "those were the days." They long for the reverence in which teachers were once held. They believe that students today are disrespectful and lack discipline. The 35th annual PDK/Gallup Poll supports their belief. For 16 of the first 17 years that the poll was conducted, when asked, "What do you think are the biggest problems with which the public schools of your community must deal?" participants most commonly answered, "lack of discipline, more control" (Rose & Gallup, 2003). In fact, lack of discipline has never left the top 10 "biggest problems" over the 35-year history of the poll. A 2001 report on teacher turnover revealed that of teachers who left the field because of job dissatisfaction, 68% identified student discipline problems and lack of student motivation as their reasons for leaving (Ingersoll, 2001). Obviously, lack of student discipline is a major concern for schools today.

With the emergence of constructivist theory and brain-based education, metaphors for the ways in which people learn have changed. No longer do we see students as empty vessels or blank slates that teachers must fill with knowledge. Now we know that students come to the classroom with a wide range of experiences and knowledge. Teachers who are able to recognize and help students make connections between their life experiences and new content are much more likely to help improve their students' academic achievement (National Research Council, 2000). This means that a different relationship must be established between teacher and student, one in which teachers know, accept, and understand their students and students trust and respect their teachers. Research shows that in classrooms where everyone feels accepted, valued, and affirmed, there are fewer conflicts, and when problems do arise, they are resolved more amicably (Elias et al., 1997; Osterman, 2000; Blum, McNeely, & Rinehart, 2002; Frey & George-Nichols, 2003). What knowledge must a teacher have to establish such an environment, and what competences must students have in order to maintain it?

This chapter examines social and emotional learning (SEL) as an approach to building respectful and trusting relationships in the classroom. It will show how the school social worker or counselor and other school-based professionals can introduce SEL skills to a classroom, and how teachers can promote transference of these skills by integrating them into classroom management and instructional strategies.

What We Know

Social and Emotional Learning

SEL plays a critical role in creating the positive learning climate in many schools today. It grows out of the theory of *emotional intelligence* developed by Peter Salovey of Yale University and John Mayer of University of New Hampshire in 1987. These two psychologists recognized that although emotions and rational thought are commonly thought to be at opposite ends of the thinking spectrum, there is a strong relationship between them. Daniel Goleman built upon their work and popularized the concept with the publication of his highly successful book *Emotional Intelligence: Why It Can Matter More Than IQ* (1995). Emotional intelligence (EQ) is a different way of being smart. Combining interpersonal and intrapersonal intelligence, two of the multiple intelligences identified by Gardner (1983), emotional intelligence refers to one's ability to know oneself and to know how one is feeling at any given time. It also means understanding and caring about others. The Collaborative for Academics Social and Emotional Learning (CASEL), a group of researchers and practitioners, looked at how schools play a critical role in disseminating and reinforcing these life skills. A book by members of the collaborative, *Promoting Social and Emotional Learning: Guidelines for Educators* (Elias et al., 1997), provides a list of skills necessary for emotional intelligence.

Key Skills in Social and Emotional Learning

Self-Awareness

- Recognizing and naming one's emotions
- Understanding the reasons for feeling as one does

Self-Regulation of Emotion

- Verbalizing and coping with anxiety, anger, and depression
- Controlling impulses, aggression, and self-destructive, antisocial behavior
- Recognizing strengths in and mobilizing positive feelings about self, school, family, and support networks

Self-Monitoring and Performance

- Focusing on tasks at hand
- Setting short- and long-term goals
- Modifying performance in light of feedback
- Mobilizing positive motivation
- Activating hope and optimism
- Working toward optimal performance states

Empathy and Perspective Taking

- Learning how to increase and develop feedback mechanisms for use in everyday life
- Becoming a good listener
- Increasing empathy and sensitivity to others' feelings
- Understanding others' perspectives, points of view, and feelings

Social Skills in Handling Relationships

- Managing emotions in relationships, harmonizing diverse feelings and viewpoints
- Expressing emotions effectively
- Exercising assertiveness, leadership, and persuasion
- Working as part of a team/cooperative learning group
- Showing sensitivity to social cues
- Exercising social decision-making and problem-solving skills
- Responding constructively and in a problem-solving manner to interpersonal obstacles

Though many educators see the importance of social skills in academic achievement, many do not know how or where to infuse instruction on social skills into their classrooms. Still others believe it is not the job of the school to teach these skills; they want children to come to school already knowing them. With the pressure of high-stakes testing and the mandates of No Child Left Behind, it is more critical than ever for classrooms to be nonthreatening, supportive, and caring. The ability to attend to academic content is directly influenced by the ability to manage emotional impulses (Salovey & Sluyter, 1997). "Researchers have found that prosocial behavior in the classroom is linked with positive intellectual outcomes (e.g., Diperna & Elliott, 1999; Feshbach & Feshbach, 1987; Haynes, Ben-Avie, & Ensign, 2003; Pasi, 2001) and is predictive of performance on standardized achievement tests (e.g., Cobb, 1972; Malecki & Elliott, 2002; Welsh, Park, Widaman, & O'Neil, 2001; Wentzel, 1993; Zins, Weissberg, Wang, & Walberg, 2004).

A recent study on managing disruptive student behavior found that effective practices for school social workers should focus not only on individual or group work but on "implementing systems change by collaborating, consulting, developing behavior plans, and training others to work with the difficult children in the context of a child's daily school experiences" (Frey & George-Nichols, 2003, p. 99). Following this train of thought, everything in the child's school environment needs to support efforts being made to change his or her behavior. Classrooms that promote the skills of SEL do not teach them just to those who appear to be lacking in them, but to all students. Everyone learns together about themselves and the people with whom they will interact. All students learn how to actively listen; how to communicate effectively, verbally and nonverbally; and how to resolve the conflicts and problems they face. Students come to see that their emotions are precursors to their actions and that controlling their emotions allows them to choose actions, especially in response to stressful situations, in a manner that preserves everyone's dignity.

As with all effective teaching, teaching these skills must proceed in an organized, well-planned, and purposeful way. Intentionality is critical because these are not just skills for occasional use; these are life skills. There is a difference between teaching a fact or concept and teaching a skill. A skill is performance based and thus requires rehearsal followed by feedback and more rehearsal (Gagne, 1965). By incorporating SEL into instructional methods, many more opportunities to rehearse can be given. As Elias et al. put this point (1997, p. 33), "It is most beneficial to provide a developmentally appropriate combination of formal, curriculum-based instruction with ongoing, informal, and infused opportunities to develop social and emotional skills from preschool through high schools."

What We Can Do

Though hundreds of packaged programs address the concept of SEL, there may be little need to purchase a program because SEL is more a philosophical approach than a program. As such, it permeates every aspect of one's life. It simply means that we treat people with respect, give them the opportunity to be responsible and caring individuals, and expect the same treatment from them. Therefore, as teachers develop their classroom management plans, discipline practices, lesson plans, and patterns of interaction between themselves and their students, SEL is an ever-present foundation. For those teachers who struggle with or may be unaware of the importance of addressing the social and emotional components of their class, the social worker or counselor can play a pivotal role in helping to create a true community of learning.

A list of programs appears at the end of this chapter for the reader to explore. What follows are tools and sample activities that represent the major components of the most effective SEL programs used in schools today (Collaborative for Academics Social and Emotional Learning [CASEL], 2003).

Tools and Practice Examples

Skills That Build Respectful and Trusting Relationships

Optimally, the time to start building respectful and trusting relationships is even before the students arrive on the first day of school. If activities are planned that allow students to begin to know each other, their likes and dislikes, their interests and the things that are important to them throughout the school year, commonalities and familiarities take root.

Class Meetings

The social worker, school counselor, or other mental health professional can be the one who introduces the concept of class meetings. Rules for conducting acceptable patterns of interaction must first be established. Common rules are: only one person will speak at a time, everyone must listen to and be respectful toward the speaker, each person will have an opportunity to speak, and put-downs will not be allowed. For young children, each of these rules will need to be explained and modeled. We should not assume that everyone knows what listening looks like or what waiting your turn to speak feels like.

Here are sample icebreaker questions for class meetings:

- If you could spend a day with someone you admire, with whom would you spend it, and why?
- If you were to be an animal instead of a human, what would you want to be and why?
- What is your favorite food, or what is your favorite restaurant?
- If you could go anywhere on a vacation, where would you most like to go, and why?
- What have you done for someone recently without expecting something in return?

These questions start out as very nonthreatening but begin to offer insight into the students' values and beliefs as the year goes on. A teacher can reinforce this personal sharing process by connecting academic material to class meetings:

- What events led up to the Revolutionary War? Which do you believe was the most influential and why?
- If you could spend a day with a character from *Tuck Everlasting,* who would it be and why?
- In reviewing for the chapter test on fractions, what was the most challenging skill for you and why?

Class meetings can also incorporate role playing of social situations. Here, students may act out a problem or conflict that has occurred or might occur among class members or between the teacher and a student. Together the students and the teacher identify the problem, generate possible situations, and act out a plan for addressing the problem in the future. If teasing is a problem in the class, for example, have the children write skits about this problem (if they are not capable of doing this, then an adult can tell them a situation) and have them act it out for the class. In the class meeting, discuss with students the feelings they see in the role playing and the things that may be done to solve the problem. Then have the actors use the solutions generated by the class to end the play.

One of the most powerful skills of communication is the ability to listen well; Daniel Goleman says it is the root of empathy (Goleman, 1995). Active listening involves being able to hear what someone has said and paraphrasing or retelling it in your own words. The retelling is a way the listener knows that he or she has understood and interpreted words the way the speaker intended. SEL also includes being able to sense what the speaker is feeling. The listener gives eye contact, pays attention to what is being said, and indicates openness to what is being said by using body language of acceptance (nodding, appropriate facial expressions, leaning forward slightly).

Active Listening Steps

1. Listen carefully to the speaker, and look for facial expressions and body language that might reveal how the speaker feels about what he or she is saying.
2. Rephrase the words you heard back to the speaker to check for accuracy.
3. State the feelings you perceive are being felt and tell why.

Examples of Active Listening

Case #1

Speaker: I hate going outside for recess. The kids never let me play kickball with them. I just end up being all by myself.

Listener: So you really don't like to go outside for recess because there is no one for you to play with, right?

Speaker: Yeah!

Listener: That makes you feel hurt and upset; I can tell because your face looks sad, and your voice is weak. That is a good reason for not liking recess.

Case #2

Speaker: My dad is going to go off the deep end when he sees my report card!

Listener: He's going to be mad because of your grades?

Speaker: Yeah, I sort of didn't tell him about the last two tests I took and got "D's" on.

Listener: I guess you must be scared because you think he's going to be mad with you, and you must also be sorry because you didn't tell him about the tests when you got them back, huh?

The social worker and teacher can co-teach active listening to students in a class meeting session. This way they can role play one of the above cases so students see the correct behavior being modeled.

When in an emotional state, a person may well find it easy to blame others for what has happened, but blaming does not move the situation toward a peaceful resolution. Using "I" messages eliminates placing blame on others and shows that you are responsible for the way you feel.

Steps

1. State how you are feeling: "I feel _____"
2. State what made you feel that way (without blaming or judging others): "when or because _____"
3. State what you want or need to happen (as developmentally appropriate): "I need or want _____"

Examples of "I" Messages

"I feel angry when I am teased about my braces; I need you to stop calling me names."

"I really get distracted when I'm trying to study and loud music is playing. Would you please turn it down?"

Emotional Vocabulary

Most children have a limited emotional vocabulary. They know that they are happy, sad, or mad. Yet, if we expect them to be able to name what they are feeling when they are feeling it, we must provide them with the words to do so.

Feelings vocabulary may be introduced in small- group sessions or to a whole class. Introduce several words from the emotions word list (see Box 7.1) (the number will vary depending on the age and development of the children). Ask if they know what the word means and if they have ever felt that way. If they have, have them explain what happened to produce that feeling. If they do not know the word, give them a definition and create a context into which the child can place the word.

Suppose, for example, that the word is *anxious*. You might say: "Do you know this word? It means to be worried about something that is going to happen or may happen. When I had to make a speech in front of a large audience, I was anxious. I was nervous because I did not want to make a mistake. Have you ever been anxious? What happened to make you feel that way?"

Again, the purpose here is to get students to accurately label what they are feeling when they are feeling it and to distinguish one intensity of an emotion

Box 7.1. Feelings and Emotions Word List*

Affectionate	Exhausted	Pleased
Afraid	Friendly	Proud
Alarmed	Frustrated	Regretful
Alert	Frightened	Relaxed
Amazed	Glad	Resigned
Amused	Gratified	Sad
Anxious	Guilty	Scared
Attractive	Happy	Secure
Bad	Helpless	Sensitive
Baffled	Hopeful	Shocked
Bitter	Horrified	Strong
Comfortable	Impatient	Tempted
Confused	Inadequate	Tender
Courageous	Inspired	Threatened
Daring	Interested	Trouble
Depressed	Joyful	Unimportant
Despised	Lonely	Unsure
Determined	Loving	Useless
Disappointed	Moody	Vengeful
Eager	Miserable	Weak
Embarrassed	Nervous	Worn out
Enthusiastic	Optimistic	Worried

*Obviously there are many words that could be added, and students can add to this list.

from another. Also, since we know that children who are very angry or aggressive tend to interpret even the most neutral facial expression or event as being hostile (Goleman, 1995), this means they often believe that they are being attacked and must defend themselves with aggression. Having children identify and share times when they experienced different emotions allow you to see how they interpret the world around them. It also allows you to make corrections to these perceptions when the need arises. It is extremely important to let children know that the emotion is neither negative nor positive. It is only the actions that one takes and the choices that one makes as a result of the emotions that are positive or negative.

Once children have acquired an emotions vocabulary, can recognize and identify what they are feeling, and have begun to make connections between their feelings and their actions, we can begin to teach ways for them to manage their impulses and negative social behaviors. The social worker may review the fact that when in a highly emotional or stressful state, it is very difficult to take in information or make good rational decisions.

"Here is a list of things we can do when we start to lose control. Is there something else you can add, something you do when you need to calm down? (Tell the children about something that you do as a model.) Look at the list and pick one or two things you have used or think would work for you so that you can stay calm." (see Box 7.2)

Box 7.2. Calming-Down Activities

Deep Breathing. People tend to breathe from the top of their lungs. Show children how to breathe using more lung capacity by expanding their diaphragms.
1. Take a deep breath in through your nose.
2. Hold it to the count of 5.
3. Blow it out slowly through your mouth.
4. Repeat as needed.

Take a walk. Physical exercise is excellent for refocusing energy.

Talk to someone.

Write. Keep a journal in which you can express your thoughts and feelings.

Draw. Use clay, color, or paint.

Listen to music.

Use visualization. Close your eyes, and imagine a quiet and calming place where you would like to be. Paint a clear picture of it in your mind. Enjoy!

Use self-talk. Change the words you are hearing by telling yourself that you are calm and in control. Whatever is happening, you are able to handle it without hurting yourself or others.

Decision Making and Problem Solving

At the heart of all conflict resolution programs is the process of decision making and problem solving. The steps of problem solving vary slightly from program to program; however, they all generally include the following steps:

1. Identify the problem.
2. Set a goal to resolve the problem.
3. Generate possible solutions.
4. Pick one solution.
5. Try it.

Each possible solution must be examined for both positive and negative consequences. "What might happen if I do this?" Planning, a step that is often omitted, requires thoughtfully designing how, where, and when one should proceed with a chosen solution. Finally, an integral step is to evaluate the action you took. Did it get you to your goal?

In effect, decision making and problem solving are the culmination of all the skills and strategies in an SEL classroom. Having a "feelings" vocabulary to accurately label what they are feeling when they are feeling it and being able to manage their emotions so that they can interact in prosocial ways and attend to content in the classroom all work together to cue into a problem that needs to be solved. Even young children can be guided through the problem-solving process with questions that will help them to think about the conflicts, problems, and decisions they face (see Table 7.1). Individuals can self-monitor behavior by using the same questions developed into a problem-solving diary. Diaries can be tools that teachers, counselors, social workers, and even administrators use when discussing progress made in behavior over time with students.

Final Thoughts

For children who are deficient in the social skills needed to function in a learning community, the classroom can be a threatening place. These are the children most likely to be involved in school conflicts (Zins et al., 2004). We now know that children are also not likely to acquire and perform these skills in any effective way unless they are generalized to the entire school environment. Administrators, teachers, and parents sometimes look for a silver bullet that will magically make schools safe and caring, protect our children, and raise the academic achievement levels so that truly no child is left behind. There is no such quick fix. What will improve safety and a sense of caring within classrooms are planned and purposeful efforts. The role of the school mental health professional is uniquely positioned to lead the way in building such a comprehensive approach to social competence.

Table 7.1 Facilitative Questioning

To Help Children Think Using Problem-Solving Steps	Consider Asking Questions Like These
1. Look for signs of different feelings.	1. How are you feeling? You look a little upset (sad, nervous, angry, etc.). Am I right?
2. Identify the problem.	2. What do you think is the problem?
3. Decide on a goal.	3. What do you want to have happen? What is your goal?
4. Stop and think of as many solutions as possible.	4. Let's stop and think of all the different ways you might reach your goal. What could you do? What else could you do?
5. For each solution, think of all the things that might happen next.	5. If you _____, what do you think might happen? What else could happen? (Prompt for both positive and negative outcomes.)
6. Choose the best solution.	6. Which of your ideas do you think is the best for you? Which idea has the best chance of getting you to your goal?
7. Plan it and make a final check.	7. What will you have to do to make your solution work? What do you think could go wrong or block your plan?
8. Try it and rethink it.	8. What happened when you tried your plan? What did you learn that might help you next time?

Source: Adapted with permission from Elias and Tobias (1996), *Social problem solving: Interventions in the schools.* New York: Guilford.

The term *social and emotional learning* is fairly new on the school scene, although the understanding that SEL skills are important to success in school and in life has been around for decades. Educators, particularly with their attention so focused on the No Child Left Behind mandates, may need a broader perspective from those who see clearly that building a mentally, socially, and academically healthy individual is precluded by first building a healthy, caring, and accepting school environment (Elias et al., 2002; Zins et al., 2004). SEL is neither a silver bullet nor a quick fix. It takes time to change human behavior, but it is time well invested and recaptured when the teacher can spend less time resolving conflicts and more time in academic pursuits.

Resources
Books
Charney, R. S. (1992). *Teaching children to care: Management in the responsive classroom.* Greenfield, MA: Northeast Foundation for Children.

Educators for Social Responsibility. (1995). *Conflict resolution workshop and implementation manual.* Cambridge, MA: Educators for Social Responsibility.

Elias, M. J., Tobias, S. E., & Friedlander, B. S. (1999). *Emotionally intelligent parenting: How to raise a self-disciplined, responsible, socially skilled child.* New York: Harmony.

Elias, M. J., Tobias, S. E., & Friedlander, B. S. (2000). *Raising emotionally intelligent teenagers: Parenting with love, laughter, and limits.* New York: Harmony.

Elias, M. J., Zins, J. E., Weissberg, R. P., Frey, K. S., Greenberg, M. T., Haynes, N. M, Kessler, R., Schwab-Stone, M. E., & Shriver, T. P. (1999). *Promoting social and emotional learning: Guidelines for educators.* Alexandria, VA: Association for Supervision and Curriculum Development.

Goleman, D. (1997). *Emotional intelligence.* New York: Bantam.

Lantieri, L., & Patti, J. (1996). *Waging peace in our schools.* Boston: Beacon.

Salovey, P., & Sluyter, J. D. (Eds.). *Emotional development and emotional intelligence: Educational implications.* New York: Basic Books.

Programs
Child Development Project (CDP): www.devs0tu.org

Don't Laugh at Me (free materials): www.dontlaugh.org

PATHS (Promoting Alternative Thinking Strategies): www.colorado.edu/cspv/blueprints/model/programs/PATHS

Primary Mental Health Project: www.pmhp.org

Resolving Conflicts Creatively Program (RCCP): www.ersnation.org/about-rccp

The Responsive Classroom: www.responsiveclassroom.org

School Development Program (SDP): www.info.med.yale.edu/comer

Second Step Violence Prevention Curriculum: www.cfchildren.org

Six Seconds Emotional Intelligence Network: www.6seconds.org

Social Decision Making and Problem Solving: http://130.219.58.44/sdm/

Social Development Research Group (SDRG): www.dept.washington.edu/sdrg

Organizations
Association for Supervision and Curriculum Development: www.ascd.org

Character Education Partnership: www.character.org

The Collaborative for Academics Social and Emotional Learning: www.CASEL.org

Social and Emotional Parenting: www.EQParenting.com

Key Points to Remember

- Helping a student to develop social skills in the classroom is more effective in the long term when the classroom culture is supportive of those social skills.

- A classroom environment that promotes caring, respectful, and responsible behaviors has fewer conflicts, and when conflicts do occur they are resolved more amicably.
- Effective communication skills such as active listening and "I" messages are critical components of a caring community.
- SEL promotes prosocial and self-management skills.
- SEL must be integrated into regular rules, routines, and academic instruction so that ample opportunities for practice arise.
- SEL teaches that emotions are neither good nor bad; they just are there. It is the actions taken while in the midst of a strong emotion that can become problematic.
- The time it takes to teach and reinforce these skills is not wasted. In fact, time for academic content is increased as time needed to resolve conflicts is decreased.

Acquaintance Sexual Assault and Sexual Harassment Among Teens

School-Based Interventions

Erin A. Casey
Paula S. Nurius

Getting Started

Nearly all youth are directly or indirectly affected by peer-to-peer sexual harassment or assault. Adolescents are more likely to be victims of sexually aggressive crimes than any other age group (American Academy of Pediatrics [AAP], 2001), and up to 15% of young women report rape (Tjaden & Thoennes, 1998). Approximately 83% of girls and 79% of boys are sexually harassed, and more than half of all adolescents of both sexes report perpetrating sexual harassment at some point during their time in school (American Association of University Women [AAUW], 2001; Fineran & Bennett, 1999). This chapter addresses adolescent peer-to-peer sexual victimization experiences, including verbal or physical sexual harassment, nonviolent verbal coercion to gain sexual contact, and physically forced sexual contact or sexual assault. Regardless of severity, sexual victimization can have immediate and long-term psychological, emotional, and physical consequences and can cause postassault reactions that interfere with school performance and other achievement (AAUW, 2001; Fineran & Bennett, 1999; Koss & Harvey, 1991). School personnel are uniquely positioned to recognize and intervene in recent occurrences of harassment or assault and to initiate prevention programs that may reduce young people's exposure to harm. This chapter summarizes recent literature on effective sexual violence intervention approaches with adolescents and offers strategies for working with youth to address and reduce harassment and assault. Chapter 10 focuses on assault and harassment prevention among teens.

What We Know

Sexually harassing behaviors between teens range from behavior such as unwanted sexual jokes, comments, gestures, name calling, antigay put-downs, pinching, grabbing, and spreading of sexual rumors to more invasive actions such as unwanted sexual touching (AAUW, 2001; Safe Schools Coalition, 1999). Sexual harassment can include *quid pro quo* harassment in which a person in a position of power or authority demands sexual contact in exchange for granting a favor or particular status, but among teens, it more commonly takes the form of "hostile environment" harassment in which ongoing physical, verbal, or non-verbal conduct of a sexual nature creates a school climate that is offensive and intimidating to one or more students (Stein, 1999). Research suggests that 30% of girls and 24% of boys experience sexual harassment "often" and that up to 68% of girls who report sexual harassment encounter it weekly or daily (AAUW, 2001; Stein, 1993). Clearly, for some youth, sexual harassment is an integral part of their daily experience at school.

Though girls and boys appear to be nearly equally involved in both sexual harassment victimization and perpetration, more serious sexual victimizations primarily involve female victims and male perpetrators (Tjaden & Thoennes, 1998). Sexual coercion and assault range from unwanted touching of sexual parts of the body to attempted or completed oral, anal, or vaginal forced intercourse. Sexual contact may be obtained through coercive behaviors such as threats, false promises, attempts to intoxicate the victim, or use of physical force or weapons. Teens are most often assaulted by acquaintances, dates, or current or former partners (Vicary, Klingaman, & Harkness, 1995).

Responses to Victim Disclosures of Sexual Harassment or Assault

Little empirical research exists related to efficacious short-term interventions with adolescent victims of rape, and virtually no studies have examined school-based interventions with targets of sexual harassment (Bennice & Resick, 2002). Substantial research has documented the immediate and long-term impacts of sexual victimization, however, and has identified important factors that can ameliorate psychological distress for victims. This section briefly reviews these empirical findings and uses them to identify potentially important aspects of short-term intervention with young people who have experienced harassment or assault.

The continuum of sexually violent behaviors from harassment to rape holds serious consequences for victims. The impact of sexual harassment on young people includes increased fear, embarrassment, self-consciousness, and self-doubt (AAUW, 2001). Many young targets of harassment begin to develop avoidance behaviors, steering clear of particular people or places in school, or skipping classes or school days to evade their harassers (AAUW, 2001). Girls tend to report more severe effects than boys, and researchers have suggested that the prevalence of harassment constitutes a gender equity issue in which hostile school environments render achievement disproportionately more difficult for girls (Fineran & Bennett, 1998). Survivors of rape or attempted rape can face more serious and long-term consequences, including posttraumatic stress symptoms, depression, suicidal ideation, anxiety, disrupted relationships, and a damaged sense of safety and self-efficacy in their environments (Koss,

Bailey, Yuan, Herrera, & Lichter, 2003; Petrak, 2002). Victimization has also been demonstrated to increase vulnerability to future physical and sexual abuse, creating the risk for compounded traumatic experiences over time (Arata, 2002). Finally, victimized youth are at risk for a range of medical consequences including physical trauma, increased risk of contracting sexually transmitted disease, and unplanned pregnancy.

The interventions we describe here are broadly applicable to victims of sexual aggression and appropriate to school-based response. However, this chapter cannot do justice to the full spectrum of potential physical health and mental health needs. Serious trauma-related needs may necessitate treatment by mental health professionals (Zoellner, Goodwin, & Foa, 2000).

What We Can Do

Factors that have been associated with reduced psychological distress and enhanced recovery among adult sexual assault victims include social support, a lack of self-blame, feelings of control over one's life and recovery, and a coping style that does not avoid or deny the abusive experience or its effect (Frazier, 2003; Koss, Figueredo, & Prince, 2002; Ullman, 1999). In addition, survivors of sexual violence appear to do better when they perceive that they are believed by support systems, when they attribute the causes of their assault to factors external to themselves, and when they feel a sense of control over the process of recovering from the assault (Frazier, 2003; Ullman, 1996). In responding, the role of school personnel is to address disclosures or rumors of sexual mistreatment, to enhance emotional and physical safety at school for identified victims, and to initiate referrals that boost a student's support network and resources outside of school. Specific strategies for responding supportively to disclosures of sexual assault or harassment are summarized in Box 8.1 and are discussed below.

Enhancing Social Support

Research consistently confirms that positive responses following a disclosure of sexual victimization are associated with decreased psychological distress, whereas negative or blaming reactions can exacerbate psychological and emotional struggles (Filipas & Ullman, 2001; Ullman, 1999). Specifically, survivors who feel listened to and believed report enhanced recovery (Ullman, 1996). Conversely, increased psychological distress is associated with others' attempts to take control of a survivor's actions or recovery process or to distract the survivor from her experience (Ullman, 1996). Research also indicates that expanding the network of positive social support available to a student is a critical aspect of intervention (Koss & Harvey, 1991). School personnel can assist survivors in identifying and expanding sources of constructive support

Box 8.1. Responding to Disclosures of Sexual Harassment or Assault

- Establish a supportive relationship.
  - Express appreciation that the student came forward.
  - Explicitly express belief in the student.
  - Demonstrate a willingness to listen to the student.
  - Respond nonjudgmentally to the student's disclosure.
  - Reaffirm that the student is not to blame for the victimization.
- Restore feelings of control.
  - Allow the student to set the pace of the interview.
  - Engage the student in collaborative problem solving about safety.
  - Attend to the student's self-identified priority concerns.
  - Ask students what kind of outcome they are hoping for, and tailor interventions to honor these wishes as much as possible.
  - Be open and clear about limitations related to mandated reporting or school sexual harassment policy.
- Provide information and referral.
  - Normalize feelings or symptoms described by the student as understandable, common reactions to an upsetting event.
  - Consider providing information about common physical and emotional reactions that someone who has been victimized may experience. Reinforce that these are normal responses.
  - Offer information about sexual assault–specific resources available in the community and how to contact them.
  - Assess interest in other referrals, such as counseling services, health and reproductive health services, legal or victim advocacy services, and cultural or community support resources.

(continued)

- Mobilize effective social support.
  - Talk with students about how or when to disclose their experience to family members or friends. Provide support, problem solving, or rehearsal about reaching out or disclosing to others.
  - Talk with the student about how she might respond or seek additional emotional support if she receives nonhelpful or victim-blaming responses from formal or informal support networks.
  - Provide family members with information about sexual harassment or assault, and about the kinds of responses that will be most helpful to teens (e.g., believing the student, being nonjudgmental, communicating support and validation).

and can provide information to friends, family members, and other network members regarding the nature and importance of positive responses to the survivor (Ullman, 1999). School personnel need also to consider the larger school environment and the potential for blaming or inappropriate responses to the student. Steps to enhance confidentiality, limit rumors, and help victimized students cope with inappropriate responses from peers, school personnel, or the news media may be helpful.

Restoring a Sense of Control
School personnel may help victims restore a sense of control by offering information regarding expected physical, emotional, and psychological symptoms associated with the sexual victimization (Calhoun & Atkeson, 1991; Koss & Harvey, 1991). Recent victims of sexual assault may experience sleep disturbances, intrusive thoughts about the event, irritability, difficulty concentrating, numbing or spacing out, fearfulness, and physical discomfort (Koss & Harvey, 1991; Osterman, Barbiaz, & Johnson, 2001). Anticipating these difficulties, knowing that these are normal responses to a traumatic event, and hearing that they subside for most people may decrease young people's anxiety and help them to restore a sense of control. Practitioners should also be aware that students' cultural backgrounds and family environments will affect the meaning that they

attach to assaults, the kinds of postassault concerns they experience, and the postassault options that they perceive as viable (Fontes, 1995). For example, some youth may feel more inclined to seek support or guidance through spiritual or community leaders than through mainstream mental health or crisis agencies. Family reactions and support needs may vary widely, underscoring the importance of staff cultural awareness in responding. Finally, the degree to which a sexually abusive experience traumatizes a victim, and the specific factors that compromise a victim's mental and physical health, vary from person to person (Gidycz & Koss, 1991; Ruch, Amedeo, Leon, & Gartrell, 1991). Thus, referral to health and mental health community services is critical.

Enhancing Safety

A primary goal with a target of sexual harassment or assault is to assess and enhance both immediate and longer term physical and emotional safety (Koss & Harvey, 1991; Resnick, Acierno, Holmes, Dammeyer, & Kilpatrick, 2000). This is especially critical for teens who have experienced sexual aggression and may have physical injuries and other medical concerns such as pregnancy and exposure to sexually transmitted diseases, or who may be at risk for further encounters with the perpetrator. In addition to medical attention, sexually assaulted students should be provided information about medical forensic services, typically available through local emergency rooms.

Once immediate physical safety is assured, targets of harassment or assault will need help in devising a plan for staying safe inside and outside school. School personnel should watch out for the student and be alert to the possibility of additional trouble, help the student find alternatives to some routines (such as using a particular walking route), identify a safe zone in the school where the student can go when feeling threatened, notify the alleged offender that he must stay away from the student, and provide ample adult supervision in places where harassment is more likely (Stein, 1999).

Responses to Perpetrators of Sexual Harassment or Assault

Appropriate school-based interventions for youth who perpetrate sexual harassment or assault are virtually absent from the literature. Bullying and aggressive behaviors tend to cluster with other antisocial conduct, placing youth at risk for a behavioral trajectory that includes delinquency (Dishion, Patterson, & Griesler, 1994; Pellegrini, 2001). Evidence suggests that boys who sexually harass or bully their peers are more likely to report being physically and verbally abusive with their dating partners (Pellegrini, 2001; Wolfe, Wurkele, Reitzel-Jaffe, & Lefebvre, 1998).

Schools should have sanctions that communicate nontolerance for violence, and they should have programs that teach alternatives to aggressive conduct. Consequences for harassing or assaultive behavior should be clearly described in school sexual harassment policy (AAUW, 2004). In addition, researchers increasingly suggest that interventions include a teaching component that provides a young person with clear definitions of inappropriate behavior and information about the effects of his or her behavior on the target (AAUW, 2004; Stein, 1999). This may be accomplished through a letter written by the target of harassment to the harasser (only in cases where this is amenable to the complaining student), tailoring activities in antibullying or sexual harassment curricula for use by the harasser, or asking the perpetrator to write an "empathy" letter detailing his or her behavior and the effects it has had on the target and on the school environment.

Additional sanctions might include in-school suspension with time devoted to completion of a harassment curriculum, required service to the school community, an "antiharassment" behavior plan meeting with parents present, an interview with criminal justice authorities regarding legal sanctions for continued or increased harassing or assaultive behavior, or school suspension or expulsion. Charges of sexual aggression pose ramifications for the perpetrator's family as well. Inclusion of parents or caretakers is essential, with an appreciation that they may well have support and legal needs beyond what the school can provide. Sibling needs should also be considered, particularly if the perpetrator's or victim's brothers or sisters go to the same school.

Legal Considerations in Responding to Sexual Harassment and Assault

Reporting to Law Enforcement and Mandated Reporting

Adolescents who experience physically abusive sexual harassment or sexual assault should receive information about reporting to local law enforcement. The decision to formally report an assault is difficult, and young people may need information about the process and help in sorting out the pros and cons of making a report. Local sexual assault programs can provide information and often offer in-person advocacy during this process. In addition, most jurisdictions mandate reporting if a minor has been assaulted or molested or is in ongoing danger of abuse. School personnel need to be familiar with mandated reporting requirements and sexual assault statutes in their jurisdictions.

Additional Obligations Related to Sexual Harassment

Sexual harassment in schools receiving federal funds is a prohibited form of sex discrimination under Title IX of the Federal Educational Amendments (Office of Civil Rights, 1997). Schools are required by the Office for Civil Rights to develop and disseminate procedures for registering complaints related to sex discrimination, including incidents of sexual harassment. In addition, many states have statutes requiring schools to develop and publish policies and procedures specifically addressing sexual harassment and/or bullying. Sample school policies on sexual harassment can be found in a free document distributed by the American Association of University Women at www.aauw.org. School policies should be disseminated to students and parents, and they must be supported by prompt response to complaints of harassment. School administrators should identify a small team of trained faculty and staff who can be available to receive and respond to incident reports or rumors. Ideally, investigative procedures should include the following elements (Northwest Womens Law Center [NWWLC], 1994): an interview with the complaining student that assesses the grievance and the student's desired outcome; an interview with the alleged harasser regarding the incident; interviews with witnesses, staff, or students to whom the victim or harasser told about the incident and witnesses to previous incidents; clear communication to all parties regarding time lines and expectations of confidentiality and nonretaliation; a determination of findings and remedies; a plan to monitor possible retaliation; and clear documentation of the process.

Resources
Countering Sexual Violence and Locating Local Programs
Rape, Abuse and Incest National Network: www.rainn.org. Provides comprehensive national list of local sexual assault programs.

National Sexual Violence Resource Center: www.nsvrc.org. Provides resources and links to educational and local organizing programs.

Arizona Rape Prevention and Education Program: www.azrapeprevention. org. Provides research, curriculum resources, and statistics related to sexual violence.

Countering Sexual Harassment in Schools
American Association of University Women: www.aauw.org. Provides free resources for educators addressing sexual harassment.

Office for Civil Rights—U.S. Department of Education: www.ed.gov (search site for "sexual harassment"). Provides information regarding schools' legal responsibilities related to addressing sexual harassment.

Safe Schools Coalition: www.safeschools-wa.org. Provides information, links, research, and resources related to sexual-orientation based harassment.

Key Points to Remember

Risk of sexual victimization is at its highest during the period of adolescence through early adulthood in one's lifetime. The high incidence of sexual victimization, together with pervasive underreporting and long-term harm to both victims and perpetrators, underscores how important it is that school personnel take an active role in the identification, intervention, and prevention of sexual harassment and assault. To the extent possible, we have built recommendations on the best available evidence, at times extrapolating from research involving people beyond adolescence. There remains, however, a serious dearth of outcome research to support strong confidence in effectiveness, particularly with respect to cultural and contextual factors, necessitating careful thought in applying recommendations. Evidence consistently indicates that young people who have witnessed, experienced, or perpetrated violence earlier in their lives are at increased risk of subsequent victimization and perpetration and tend to be less responsive to universal interventions. These background factors should remain at the forefront while planning interventions.

Although separated into different chapters here, there are many interlocking themes between intervention with and prevention of teen sexual assault and harassment. Early intervention, for example, can serve not only to ameliorate the effects of victimization but also reduce risk of future perpetration and repeat victimization. Similarly, prevention activities will undoubtedly be received by students who have already perpetrated or experienced sexual victimization by a peer, potentially increasing the likelihood of identifying unmet needs. Moreover, there is considerable overlap among forms of relationship abuse. Other chapters in this book on topics such as bullying, dating violence, and domestic violence provide guidance complementary to ours.

Finally, as we focus here on individual students and their families, we urge recognition that intervention with sexual violence inherently involves complex and often conflicting perspectives, expectations, and emotions of all involved—those of school personnel in addition to students and their support communities. The societal attitudes, norms, and structures that give rise to sexual violence are part of and shape intervention solutions. Schools need to make an unambiguous commitment to antiviolence messaging and response readiness.

Enhancing Conflict Resolution Through Family and School Staff Alliances

Planning for Parent or Guardian Participation in Conferences

Martha J. Markward

Getting Started

School personnel are challenged to enhance alliances between parents or guardians and school staff at a time when great emphasis is placed on students' academic and behavioral outcomes. A variety of studies suggest that parent or guardian involvement in schools, especially school–home communication, accounts for a 10% to 20% improvement in achievement (Thorkildsen & Stein, 1998). When one considers that school–home communication has also been identified as an important means of preventing conflicts between parents or guardians and teachers (Hoberecht, 1999; McDermott & Rothenberg, 2000; Penney & Wilgosh, 2000), planning conferences to meet the unique needs of families takes on even more importance.

What We Know

Grimmett and McCoy (1980) found that educational outcomes were positive when teachers described to parents or guardians their child's reading program and informed them of the child's progress in the program. Fantuzzo (1993, 1995) found that students' mathematics scores were higher when school staff used notes and phone calls to communicate with parents or guardians and when both teachers and parents rewarded children for activities. Evans, Okifuji, Engler, Bromley, & Tishelman (1994) used home visits to improve academic achievement and to reduce the number of children placed in special education.

Ames (1993, 1995) asked teachers in experimental schools to implement a variety of school–home communication strategies over time and found that these strategies advanced children's motivation to achieve in school; these findings held even for children with learning disabilities. Ialongo, Poduska, Werthamer, and Kellam (2001) implemented a family–school partnership (FSP) intervention that included a parent–teacher and partnership building component with a subcomponent that involved training teachers to conduct problem-solving conferences with parents. The overall FSP intervention with children in first grade resulted in positive academic and behavioral outcomes for those children when they were in the sixth grade.

What We Can Do

Despite the salience of these findings, planning adequately for parent or guardian participation in school conferences takes on importance at a time when families in the United States are so diverse. Although it is commonly believed that enhancing parent–teacher communication prevents conflicts between school staff and parents and guardians, much more information is needed to understand the extent to which planning conferences to meet the needs of families enhances alliances between school staff and parents. Many school social workers, counselors, and other support personnel who practice in schools would likely agree that poorly planned school conferences result in conflicts between parents and teachers that place students in a stressful position. Teachers in most schools hold conferences twice a year; the extent to which these attract parents can be crucial to whether or not parent–teacher alliances are forged. Coleman (1991; see also Coleman, 1997a, 1997b) identifies the following steps in planning adequately for parent participation in parent–teacher conferences.

Steps in Planning for Parent Participation in Conferences

1. Identify barriers to parent participation in school conferences.
   - Which parents/guardians should participate in the conference?
   - When should the conference be held? (Before, during, or after school?)
   - How should the conference be conducted? (Face-to-face, telephone, e-mail, or with small groups of parents?)
   - Where should the conference be held? (School, home, neighborhood center, or parents' place of employment?)
2. Create a comfortable environment for offering information, asking questions, and making recommendations.
   - Schedule an adequate amount of time for the conference so that parents do not feel rushed.
   - If the conference is held at the school, point out to the parents the projects that involved their child; if held elsewhere, take examples of the child's best efforts.
   - Begin and end the conference by emphasizing something positive about the child for whom the conference was planned.
   - Communicate in a way that matches, yet shows respect for, parents' background. Be careful not to make assumptions about parents' level of knowledge or understanding, and do not talk down to parents.
   - Send nonverbal messages of respect and interest, sit facing the parent and maintain eye contact except in situations where the cultural norm is to avoid eye contact. Put aside paperwork, and postpone taking notes until after the conference.

- Instead of offering advice, ask parents for information and suggestions about the child; offer your own impressions as a basis for negotiation.
- Limit the number of objectives to be achieved in the conference to one or two of the most important ones that can be addressed with some ease; then break each objective into very simple steps; assign tasks to both teacher and parents that meet each objective in the home and school, respectively; plan a strategy for evaluating the objectives from the perspectives of teacher, parents, and student.
- Follow up the conference with a thank-you note to parents This is a good opportunity to summarize the important points addressed in the conference.

3. Implement the strategy for evaluating the impact of having planned for parent participation in the conference on the educational and behavioral outcomes of students; this plan will often need to be developed before the conference to establish a baseline for change from the perspectives of parents, teachers, and students.

Tools and Practice Example

Juan Gonzalez: A Case Example

Juan Gonzalez is a fourth grader in an elementary school of a community in one southeastern state that serves a largely Mexican population. Juan's mother works as a domestic, and his father is a laborer with a tree-trimming firm. The school social worker identified, when he conducted a needs assessment at the beginning of the year, that the Mexican parents in this community prefer services provided in the neighborhood/home rather than in the school.

Because Juan's father leaves for work very early in the morning, the teacher, interpreter, and school social worker arranged with Juan's parents for the conference to be held in the home at 4:30 in the afternoon. The teacher and school social worker made face-to-face contact with Juan's parents while the interpreter translated the teacher's comments about Juan's schoolwork and behavior for the parents; the teacher's comments were positive, and she showed his parents worksheets he had completed to accompany an exercise in comprehension. Via the interpreter, Juan's teacher told his parents that the main objective of the conference was to inform them of his academic performance and behavior. She told them that another objective was to consider their concerns and suggestions about his schoolwork.

After Juan's parents were told how well the teacher thought Juan was doing in school, she asked the parents how they thought he was doing in school. Although Juan's parents said that they thought Juan was doing okay in school, they were concerned about his being shy because they think he has few friends in the neighborhood. The teacher assured them that even though Juan is shy, he has two friends with whom he interacts at school much of the time. They were very happy to hear this, and both Juan's teacher and the social worker could tell that they were relieved to receive this news.

The teacher closed the conference by telling the parents that Juan was doing quite well overall. She thanked his parents for allowing the conference to be held in their home, and they responded that this was more comfortable for them than meeting elsewhere. She told them that she would send them a thank-you note in a week and indicated that she would send a progress note home with Juan at the end of each week regarding his academic progress and peer relationships. She asked Juan's parents to send her a note if they ever have any concerns about him.

Tools and Forms

Hughes, Oakes, Lenzo, and Carpas's (2001) book, *The Elementary Teacher's Guide to Conferences and Open Houses,* provides excellent tools for planning for parent participation in conferences. These include (a) a preconference student survey form that asks students what they want parents to know about their work, classroom, and what questions they want parents to ask the teacher; (b) a conference invitation form; (c) conference confirmation and reminder forms; (d) receipt of reminder form; and (e) a preconference parent survey form that asks parents what they want to know about their child's progress and what other questions and concerns they may have.

Most important, Hughes et al. provide forms that can be used by practitioner-researchers to evaluate the plan for parent participation in conference. Those include: (a) the teacher conference reflection form, (b) conference evaluation form, and (c) family evaluation form. For example, the conference evaluation form asks parents to use a Likert-type scale (4 = Very much; 1 = Not at all) to rate the extent to which the meeting (a) helped them understand policies and procedures of the classroom; (b) helped them understand their child's work; (c) increased their willingness to help their child at home after this meeting; (d) allowed their questions and concerns to be addressed; (e) encouraged them to meet again; and (f) lasted an appropriate length of time and was scheduled conveniently for them (p. 39).

In addition, student performance should be measured before and after the meeting so that the effect of planning for parent participation can be assessed. For example, the revised edition of *Teacher Observation of Classroom Adaptation* (TOCA-R; Werthamer-Larsson, Kellam, & Wheeler, 1991) can be used to assess the student's performance on the core tasks in the classroom as rated by the teacher before and after the conference. Numerous reliable and valid measures can be used before and after the conference to assess the effects on various behavioral and mood outcomes, if behavioral and affective domains of functioning are of concern.

The conference evaluation form is shown in Box 9.1.

Box 9.1. Parent or Guardian Conference Evaluation

Please fill out the following evaluation form to help me plan for and improve future conferences and open houses. Please sign and return this form by [date]. Thank you for your help!

_____ [sender's signature]

1. This meeting helped me understand policies and procedures of the classroom.
   very much   somewhat   a little   not at all

2. This meeting helped me better understand the work my child is doing/will do in class.
   very much   somewhat   a little   not at all

3. I am more prepared to help my child at home after this meeting.
   very much   somewhat   a little   not at all

4. My child is better prepared to complete his or her work after this meeting.
   very much   somewhat   a little   not at all

5. My questions and concerns were addressed during this meeting.
   very much   somewhat   a little   not at all

6. I would like to attend another meeting like this.
   very much   somewhat   a little   not at all

7. The length and scheduling of this meeting were satisfactory.
   very much   somewhat   a little   not at all

Please list any additional comments below or on the back of this sheet.

_____Parent Signature_____Date

The easy-to-use *Behavior Rating Index for Children* (BRIC; Stiffman, Orme, Evans, Feldman, & Keeney, 1984) is shown in Box 9.2. This scale can be accessed in the journal article cited in references at the end of this chapter.

Resources

www.aft.org/parentpage/communicating/parent_teacher.html
www.bridges4kids.org/articles/10–03/IDEApractices10–03.html
www.carsondellosa.com
www.kidsource.com/kidsource/content3/parent.teacher.3.html
www.ncrel.org/sdrs/areas/issues/envrnment/famncomm/pa31k9.htm
www.nea.org/parents/schoolinvolve.html
www.npin.org/library/pre1998/n00318.html

Box 9.2. Behavior Rating Index for Children

For each item, please record the number that comes closest to your observations of the child. Record your answer in the space to the left of each item, using the scale: 1 = Rarely or never; 2 = A little of the time; 3 = Some of the time; 4 = A good part of the time; 5 = Most or all of the time.

In general, how often does this child

____ feel happy or relaxed?
____ hide his/her thoughts from other people?
____ say or do really strange things?
____ not pay attention when he/she should?
____ quit a job or task without finishing it?
____ get along well with other people?
____ hit, push, or hurt someone?
____ get along poorly with other people?
____ get very upset?
____ compliment or help someone?
____ feel sick?
____ cheat?
____ lose his/her temper?

www.pta.org/parentinvolvement/helpchild/hc_gc_teachers_best.asp
www.topnotchteaching.com

Key Points to Remember

Planning for *meaningful* parent participation is an important means of enhancing parent and school staff alliances. The steps outlined in this chapter allow any member of a school's staff to plan conferences with parents that take into account the diversity of families in today's society, whether diversity is related to ethnicity, family structure, work schedules, or other factors. In planning conferences, staff should

- identify and anticipate the barriers that might prevent parents from attending conferences
- create an atmosphere that will be comfortable for parents from all types of families and backgrounds
- implement evaluation strategies to measure whether the conference positively influenced the academic and behavioral outcomes of students and whether it satisfied the needs of parents

Social workers, school counselors, and other mental health personnel who practice in schools can play a key role in enhancing alliances between parents and school staff, particularly teachers. More important, they can determine under what circumstances planning for parent participation results in positive educational and behavioral outcomes for students with particular characteristics.

10 Engaging Adolescents in Prevention of Sexual Assault and Harassment

Erin A. Casey
Paula S. Nurius

Getting Started

Schools place a high premium on creating safe learning environments for their students, and they possess exciting potential to foster climates of respect that render hurtful or harassing behavior rare and unacceptable. With their ability to draw staff, teachers, youth, and parents into schoolwide prevention efforts, school personnel are uniquely situated to proactively address issues of sexual mistreatment and to reduce students' exposure to this harmful conduct.

Given that more than 75% of all high school students report experiencing some form of sexual harassment at school and that approximately 5% of all youth report being sexually assaulted by other youth on school grounds at some time in their school careers (American Association of University Women [AAUW], 2001), purposeful primary prevention is critical to maintaining a safe school atmosphere. This chapter reviews approaches to the prevention of sexual harassment and assault among adolescents and is a companion to Chapter 8, which focuses on interventions used with victims and perpetrators of sexual mistreatment.

What We Know

Research on prevention efforts in schools typically highlights the importance of multilevel, ecological approaches. Sexual harassment and violence prevention is best supported by strong, enforced antiharassment policies, staff who are trained to intervene in witnessed or reported incidents of harassment, parent education, and clear, schoolwide systems for addressing inappropriate behavior (Olweus, 1994; Sanchez et al., 2001; Stein, 1999). Indeed, training of all staff on procedures for handling episodes of sexual harassment or violence is critical, as classroom presentations about sexual violence may increase reporting among participants. In addition to the resources listed near the end of this chapter, school district curriculum offices, local sexual assault programs, or community agencies are often able to provide staff with in-service training on preventing violence and intervening with perpetrators and victims. Further, prevention approaches may be strengthened by engaging youth in the process of planning and implementing antiviolence programs and complemented by efforts to actively support and reward respectful behavior among students.

This chapter briefly reviews literature on effective classroom interventions used to prevent sexual violence, and it provides resources that staff can use to tailor programs for their schools. Three types of prevention programs are addressed:

1. acquaintance rape prevention programs for mixed-sex or male-only audiences;
2. rape avoidance programs for female audiences; and
3. schoolwide sexual harassment prevention interventions.

Unfortunately, few widely available antisexual violence curricula for adolescents have been empirically tested, and those that have tend to address the related issues of dating violence or bullying (Foshee et al., 2000; Sanchez et al., 2001). (For guidance on those behaviors, readers should see Chapter 11 on dating violence and Chapter 4 on bullying.) However, empirical literature on sexual violence prevention among college students and others identifies some elements of preventive interventions that appear to increase awareness of sexual assault and decrease rape. We apply these findings to recommendations for adolescent audiences. Additional prevention resources and curricula references can be found in the Resources section below.

What We Can Do

Sexual Assault Approaches for Mixed-Sex or Male-Only Groups

Sexual violence prevention programs that target young audiences tend to consist of educational and interactive presentations in the classroom or other group settings. Although schools may invite experts from local sexual assault programs or other community agencies to provide presentations, prevention efforts are perhaps best led by teachers or other school staff who can be available for follow-up discussions and to handle disclosures or integrate prevention learning objectives into ongoing lesson planning. Prevention approaches are most effective when they involve multiple sessions, later "booster" sessions, or integration into ongoing academic curricula rather than a single encounter (Foshee et al., 2000; Lonsway, 1996). Many researchers now conclude that single-sex sessions are more effective than mixed-sex groupings, although both approaches can be successful in increasing knowledge and decreasing victim-blaming or rape-supportive attitudes among participants (Heppner, Neville, Smith, Kivlighan, & Gershuny, 1999; Lonsway, 1996).

Presentations aimed at a single sex provide the advantage of tailoring presentations for males that address risk factors for perpetration and for females that enhance self-protective capacity. Further, male-only groups allow boys to talk frankly about their attitudes, concerns, or misconceptions about sex without fear of ridicule or hostility from female participants, and single-sex interventions prevent previously victimized girls from hearing rape-supportive talk from their male peers (Berkowitz, 2002). Whether designing programs for male-only or mixed-sex audiences, it is important to defuse the defensiveness that the subject matter can raise for young men. Approaches that address males as potential allies in ending sexual violence and as part of the "solution" are more effective in changing attitudes than approaches that focus on males as perpetrators (Berkowitz, 2002; Heppner et al., 1999). (For additional resources related to engaging boys and men as partners in antiviolence work, see the Resources section.) Finally, presenters, educational materials, content, and activities that reflect and are relevant to the cultural diversity of participants enhance the likelihood of student engagement (Heppner et al., 1999).

Classroom presentations that incorporate interactive elements have been shown to be more effective than strictly didactic or lecture approaches (Heppner et al., 1999; Lonsway, 1996). Interactive features of existing prevention programs have included theatrical skits performed live or on video, student role plays of assisting a victim or confronting someone on inappropriate behavior, classroom discussion based on videotaped vignettes or stories of sexual assault, or classroom exercises such as asking students to collectively generate a letter to the editor of the local paper or other periodical or an antirape brochure for younger students. Resources for locating videos on sexual assault and harassment are included at the end of this chapter.

Research demonstrates that providing clear definitions and concrete examples of what constitutes sexual assault can create lasting gains in students' knowledge of sexual violence (Heppner, Humphrey, Hillenbrand-Gunn, & DeBord, 1995). Addressing "rape myths" (beliefs about rape that are widely held but untrue, such as "women say no when they really mean yes" or "girls who wear revealing clothing are asking for sex") has been shown to be an effective element of reducing attitudes that are consistent with sexually aggressive behavior (Schewe, 2002). Box 10.1 offers concrete strategies for addressing rape myths in classroom settings.

Additional aspects of prevention programs that have yet to be fully empirically validated but are recommended by researchers include generating conversation about gender roles and gender socialization, defining and discussing consent in sexual relationships, building skills for bystanders to intervene on a potential victim's behalf, and building empathy for victims through information about the effects of sexual violence (Banyard, Plante, & Moynihan, 2004; Berkowitz, 2002; Schewe, 2002). A sample educational presentation outline can be found in Box 10.2.

Box 10.1. Sample Rape Myths Activities

There are many approaches to surfacing, discussing, and challenging misperceptions about sexual assault. Common "myths" about rape include:

- Most sexual assaults are committed by strangers in dark, isolated places.
- In sex, "no" can really mean "maybe" or "yes."
- People would not be raped if they didn't wear sexy clothing or drink.
- Girls who accept rides from guys, go to their homes alone, or drink on dates are signaling that they want to have sex.
- If someone has had sex with a partner before, she can't say "no" to sex later.
- During sexual activity, there is a point at which it is too late to say "no."

Strategies for discussing rape myths and facts:

- Create a true/false quiz: Transform the above myths into true/false statements and supplement with other statements about rape, such as prevalence rates, definitions, and so on. After students take the quiz, discuss each answer, providing accurate information.
- Use an "attitude continuum." Designate one side of the room as the "agree" area, and the other side of the room as the "disagree" area. Pose one or more of the above statements and ask participants to physically indicate their opinion by standing in a place that reflects their beliefs (students who are unsure or who think "it depends" can stand in the middle of the room). Ask students to describe why they are standing where they are. Let students know that they can move around and change their minds after hearing their classmates speak. If rape myths are not effectively challenged by the students themselves, suggest factual information that challenges rape myths. (Adapted with permission from King County Sexual Assault Resource Center (1992), Ending Sexual Violence Workshop.)

(continued)

Critical issues in facilitation:

- Keep in mind that you will have students in the room who have already been sexually assaulted. Monitor discussions for victim-blaming statements, and gently challenge them when they arise. Ensure that "hidden" victims in the room hear clear messages from you that reinforce that victims are not to blame. Consider starting activities such as the attitude continuum with a statement such as "Everyone has valuable and important opinions to share, and we want to hear what everyone thinks. Before you share your ideas about these statements, however, consider how your words would sound to a classmate who has been sexually assaulted. We also want everyone here to feel safe."
- Reinforce ground rules with students, particularly confidentiality. Remind students not to use names or tell stories about other people that would disclose private information.
- Rape-supportive attitudes are very likely to emerge during these discussions. Anticipate these responses and prepare additional questions or information that would support a student in reconsidering his or her statements.

Reducing Adolescent Girls' Vulnerability

Sexual assault prevention programs for all-female audiences typically focus on enhancing young women's ability to reduce exposure to potentially assaultive situations and to respond self-protectively when faced with the threat of rape. These programs should be designed with an understanding that some audience members will already have been assaulted and that the content of presentations should in no way suggest that victims are responsible. Factors associated with rape-avoidance for women include reducing exposure to known risks and using active, physical resistance to a potential assailant (Schewe, 2002; Ullman, 2002). Situational risk factors for sexual violence include settings involving alcohol or drug consumption, being in an isolated or vulnerable setting with a male, and being in the company of a male who is derogatory toward women, ignores boundaries, or attempts to assert control (Marx, Calhoun, Wilson, & Meyerson, 2001; Ullman, 2002). In addition, passive or negotiating approaches to resisting a potential perpetrator are less effective than physical resistance or yelling

Box 10.2. Sample Outline for Basic Sexual Assault Presentation

I. Make introductions, set ground rules, acknowledge difficulty of topic.

II. Sexual assault: Give definitions and statistics.
   A. Provide clear, behaviorally specific definitions of assaultive behavior.
   B. Offer statistics about how many teens are assaulted.

III. Rape myths: See Box 10.1.

IV. Define consent: Understanding what one is consenting to and not fearing for physical or emotional safety if one says "no."
   A. Brainstorm ways someone indicates consent.
   B. Brainstorm ways someone indicates nonconsent.
   C. List ways that someone might undermine another person's ability to give consent, and reinforce that these tactics are sexual assault.
   D. Provide information about warning signals that someone might try to sexually coerce or undermine consent (female or mixed-sex audiences).
   E. Discuss options if someone is unsure whether his partner is consenting.

V. How to get help.
   A. Provide information about resources for victims, including resource people in school.
   B. Provide information about how to help a friend.

VI. End sexual violence: Brainstorm ways for all young people to help end sexual violence.

in avoiding assault (Ullman, 2002). Effective preventive interventions with girls may therefore include information about recognizing the above risk factors and about self-defense techniques in the face of threat.

Research also suggests that prevention approaches should attend to the fact that the vast majority of victimized young women are assaulted by someone they know and perhaps trust, and that assaults often occur during normative socializing and dating. Young women in these settings can face psychological and emotional barriers to resistance such as fear of embarrassment or rejection, concerns about preserving a relationship, and fears about physical safety if resistance is escalated (Norris, Nurius, & Dimeff, 1996). In addition, even though research shows that women assign more blame to their assailants than to themselves in assault situations, self-blame continues to hurt women's ability to actively resist (Nurius, Norris, Macy, & Huang, 2004). Prevention education with young women can help women to anticipate these psychological responses and build active resistance skills in the face of a known assailant. Building on the work of Nurius, Norris, and Young (2000), Rozee and Koss (2001) propose providing young women with the "AAA" (Assess, Acknowledge, Act) model of recognizing and responding to sexual threats. This approach would provide girls with tools (such as information about risk factors) to assess a situation as potentially dangerous, empowerment in acknowledging this threat, and practice with behavioral options for acting on their assessment. See the Resources section for additional prevention education resources for girls.

It is important to note the repeated finding that prevention programs within colleges have been significantly less effective for students with histories of sexual assault victimization or perpetration (Hanson & Gidycz, 1993; Lonsway, 1996). Thus, early detection and intervention using tailored approaches is likely needed to address the special needs of previously victimized or perpetrating students. There are several inherent challenges to implementing prevention programs. One is the "illusion of invulnerability" inherent to the developmental stage of adolescence as well as the dissonance between simultaneously pursuing safety and social goals—for example, developing habits of vigilance and resistance in the same circumstances that students are seeking friendship, popularity, experimentation, and intimacy (Nurius, 2000). Prevention efforts can be enhanced by giving young women the opportunity to explore these complexities and to role play and practice feasible verbal and physical responses to threats of sexual assault (Marx, Calhoun, Wilson, & Meyerson, 2001).

Sexual Harassment Prevention

Although awareness about sexual harassment in schools has increased dramatically over the past decade, empirically tested sexual harassment prevention curricula are nearly nonexistent. Safeplace's Expect Respect curriculum (see Resources), which addresses both bullying and sexual harassment with elementary and middle school students, is one of the few evaluated programs discussed in the literature (Sanchez et al., 2001). Effective principles for addressing dating violence and sexual assault have emerged, however, and are likely to apply to educational programs aimed at preventing harassment:

1. Providing concrete definitions and examples of sexually harassing behavior, as well as challenging sexual harassment "myths" (such as that people

invite harassment by their dress), can increase students' awareness of inappropriate behaviors.

2. Because many students who engage in harassing behavior are unaware of the effects of their conduct or see such behavior as routine (AAUW, 2001), educating them on the emotional and psychological effects on the targets of harassment may support behavior change.

3. Many bullying curricula include "bystander" education components that aim at enhancing nontargeted students' ability to speak out against harassment, intervene on behalf of a peer, or seek adult assistance. The Expect Respect program produced a positive change in young people's intention to intervene in bullying (Sanchez et al., 2001), and these findings lend support to the inclusion of bystander skill building in sexual harassment prevention education.

A sample sexual harassment presentation outline is presented in Box 10.3.

Box 10.3. Sample Outline for Basic Sexual Harassment Presentation

I. Make introductions, set ground rules.

II. Define sexual harassment.

  A. Provide a sample definition from school policy.

  B. Brainstorm list of behaviors that could be considered harassment.

  C. Discuss difference between flirting and harassment: Brainstorm characteristics of flirting vs. characteristics of harassment, and note differences (i.e., flirting is mutual, respectful, complimentary, fun; harassment is one-sided, repeated, demeaning).

  D. Address behaviors that are both antigay harassment and sexual harassment (such as using the word *gay* as a put-down, using derogatory words for sexual minorities, threatening to harm students who identify as sexual minorities).

  E. Provide information about the prevalence of harassment in schools.

(continued)

III. Address myths associated with sexual harassment, such as the ones listed below, through discussion, attitude continuum exercises, or small-group discussion.
  A. People invite harassment through their dress or actions.
  B. Harassment isn't harmful if the intention is to joke around and have fun.
  C. People who complain about harassment have no sense of humor or are too sensitive.
  D. Only girls get sexually harassed.
IV. Explore the effects of sexual harassment. Goal of discussion is not only to enhance participants' knowledge of the effects of harassment but also to increase empathy and understanding that harassment can be very hurtful, regardless of the harassers' intent.
V. What to do?
  A. Brainstorm options for bystanders/witnesses of incidents. Role play potential bystander responses.
  B. Brainstorm options for targets of harassment. Provide information about reporting procedures.
  C. Brainstorm options for what people can do if they realize they have offended someone.
  D. Brainstorm options for what students in general can do to end harassment and mistreatment.
VI. Provide resources for follow-up, reporting, and community referrals.

In designing sexual harassment prevention interventions, it is particularly critical to address overall school climate and responsiveness in addition to student behavior (Stein, 1999). Classroom interventions alone may be ineffective if the larger school atmosphere contains overt or subtle support for harassing behaviors or fails to respond to incident reports. Although no multilevel interventions specific to sexual harassment have been evaluated, research from related fields highlights the importance of an ecological approach to prevention (Olweus, 1994; Sanchez et al., 2001). Elements of such an approach might include the following: conducting a schoolwide survey of students' experiences of harassment and disseminating the results among staff, students, and parents as a way of highlighting the importance of prevention and of tracking progress; sponsoring a sexual harassment awareness week with antiharassment poster contests, speakers, essay contests, or student-planned educational activities; pulling together an antiharassment advisory committee of staff, students, and parents to plan schoolwide "respect" promotion campaigns; conducting a review and revision of existing sexual harassment policy with participation of students and parents; and inviting parent organizations to sponsor or attend educational opportunities for parents regarding bullying and harassment. Finally, it is critical to provide ongoing opportunities for staff to discuss approaches to addressing harassment, to collectively examine and challenge attitudes that prevent active intervention, and to receive training on responding.

Resources

Sexual Assault

Fink, M. (1995). *Adolescent sexual assault prevention curriculum and resource guide.* Learning Publications. Available through online booksellers and bookstores.

Marx, B. P., Calhoun, K. S., Wilson, A. E., & Meyerson, L. A. (2001). Sexual revictimization prevention: An outcome evaluation. *Journal of Consulting and Clinical Psychology, 69*(1), 25–32: This article describes a prevention intervention for previously victimized college women.

Men Can Stop Rape: www.mencanstoprape.org. This Washington, DC–based organization offers strategies and tangible tools for engaging boys and men in sexual violence prevention and antiviolence work.

Safe Dates. An empirically evaluated dating violence prevention curriculum by Vangie Foshee. Distributed through the Hazeldon Foundation at www.hazeldon.org.

The White Ribbon Campaign: http://www.whiteribbon.ca/. This organization's Web site details an international campaign to involve boys and men in antiviolence work. The Web site includes tangible classroom activities to address sexual and domestic violence.

Sexual Harassment

American Association of University Women: www.aauw.org

Expect Respect. For more information about this comprehensive approach to bullying, harassment, and violence prevention, see www.austin-safeplace.org

Flirting or Hurting? Curriculum for students in grades 6–12 by Nan Stein and Lisa Sjostrom. Distributed by Wellesley College Center for Research on Women: wcwonline.org

Steps to Respect. Antibullying and harassment curriculum for grades 3–6, currently being empirically evaluated. Distributed by Committee for Children: www.cfchildren.org.

Producers of Educational Videos Addressing Sexual Assault and Harassment

Intermedia: www.intermedia-inc.com

Coronet/MTI Film and Video: 1–800–621–2131

Key Points to Remember

School personnel can enhance their impressive efforts to foster positive, safe school climates by incorporating intervention and prevention programs that both ameliorate the effects of sexual mistreatment and reduce its occurrence. Though there remains a serious dearth of outcome research on best practices in intervention and prevention among adolescents, the preceding recommendations have been built on the best available evidence. It is worth reiterating the importance of supporting classroom prevention curriculum with efforts at every level to consistently communicate expectations of respectful treatment among members of the school community and to challenge sexually aggressive attitudes and behavior. When students are embedded in a climate characterized by equity, respect, and safety, they can more easily apply the skills and knowledge gained through prevention curricula and can assist school staff in undertaking the vital task of proactively creating violence-free schools.

Effective Interventions With Dating Violence and Domestic Violence

Beverly M. Black
Arlene N. Weisz

Getting Started

This chapter emphasizes the development of dating violence prevention programs in schools and briefly discusses interventions for victims and perpetrators. We have selected this emphasis because of the advantages of presenting prevention programs in schools. Schools present an ideal opportunity for offering prevention programs, because they offer universal education (prior to the legal dropout age) and have repeated contact with youth (Jaffe, Wolfe, Crooks, Hughes, & Baker, 2004). Presenting programs to all youth rather than those considered vulnerable or at risk decreases the stigma of attending the program (Durlak, 1997). Youth may be more receptive to messages that are received under less stigmatizing conditions. Some experts suggest that youth who are most at risk are the least likely to seek formal help (Avery-Leaf & Cascardi, 2002), so universal programs are advantageous for them. Since victims and perpetrators are unlikely to seek help about dating violence from adults (Bergman, 1992; Henton, Cate, Koval, Lloyd, & Christopher, 1983), it is very important to reach peers with knowledge of how to help a friend who is involved in dating violence. Having contact with adults who are clearly open to discussing dating violence may also increase youths' willingness to seek help from adults when a violent incident occurs (Weisz & Black, n.d.).

This chapter is written for school staff who wish to conduct prevention programs. However, readers should also consider contacting a local domestic violence program or free-standing youth prevention program for assistance. Many of these agencies present prevention programs at no charge to the schools. Collaborating with an external prevention program offers the advantage of having the program presented by specialists. Staff members from an outside agency will bring experience in presenting prevention and education programs, and they often bring ample experience in working with survivors and/ or perpetrators that can enrich their educational programs. For schools that do decide to work with an agency to conduct a dating violence education program, the following material will help school staff think about how they would like the program to be conducted and will help staff engage in knowledgeable dialogue with an agency's staff to prepare for the program.

What We Know

The Importance of Dating Violence Prevention

Dating violence, the perpetration or threat of violence by a person in a relationship, has emerged as a significant social problem and public health concern among American youth. Studies suggest that about one third of U.S. high school students have had experiences with dating violence (Foshee, Linder, Bauman, Langwick, Arriaga, Heath, McMahon, & Bangdiwala, 1996; Jezl, Molidor, & Wright, 1996; Malik, Sorenson, & Aneshensel, 1997; Molidor & Tolman, 1998). Dating violence occurs among youth of all racial and ethnic backgrounds (O'Keefe, 1997; O'Keefe & Treister, 1998). Both girls and boys are victims and perpetrators of dating violence; perpetrating dating violence and being a victim of dating violence are often correlated with each other.

Adolescents who have experiences with dating violence are at increased risk for physical and psychological harm (Callahan, Tolman, & Saunders, 2003; Jezl et al., 1996; Molidor & Tolman, 1998) and serious health risk behaviors (Silverman, Raj, Mucci, & Hathaway, 2001). Girls are particularly at high risk; they are three to four times more likely than boys to experience emotional or physical injury from dating violence (Sugarman & Hotaling, 1989). Many times, girls, in particular, fail to recognize the injuries and harm being inflicted upon them (Banister & Schreiber, 2001).

Youth increasingly appear to accept violence in their dating relationships as normal and as a version of love (James, West, Deters, & Armijo, 2000; MEE Productions, 1996; Vezina, Lavoie, & Piche, 1995). Adolescents' tendency to exaggerate gender-specific roles and accept mythical notions about romance makes them particularly vulnerable to violence in their relationships (Prothrow-Stith, 1991). Adolescent relationships may also be prone to violence because of the dependency that they place on each other for social acceptance and for social conformity (Levesque, 1997). The majority of adolescents report approval of violence toward a dating partner under some circumstances (Carlson, 1990), and the majority of those who have experienced violence in their relationship continued to date the perpetrator of the violence against them (Bergman, 1992; Bethke & DeJoy, 1993). Banister, Jakubec, and Stein (2003) found that girls' desire to have a dating partner outweighed their health and safety concerns.

Empirical Support for Dating Violence Prevention Programs

Despite the fact that numerous prevention programs have been developed, empirical evaluations of prevention programs remain rare. Among the relatively few evaluation studies of prevention programs examining change beyond the immediate effects, only a handful of studies have examined behaviors in addition to attitudes and knowledge (Foshee et al., 1998; Wolfe et al., 2003). Even fewer evaluation studies have been conducted using samples of minority youth in the inner city. In particular, we know little about the characteristics and content of prevention programs that relate to program effectiveness. Table 11.1 summarizes current empirical research on the characteristics of dating violence prevention programs related to effectiveness.

Few research projects have examined which program components contribute to effectiveness in youth dating violence prevention (Avery-Leaf & Cascardi,

Table 11.1 Programs That Conducted Research on Best Practices in Youth Dating Violence Prevention

Study: Jaffe, Sudermann, Reitzel & Killip, 1992
Format: School based; students received full-day or half-day program consisting of community speakers.
Target: High school students
Evaluation Design: Pre-, post-test, 5–6 week follow-up
Results: Significant improvement for participants in attitudes, knowledge, and behavioral intent; some males had a "backlash effect" in attitudes.
Explanation of Results: Use gender-neutral materials to prevent defensiveness among males.

Study: Lavoie et al., 1995
Format: School based; schools received 2 sessions or 2 sessions plus film; wrote fictional letters to victims and perpetrators.
Target: 10th grade
Evaluation Design: Pre-, post-test
Results: Students improved to a similar degree in attitudes; students receiving shorter version improved more on knowledge; boys and girls comparably gained in shorter program. Girls improved more in the longer program.
Explanation of Results: Short programs can modify knowledge and attitudes. Short-version improvement may relate to school differences at pretest.

Study: Foshee, Bauman, et al., 1998
Format: School based; 10 sessions, with theater production, poster contest, community component.
Target: 8th and 9th grades
Evaluation Design: Pretest, follow-up Control group
Results: Youth in prevention program reported less psychological abuse and sexual violence perpetration than control group.
Explanation of Results: Program effects due to changes in dating violence norms, gender stereotyping, and awareness of services.

(continued)

129

Table 11.1 (Continued)

Study: Cascardi, Avery-leaf, O'Leary & Slep, 1999
Format: School-based program with students receiving the 5-session program either once or twice.
Target: Inner-city middle schools
Evaluation Design: Pre-, post-test Control group
Results: Program increased knowledge and help-seeking intentions, decreased intent to use aggression. Double dose showed greater attitude change and behavioral intentions.
Explanation of Results: Single program dose can decrease verbal aggression and jealous and control tactics.

Study: Wolfe et al., 2003
Format: Community based; 18 sessions; focus on abuse dynamics, skills, and social action.
Target: 14–16 years
Evaluation Design:
Results: Physical and emotional abuse decreased; listening skills and group involvement related to a decline in physical abusiveness.
Explanation of Results: Didactic and interactive interventions are effective in changing attitudes (at least in the short run).

Study: Schewe, 2003
Format: School-based programs with variations in length, format, and content.
Target: 5th–12th grades
Evaluation Design: Pre-, post-test
Results: Effective programs had more sessions of shorter duration; male/female cofacilitators, homework, role plays, discussions, healthy relationship skills, warning signs. Ineffective programs had gender role and self-defense content, videos, quizzes, anonymous question boxes, games, artwork.
Explanation of Results: Program length, content, format, and characteristics can positively and negatively relate to program effectiveness.

2002; Schewe, 2003). Therefore, this chapter presents the decisions that developers of prevention programs must make and, where possible, presents evidence supporting particular approaches. In some cases, knowledge gained from other types of youth prevention programs, such as substance abuse and AIDS prevention (Durlak, 1997), may be logically extrapolated to dating violence prevention without specific empirical validation. Similarly, knowledge from social learning theory (Bandura, 1977) and persuasion theory (Hovland, Janis, & Kelley, 1953; Insko, 1967) can be applied to youth dating violence prevention, but evidence to support these applications is rarely available.

What We Can Do

Steps and Issues to Consider When Beginning a Dating Violence Prevention Program

Prevention Educators

- Because dating violence issues are so sensitive, your school may require some orientation regarding the need for this program. Sudermann, Jaffe, and Hastings (1995) present some excellent suggestions of content for orienting administrators and faculty.
- School staff should have training to conduct prevention sessions (Avery-Leaf & Cascardi, 2002). Presenters need thorough knowledge of the issues, because youth will ask many questions. They also need to be trained to avoid the victim blaming that is so common in our society. School staff may seek training from a local domestic violence program to help them become more knowledgeable on dating violence issues.
- Many experts believe knowledge of youth culture or willingness to learn from youth about their culture is also necessary (Weisz & Black, n.d.). The educators must be able to help youth feel comfortable talking about sensitive issues. Because youth are reluctant to tell adults about dating violence victimization, educators must overcome this obstacle by making it clear that they are approachable and nonjudgmental.
- There is no research demonstrating the superiority of using mixed-gender versus single-gender program presenters (Avery-Leaf & Cascardi, 2002). Black (2004) found no outcome differences in youth participating in mixed-gender versus single-gender programs. Experienced prevention practitioners often report advantages of having male presenters, but many believe females can be very successful addressing male and female youth (Weisz & Black, n.d.). Similarly, expert prevention practitioners believe an ethnic match between youth and presenters is a good idea but far from essential for a successful program (Weisz & Black, n.d.).

Recruitment of Youth

- Start before they date. Many educators believe middle school is an ideal time to start prevention programs because students have not yet established dating patterns (Avery-Leaf & Cascardi, 2002). Though middle school youth may not be officially "dating," they may be forming romantic attachments and developing patterns of behavior within these attached relationships.
- Determine whether your school requires parental consent for youth to participate in the program or in program evaluation.

- Target all youth, not just those particularly at risk (Avery-Leaf & Cascardi, 2002; Weisz & Black, n.d.). Programs generally address all youth in particular classes, operating on the principle that making programs voluntary eliminates those most in need of the program.
- Decide whether you want to separate or combine girls and boys (Weisz & Black, 2001). Some experts believe that youth are more open when they can talk in separate groups, while others believe that dialogue between genders is essential. One option is to separate genders for some sessions or some small-group exercises and combine them for others.
- Consider the optimal group size. Most educators try to avoid addressing assemblies (Hilton, Harris, Rice, Krans, & Lavigne, 1998) because they believe smaller groups enable discussions that truly capture youths' attention and enable them to participate in active learning (Weisz & Black, n.d.).

Steps to Guide Program Structure, Content, and Evaluation

Program Structure

- Plan multiple sessions. Although some programs of short duration have been found to be effective (Lavoie, Vezina, Piche, & Boivin, 1995), multiple-session programs are generally more effective (Avery-Leaf & Cascardi, 2002; Schewe, 2000; Weisz & Black, 2001). Experts recommend presenting at least three to four sessions.
- Decide how you want the sessions to be spaced. Weekly sessions allow students time to integrate the material. However, some experienced practitioners prefer presenting one session per day for several days to increase chances of students' retaining and using information from one session to the next (Weisz & Black, n.d.). Between sessions, some educators ask students to do assignments that reinforce their message.
- Make the sessions interactive. Experts recommend devoting time to discussion, role plays, and skill development (Durlak, 1997; Schewe, 2003). Practitioners agree that discussion of issues that students raise seems to attract their attention and enables the content to be locally relevant (Weisz & Black, n.d.). Empirical evaluation does not support the use of videos, games, artwork, or anonymous question boxes (Schewe, 2003). However, expert practitioners believe that judicious use of short videos attracts youths' attention and raises important issues for discussion (Weisz & Black, n.d.).
- Set guidelines for discussion at the beginning of the program. Examples of guidelines included in the curricula listed at the end of the chapter show that these guidelines are based on sound principles of group leadership, such as respect for everyone's opinions and feelings.

Content

- Find out whether the prevention material must be reviewed by anyone in your school or district. Sometimes, content about dating or violence is considered controversial and must be reviewed before it is presented.

- Use a curriculum developed by experts. These people will have experience presenting their material to many school groups. Box 11.1 includes a sample lesson from "Expect Respect" (Rosenbluth & Bradford-Garcia, 2002), and the reference list includes other recommended curricula.

- Choose a program that matches your audience. The curriculum and audiovisual materials should be sensitive to the primary cultural group of the youth who participate in your program. Youth are more likely to pay attention to images and stories about people who seem similar to them (Hovland et al., 1953). The material should address youth in sexual minorities, because dating violence is not limited to heterosexual couples. It should also address the vulnerabilities of youth with disabilities.

- Develop wide-ranging content. Content should include: forms of violence, information about the magnitude of the problem, relationship myths, power and control versus equality, warning signs and red flags, definitions of consent, healthy and unhealthy relationships, relationship rights and responsibilities, resources for seeking help, healthy relationship skills, and how peers can help friends.

- Consider whether you want your program to address larger, societal violence issues that contribute to dating violence.

- Consider combining content. Some programs combine content on sexual violence with content on dating violence prevention, but other programs separate them.

- Train students to be educators. Incorporating peer education requires training and supervision of peer educators, but it can increase the number of students that are reached. In addition, students may pay more attention and respond better to their peers (Sudermann et al., 1995). The peer educators themselves will learn a great deal. They can be influential in changing the school's atmosphere, and they will be prepared to help friends who consult them about an incident of dating violence. One approach to peer education is to train high school students to address middle school students. Other programs recruit youth to perform in interactive theatrical presentations about dating violence.

- Select gender-neutral materials. Research suggests that these are more effective than materials that consistently describe males as perpetrators and females as victims. No program will be effective if it alienates the male students (Avery-Leaf & Cascardi, 2002; Weisz & Black, n.d.).

- Include information on peer intervention. Programs using the "bystander approach" of teaching students how to intervene in peers' abusive relationships can convey a nonblaming, empowering approach to nonviolence.

Goals and Program Evaluation

- Do conduct an evaluation. This will help you to measure how effective your program is. An evaluation can also identify aspects that need improvement. It is considered optimal to test students at the outset and after the program has run its course. Conducting a 3- to 6-month follow-up on knowledge, attitudes and behaviors would be ideal. The presenters might ask classroom teachers to administer the surveys so that time is not taken away from presentation and discussion.
- Get feedback from students. Process evaluation that asks students to recommend improvements to the program can also be very helpful.

Galvanizing the School and Involving Stakeholders in Dating- and Domestic-Violence Prevention

Schoolwide Involvement

- Give the program visibility outside the classroom. Programs that create an atmosphere in the school that supports the prevention program's norms are considered most effective (Foshee, 1998). You might organize students to put up posters that are purchased or created by youth for a contest. Musical events featuring musicians who promote nonviolence can be very appealing to youth (Center for Prevention and Study of Violence, 2000).
- Offer a training session for faculty so they understand and can reinforce the information you are presenting to the students. This session can inform faculty that they might be confusing youth by expressing attitudes that are contrary to those taught in your prevention program (Sudermann et al., 1995).

Parental Involvement

- Let parents or guardians know what their children are learning. Given their influence in their children's lives (Black & Weisz, 2003), parents can be your program's most important allies and can reinforce its messages. A parent meeting can be an ideal forum in which to present information and to influence parents' own knowledge and attitudes. The information may help parents who are dealing with domestic violence and may decrease students' exposure to parental violence, which researchers think predisposes youth to violent actions (Skuja & Halford, 2004).

- Publish a newsletter. If your program is more than one or two sessions, it is helpful to send home a newsletter periodically to inform parents about the content of the program.
- We include in this chapter (Box 11.2) an exercise intended to supplement or replace a parent orientation if parents are unable to attend. This exercise asks youth to interview their parents about dating violence issues.

Preparation for Unintended Consequences of Programs

- Be prepared to help youth decide what they should and should not disclose during programs. Even though youth should be reminded about confidentiality and respect, it is important to protect survivors from revealing information that may become the source of gossip or ridicule after the program is over.
- Inform the students of your professional obligations to report child abuse or threats to harm.
- Have a plan and resources in place to respond to disclosures of child abuse or dating violence, because youth frequently approach prevention educators for help after a presentation.

Working With Survivors and Perpetrators of Dating Violence and Domestic Violence

It can be difficult to employ the best counseling and social work skills when presented with a teen survivor of dating violence, because it is upsetting to see harm inflicted on someone so young. However, it is very important for helpers to listen with empathy instead of telling survivors what to do (Sudermann et al., 1995). Otherwise, the helper risks repeating the same type of controlling behavior used by the abuser. Within state legal guidelines, it is important not to force survivors to tell their parents or legal authorities about dating violence. It is better to help them explore the advantages and disadvantages of telling someone. Similarly, pressuring them to break up with an abuser is not empowering. The idea of breaking up with an abuser may seem very complicated and troubling to survivors and, furthermore, does not guarantee their safety. Again, it is better to explore the survivor's thoughts about safety and about remaining in the relationship versus leaving it (Davies, Lyon, & Monti-Catania, 1998). It is important for a helper to express concerns about a survivor's safety and to urge the survivor to develop a safety plan for use if violence occurs again or is imminent. Group work with survivors of dating violence can be very powerful in decreasing isolation and helping youth share safety planning ideas with each other (Levy, 1999).

Couples counseling is not recommended for abusive intimate partner relationships (Hansen & Goldenberg, 1993) because the victim cannot speak freely in a joint session—the abuser may punish her later for what she said. Most domestic violence experts recommend couples counseling only after perpetrators have received ample intervention to help them accept responsibility for their decisions to use violence and have learned not to use it.

Research supports the practice of group treatment for perpetrators. Groups decrease isolation and increase youths' openness to learning new behaviors from peers rather than from an individual adult therapist (Davis, 2004). Because many regions do not have agency-based groups available for adolescent dating violence perpetrators, you may want to consider developing a group within your school (Davis, 2004). The focus of intervention should be psychoeducational with an emphasis on learning new coping strategies and on increasing accountability for one's behavior (Peacock & Rothman, 2001).

Tools and Practice Examples

Sample Interview

Box 11.1. Sample Lesson From the Expect Respect Curriculum

Session #11 Jealousy and Control

Society is saturated with images that equate jealousy with love. As a result, many young women excuse extremely controlling behavior as a normal expression of love. Girls who are dating jealous partners may eventually withdraw from their friends and families. They may give up opportunities such as going to college or taking a good job because they don't want to upset their partner. Ultimately, they may become afraid that if they end the relationship, the abuser will hurt them, their friends, family members, pets, or children.

In an abusive relationship, the abuser wants to dominate or control his or her partner. The abuser may be extremely jealous of anyone or anything that interferes with his or her influence or ability to control his or her partner. Abusers will try to restrict a partner from people or activities that increase that person's self-esteem. The abuser is likely to feel most secure when his or her partner is physically and emotionally isolated.

(continued)

Objectives

Identify words and actions that signal extreme jealousy.

Identify ways to handle jealousy without violence.

Understand that jealous and controlling behaviors are warning signs for further abuse.

Materials: Handout: "Is Your Relationship Based on Equality?"

Check-In: A time when I felt jealous was _____.
I handled it by _____.

Activities: Jealousy

Using one or more of the situations described during the check-in, have group members create a role play about the situation and how it was handled.

Discuss and role play healthy ways of handling jealousy or responding to someone else's jealousy.

Emphasize to group members that jealousy is a normal feeling but that trying to control someone because of it is abusive. Extreme jealousy is a warning sign of dating violence.

Discussion Questions

1. What did the abusive person in the role play say or do to indicate he or she was jealous?
2. What does the abusive person want from his or her partner when he or she becomes jealous?
3. What are some things that an abusive partner might do to control his or her partner when he or she feels jealous?
4. Do people have a right to feel jealous?
5. What can the jealous person do to handle his or her feelings without violence or control?
6. How do boys control girls, girls control boys?
7. How do you know when someone is trying to control you?
8. How do you know when you're trying to control someone else?
9. Why are jealous and controlling behaviors warning signs for further abuse?

Source: From *Expect respect: A support group curriculum for safe and healthy relationships*, 3rd. ed., by Rosenbluth & Bradford-Garcia. Austin, TX: Safe Place. Copyright 2002. Reprinted with permission.

Box II.2. Exercise for Students to Interview Parents

Parent Interview: Dating Violence Prevention Program

Interview Feedback Form*

The goal of this exercise is to enhance the communication between student and parent(s) and share in a dialogue about relationships. Students should read the question to their parent(s) and allow them time to give a response. The student then shares his or her response with the parent(s) and discusses similarities and differences that occur.

1. What components do you think contribute to a healthy relationship?
   Student shares response:
   Parents share response:

2. What do you understand dating violence to be? What are the warning signs of dating violence?
   Student shares response:
   Parents share response:

3. What steps can you take toward ending dating violence?
   Student shares response:
   Parents share response:

---

*This form is shortened to preserve space. Create a form with spaces for student to record their own and their parents' responses. You might want to offer an incentive for students to bring back completed forms.

Source: This interview was developed by James Ebaugh and Beverly Black.

Resources

Curricula

Expect Respect. For more information about this curriculum, see www.austin-safeplace. org. For information about conducting the program, consult http://www.vawnet. org.

Safe Dates. For more information, contact Vangie Foshee, University of North Carolina at Chapel Hill School of Public Health, Campus Box 7400, Chapel Hill, NC 27599-7400.

Reaching and Teaching Teens to Stop Violence. For more information, contact the Nebraska Domestic Violence Sexual Assault Coalition, Lincoln, Nebraska, through http://www. ndvsac.org.

In Touch With Teens: A Relationship Violence Prevention Curriculum for Youth Ages 12–19. For more information, contact the Los Angeles Commission on Assaults Against Women through http://www.lacaaw.org/.

Videos and Other Aids

Dating in the Hood, available at http://www.intermedia-inc.com
Dangerous Games, available at http://www.intermedia-inc.com
In Love and in Danger, available at http://www.intermedia-inc.com
A list of videos is available at: http://www.nrcdv.org
Teen Power and Control Wheel, which describes different types of dating violence abuse, is available at http://www.ncdsv.org/images/Teen_PC_wheel_NCDSV.pdf. This Web site also includes power and control and equality wheels in Spanish.

Key Points to Remember

Dating violence—experienced in some form by about one third of all U.S. high school students—is the perpetration of violence or threats of violence upon a partner in a relationship. Although many prevention programs have been developed to confront this issue, few have been subjected to empirical evaluation. However, by comparing the multiple programs currently in use and the evaluation studies that are available, it is possible to establish a set of guidelines for implementing new dating violence prevention programs in a school setting:

- Staff should receive orientation regarding the need for and benefits of such a program. Though few may be needed to present the programs, all staff must be trained to handle questions from students.
- Current practice suggests that youths should be targeted for prevention programs as early as middle school, when romantic relationships may be beginning to form. Whether the program is being presented to all youths or just those in an at-risk population, parental consent may be needed for the child's participation.
- Experienced practitioners tend to advocate a program consisting of multiple sessions over a short period of time. These sessions may be presented weekly or daily, with support existing for both.
- The curriculum for the program should be chosen carefully to represent the school's primary cultural makeup, address minority sexual lifestyles, and be gender neutral.
- Parents should be kept involved with the program and their child's progress by means of parent sessions and/or newsletters (for longer programs).
- Program presenters should be trained and ready to deal with issues requiring immediate attention (e.g., children currently being abused) or exceptional care (e.g., children who have been abused or otherwise victimized).

Effective Intervention With Gangs and Gang Members

Timothea M. Elizalde
Gilbert A. Ramírez

Getting Started

Gang presence in public schools is a growing issue across the United States. The growth of drug sales, drug use, and gun possession on school grounds is alarming. The correlation between gang presence and crime on school grounds is significant (Howell & Lynch, 2000). Research suggests that some intervention measures can be successful in working with gang members and decreasing gang-related crime and violence in schools. This chapter reviews several studies that clearly show the need for gang intervention in schools. It introduces an evidence-based program that can be used in schools with middle school and high school students who are gang members or on the verge of becoming involved with gangs. The focus of the chapter is a step-by-step guide to assessing the need for a gang intervention group, gaining support from school administration and staff, and creating a successful school-based gang intervention program.

What We Know

Research on gangs and gang prevalence in U.S. schools continues to grow. A study conducted by the U.S. Departments of Education and Justice (Chandler, Chapman, Rand, & Taylor, 1998) suggests that gang presence in schools now extends from metropolitan urban districts to suburbia, small towns, and rural areas. Although gang involvement is associated with lower income households (less than $7,500 a year), it is increasingly noted in households with income levels of $50,000 and higher (Howell & Lynch, 2000). Student self-reports of victimization at school such as theft, theft by force or with use of weapon, and physical assault all appear to be more prevalent when gangs have been identified in a school. Although gang involvement is commonly identified in students age 13 and older, it is seen in all levels of education, including elementary through secondary levels. It is apparent that regardless of household income, residence, or school grade level, gang presence in public schools is abundant.

The Importance of Collaboration

A collaborative effort can ultimately lead to more successful reduction in gang prevalence in schools and the community. For example, increasing school security and suppression alone is not typically as successful as when they are combined with intervention and prevention measures. Research suggests that gang violence can be reduced through a comprehensive gang initiative that includes a combination of suppression, prevention, and intervention (Police Executive Research Forum, 1999). School security/suppression efforts can be effective if used in conjunction with community involvement and intervention programs that take place during school hours (Gottfredson & Gottfredson, 1999).

The Social and Psychological Paradigm of Gang Involvement

Human beings have basic social and emotional needs, for love, protection, identity, respect, friendship, loyalty, personal power, responsibility, rewards, and consequences, and rituals/rites of passage. These needs are often met for teenagers through their connections with family, schools, peers, and peer organizations. For gang members, needs such as belonging, protection, power, and family tradition are met through gang affiliation. The need to connect with others who share a common language or culture can be a strong factor, as well as the need to identify with others who share the common experience of poverty, violence, racism, and poor access to economic and educational opportunities. The primary goal of gang intervention programs is to have more of these needs met by family, school, and community, and fewer by gangs.

Through a school-based gang intervention program, youth can be helped to redefine how they use their value system and their innate social and leadership skills to get their needs met in a prosocial manner. Many gang-involved youth have such skills but are using their abilities to lead themselves and others down a dangerous path. The skills they use to participate in illegal and dangerous behaviors are the same skills they can use to complete high school, get a job, have positive relationships, and seek postsecondary education. An effective intervention program can guide them to discover better uses for these skills and shift them to activities that will provide better outcomes for their lives.

Many gang-involved youth come from disadvantaged backgrounds, and a frequent misconception is that their parents do not care about their education and are neglectful and unfit. This is not usually the case. The case is usually that one cannot know what one does not know. Thus, if parents did not attend high school or college themselves, it is difficult for them to guide their children through experiences that they themselves have not had. This is where the social worker can be crucial in engaging the family with exposing the youth to as many career and educational opportunities as possible and exploring activities that can positively channel the incredible adolescent energy.

Gang-involved populations are often completely disengaged from traditional school roles and activities such as student government, athletics, band and chorus, and drama. There are many opportunities within a comprehensive gang intervention program to assist youth in redefining their school experience and reengaging them in the school culture. As the intervention program expands and a greater sense of belonging and self-worth begins to manifest, opportunities build upon each other, and changes become more rapid and remarkable.

What We Can Do

A survey of school-based gang prevention and intervention programs by Gottfredson and Gottfredson (1999) offers a look at the gang prevention and intervention methods that have been most successful and productive across the nation. In particular, their report outlines areas that were considered to be rated as best practice when included in a prevention or intervention program. This chapter will highlight models provided by social workers, counselors, psychologists, and other therapeutic professionals. Gottfredson and Gottfredson (1999) found that programs that include these features were more effective:

- A formal assessment or diagnosis
- Written treatment goals that are agreed to by the client
- A system that monitors or tracks behavior

Table 12.1 from the report of Gottfredson and Gottfredson (p. 11) describes these and other characteristics that received higher scores in the effectiveness portion of the study.

Table 12.1 Measuring Best Practice (*Methods*)—Counseling, Social Work, Psychological, or Therapeutic Activity

- *Sometimes, usually,* or *always* makes formal assessments to understand or diagnose the individual or his/her situation.
- *Always* prepares a written diagnosis or problem statement for each participant.
- *Always* develops written treatment goals for each participating student.
- Student *usually* or *always* agrees to a treatment plan contract.
- A contract to implement a treatment plan is *always* agreed to by the client.
- Specific treatment goals for individuals depend on *individual needs as indicated by assessment.*
- When referrals are made, school-based personnel *contact the provider* to verify that service was provided or to monitor progress.
- The counseling or social work plans *always* include a method for monitoring or tracking student behavior over time.

Source: Gottfredson & Gottfredson (1999), p. 11.

In addition to this table, Gottfredson and Gottfredson examined program adequacy and program quality for pertinence to program effectiveness. The "overall program adequacy" of programs and models was judged on a score-card. Those with some or all of the practice measures identified in Table 12.1, in addition to counseling or therapy services offered weekly over a period of several months, were given higher program ratings.

Regarding program quality, Gottfredson and Gottfredson identify numerous factors that should be in place for a program to meet the requirements of a quality program. These factors include the following:

- Extensive training of facilitator
- Adequate supervision of clients during activity
- School administrative support for the proposed activity
- Integration of multiple sources of information and utilization of field experts
- Structured activities that have a sense of "scriptedness"
- Activities that are part of the regular school day and not scheduled as an after-school program or in addition to the regular school day

The study goes on to address curriculum-based intervention programs and the areas each curriculum should have in place to be considered a best practice method. Overall, the study is a preliminary report, and much of the research on gang prevention or intervention effectiveness examines numerous factors depending on the type of model utilized. It is strongly recommended that this report be reviewed by practitioners to better understand the scope of factors that need to be considered when looking at best practice models.

Preparing the Ground

Conduct a Comprehensive Assessment

It is essential, in assessing the school for a gang intervention program, to identify the extent of gang presence and the amount of administrative and staff support needed to move forward. Table 12.2 presents a checklist of conditions that can be used as a general assessment tool to help determine the severity of gang activity in a particular school.

The data that schools maintain on student activity can also reveal conditions leading to an environment vulnerable to aggression, violence, or gang prevalence and can assist in securing administrative support needed to initiate a gang inter-vention program. The more the data demonstrating the need for intervention services, the more is the support for moving the school toward a proactive approach to reducing or eliminating the chance of gang violence on or near the school campus.

Table 12.2 Gang Assessment Tool

1. Do you have graffiti on or near your campus?	5 points
2. Do you have crossed-out graffiti on or near your campus?	5 points
3. Do your students wear colors, jewelry, clothing, flash hand signs, or display other behavior that may be gang related?	10 points
4. Are drugs available at or near your school?	5 points
5. Has a significant increase occurred in the number of physical confrontations/ stare-downs within the past 12 months in or near your school?	5 points
6. Are weapons increasingly present in your community?	10 points
7. Are beepers, pagers, or cellular phones used by your students?	10 points
8. Have you had a drive-by shooting at or around your school?	15 points
9. Have you had a "show-by" display of weapons at or around your school?	10 points
10. Is your truancy rate increasing?	5 points
11. Are an increasing number of racial incidents occurring in your community or school?	5 points
12. Does your community have a history of gangs?	10 points
13. Is there an increasing presence of "informal social groups" with unusual (aggressive, territorial) names?	15 points

Scoring and Interpretation

15 or less	No significant gang problem exists.
20–40	An emerging gang problem; monitoring and development of a gang plan is recommended.
45–60	Gang problem exists. Establish and implement a systematic gang prevention and intervention plan.
65 or more	Acute gang problem exists, meriting a total prevention, intervention, and suppression effort.

Source: Gangs in schools: Signs, symbols, and solutions by Arnold P. Goldstein and Donald W. Kodluboy, 1998, pp. 31–32. Adapted from "Gangs vs. schools: Assessing the score in your community" by Ronald D. Stephens, March 1992, *School Safety Update* (National School Safety Center, 141 Duesenberg Dr., Suite 11, Westlake Village, CA 91362; www.nssc1.org), p. 8.

School enrollment rates and dropout rates should be examined, and staff should be alert to pockets of students detached or isolated from general school activity. Mental health staff should become familiar with the dynamics of the surrounding community by examining crime rates and incidence of drug trafficking, violent assaults, gang arrests, and domestic violence. Also significant is the number of child protective service responses to neglect or abuse calls in the area.

Finally, it may be beneficial to notice the degree of family transition and ethnic composition in the local area. This knowledge will assist in gaining a clear portrait of the community. Since "zero tolerance" policies do not exist beyond the school, conflicts created in the community often spill onto campus grounds. A well-informed community portrait provides a framework for understanding issues that the school may encounter currently and in the future.

Establish a Foundation: Initiating the Group Process

Implementing a gang intervention program provides a good opportunity to do important work in the organizational systems of the school. In evaluating the effects of gangs on the climate of your school, it is important to meet the staff at their current tolerance level. If they are fed up with constant disputes and violence and believe that the current policies are not working, they may be ready to support a comprehensive intervention program. However, if they are resistant, you must advance more slowly, perhaps by starting a small support group or offering assistance with mediation after a conflict. In either case, it is important to use the assessment tools (refer to Table 12.1) to gather and organize baseline community and school data to use in advocating for an intervention program.

Program Components

Gang intervention and prevention programs employ multiple levels of practice, including individuals, groups, and larger family, organizational, and community systems. Gang-involved student support groups are the initial and core activity for most school-based gang intervention programs. The following additional components and activities are added as the program expands:

1. Parent involvement
   - Parent support groups and/or family therapy
   - Fund raising
   - Award ceremonies
2. Case management
   - Referrals to health/mental health/psychiatric services
   - Referrals to income support agencies and housing
   - Links to employment opportunities and job training
   - Links to sports organizations, clubs, tutoring programs, mentor programs, art programs, theater programs, and so on

3. Mediation and conflict resolution training
   - Conflict resolution training for youth and opportunities to use new skills
   - Mediation in gang disputes
4. Culturally relevant activities and exposure to new experiences
   - Sales of ethnic snack foods that students and parents jointly prepare
   - Cultural events such as plays, musical productions, art exhibitions, and so on, especially those that provide strong ties to cultural traditions
   - Introduction to established clubs that help students to connect to and have pride in their cultural traditions (BSU [Black Student Union], MEChA [Movimiento Estudiantíl Chicanos de Atzlán], Asian club, and so on)
   - Sporting events, car shows, and other events of interest to the youth
   - Visits to universities, community colleges, technical/vocational schools
   - Attendance at job/career or college fairs
   - Participation in school dances, celebrations, and theme days
   - Planning of an end-of-year event; use fundraisers to help youth meet their goal
   - Exposure to fine dining, museums, and cultural centers
   - Introduction to ropes courses, rock climbing, and challenging events
5. Service learning
   - Volunteer drives for local programs for homeless, children, animals, and so on
   - Food drives for the holidays; have the youth help deliver food to families in their neighborhoods (include their families in the giving and receiving of the food)
   - Prevention presentations: As the group becomes more established and builds credibility as leaders in their community, have them make presentations to professional groups, college classes, community groups, and children advocacy groups about how to work with gang-involved youth
   - Service on a youth advisory board for a community organization
   - Preparation of a meal that the youth serve to their families at an award ceremony that celebrates their achievements, both big and small
6. Community collaborations
   - Media coverage for an activity that highlights the youth's strengths and service to community
   - Solicitation of financial and in-kind donations from community merchants for scholarships or for entry into an event/place such as a baseball, basketball, or hockey game; zoo; water park; restaurant; or cultural/musical/artistic event
   - Links with adult mentors in the community

- Partnerships with local businesses to provide jobs or job mentor opportunities
- Collaboration with all outside providers who are working with the youth to provide continuity of care and to avoid duplication of services
7. Collaboration with school staff and administration
   - Maintenance of open communication with the students' teachers. If there is a problem, this is an opportunity to assist the youth in problem solving
   - Maintenance of open communication with administrators so that you are included in the loop of communication when discipline issues arise. Also, take time to communicate individual and group successes
   - Collaborations with school counselors, who can provide educational guidance and information about postsecondary options
   - Help from staff for securing caps, gowns, graduation invitations, yearbooks, and other things students may not be able to afford

With numerous other priorities in the school competing for funding and staff resources, such a comprehensive program can be challenging to start. The list above is the ideal one.

Additional Training for Practitioners

In establishing a support group and other services for gang-involved students, practitioners may consider professional training in areas specific to this kind of program. Mediation and conflict resolution, multiparty dispute resolution, and aggression replacement training are excellent tools for leaders. Cultural awareness/competency and bilingualism are also assets for staff involved in gang intervention services. Experiential education is a group model that we have found to be a good fit with our gang intervention groups.

Experiential education is a unique teaching and learning process that is applicable to many learning environments, including therapeutic groups. In experiential education, participants learn by doing rather than by being given answers to questions. Participants are asked to actively explore questions and solve problems through direct hands-on experience.

Experiential education is most often understood as a specific set of activities such as outdoor adventures, cooperative games, challenge courses, and ropes courses. The basic experiential learning cycle consists of goal setting, experiencing, processing, generalizing, and applying. The group begins by setting goals and then is given a challenging activity to meet those goals, thereby providing concrete experiences. After the activity, the group processes its observations and reflections. Participants are then able to form abstract concepts and generalize the learning to their own life experience. Once the experience is generalized, they can test it out in new situations.

Establishing a Student Support Group

Here are some guidelines for establishing a support group for gang-affiliated youth in the school:

1. Use a cofacilitation model to provide continuity and support for leaders.
2. Get referrals from an administrator familiar with the discipline history of students involved in gang behaviors on campus.
3. Limit group to 10 people. It should consist of students in the same gang or students associated with the same gang to ensure higher levels of trust.
4. Meet with students individually about interest in participating in a support group.
5. Check the students' class schedules. Find a time that does not take students out of a core class.
6. Speak individually with teachers about what you are doing and gain their support.
7. Contact parents in person or by phone to tell them about the support group and activities. Send a permission form home (in parents' first language) to obtain parental consent.
8. Meet again with the student for an intake interview and assessment of needs. Talk about the short-term and long-term goals he or she would like to reach. Explain the basics of confidentiality and ask for a commitment to attend at least three group sessions before making a decision about staying or leaving the group. Give students freedom to decide about their own participation in the group.
9. Collect baseline data on behaviors you want the group to affect, such as grades, absences, suspensions, and discipline reports. This will help you and the student to better evaluate his or her progress throughout the year.
10. Find a consistent private space where there will be no interruptions during the group process. It is important that youth in the group feel they have the position of priority.
11. Set a schedule. Once established, groups can meet all year, and a session should last 1.5 hours.

Session Format and Content

The first session should be devoted to orientation. After making introductions, defining the limits of confidentiality, and getting the group started on initial activities, allow participants to be the key players in determining the rules, topics of interest, and activities. It is essential that the group members feel a sense of ownership.

Sticking to a predictable format lends stability and consistency to the group process, though the topics and activities will vary. This provides a sense of safety among participants, and the process of following positive rituals may transfer into participants' lives.

This is the format that we have found effective in our own school-based practice:

Snack and Settle: As group members arrive, providing them with a snack and time to settle in is a good way to get things started. (Snack food often can be obtained through local donations.) This beginning provides for informal interaction and building ritual into the group session. It meets basic needs for food and safety.

Brain Gym: Once everyone is seated, begin a brain gym activity (for more information, see Brain Gym International in the Resources section below) or have a couple of minutes of deep breathing or 2-minute melt (Goldstein, 1998). These activities help the youth to get focused as well as provide ritual for the beginning of the session.

Positive Peer Feedback: Have students design their own cards with their names. At the beginning of each session, have participants select a name card randomly. Ask the students to remember the name on the card and to notice something positive that the person does, says, or contributes during the session.

Check-in: Go around the room and have the youth check in by using a feeling word or two that best describes their feelings at that point in time and the reason they are feeling this way. This check-in gives facilitators an opportunity to see if there is a pressing issue that needs to be addressed immediately or if the scheduled topic or activity can proceed. It also often provides information about an impending dispute that requires intervention.

Business: Next, take a brief time to discuss coming activities, set group goals, or plan a community project. Keep this brief and schedule alternative times to go into more detail or actually participate in the activities.

Topic/Activity: Facilitators should have a menu of activities planned for the session, and this menu should draw from concerns of the youth present and the needs assessed for the group. However, be flexible and ready to change the plan if a gang conflict is arising. Use the session to help the youth understand their feelings about the conflict and identify strategies to confront the situation in a manner that will provide them with dignity, respect, and a way out. The leader can help the group explore the pros and cons of mediation versus a violent confrontation. Some topics and issues that are important to gang-involved youth:

- *Relationships:* family, friends, legal, gang conflicts
- *Social and economic issues:* sexuality, teen pregnancy, parenting, jobs, money, hobbies, youth activities

- *Academic issues:* goals, conflict with teachers, conflict with peers, tutoring, truancy, grades, achievement, postsecondary education plans
- *Self-esteem issues:* self-care, goal setting, acknowledgment
- *Grief and loss issues*
- *Communication and conflict resolution skills*
- *Substance abuse*
- *Aggression and anger management issues*

Once the group has defined goals and decided on topics, as cofacilitators you will plan your group sessions accordingly. For gang-involved participants, experiential education is a group method that tends to feel less intrusive to youth who have been guarded about their feelings and also provides many physical challenges. Leaders must be well trained in experiential education before working with this population. Given that experiential education provides fun, challenge, and opportunities for personal growth, students become quickly enthusiastic about attending group sessions.

Debrief: Use this time to go around the group and ask the participants about one thing that they learned or are taking away from the group session.

Positive feedback: Have the participants take turns giving positive feedback to the person whose name card they selected at the beginning of the session.

Check-out: At the closure of the session, have each member briefly disclose their feelings once again. This allows the practitioner to gauge the immediate effect of the group session, and it allows the participants to take note of any shift in their own attitudes or feelings.

Working Within the System

In order to foster change at the micro level for gang-involved youth, working toward systemic change is vital. For example, a youth may show a positive change in attitude toward resolving personal conflict during a group or individual session, but if other gang members are threatening him or he is subject to violence at home and these larger conflicts are not addressed or mediated, the individual may feel unable to make this change.

Collaboration With Juvenile Probation and Parole System

Since many gang-involved youth have criminal records, they often have a court-mandated probation agreement and a juvenile probation and parole officer to monitor their adherence to the agreement. Collaborating with the JPPO will help your interventions coincide with probation mandates and support the youth in reaching their set goals. The group support you are offering, along with individual and family therapy and other culturally relevant activities, may also help the youth meet mandates set forth in their probation agreement, such as counseling, community service, employment, curfew, school attendance, positive interaction with peers, and abstinence from drugs and alcohol. When youth are consistently engaged in positive activities of their choosing, there is much less free time to be involved in negative behaviors. Likewise, there is a positive connection between meaningful participation and other important protective factors for the youth.

Collaboration With Other Stakeholders

Developing collaborative relationships with the school resource officer, security or police officers, school staff, parents, and administration is crucial to your ability to offer appropriate prevention and intervention strategies before, during, and after a conflict. Suppose, for example, there has been a gang altercation on campus, and students have been suspended. Because suspension deals only with immediate discipline issues and does not help resolve the original dispute, the conflict may have grown in magnitude by the time the suspended students return to campus. This is where your credibility with the youth, the police, the administration, and parents is paramount. This rapport will enable you to offer mediation to help resolve the conflict in a socially acceptable and legal manner and may help prevent a lethal altercation. Most youth who are provided with a dignified way out of the situation will want to mediate the conflict.

School social workers play an intricate role in balancing the roles of each stakeholder in the process: police, administrators, parents, and social workers. Police officers have the role of suppression and legal direction; administrators have the role of maintaining school policy, procedure, and discipline; parents have the role of advocating and caretaking of their child, and the social worker has the role of offering therapeutic intervention strategies and coordinating efforts. All these roles must be respected as separate, yet equally important, in ultimately serving the best interest of students and the safety of the school. Working toward this end is often challenging, but the ultimate outcome is worth the collaborative effort.

When there is a peaceful agreement at the end of multiparty gang mediation, gang-involved youth, their parents, school staff and administrators, and the school community experience a sense of relief and safety. This may also demonstrate to the judge, the probation officer, and the police that the disputants are learning nonviolent ways to deal with their conflicts. These skills inevitably provide a benefit to the youth in their probation status. They learn that as they use new skills to confront their conflicts, they earn trust and freedom, something that adolescents highly value. Many of these conflict resolution skills also transfer to interactions with their families, and many experience improved relationships at home.

After the gang members have taken part in the program for a while, you'll begin to see a metamorphosis occur in them. You will be able to see the paradigm shift (Table 12.3). *Respect,* which was gained by threats, manipulation,

Table 12.3 Paradigm Shift

Gang Definition	Individual Needs	Redefining Through Support Group and Intervention Program
Jealousy, possessiveness, manipulativeness	Love	Unconditional, supportive, caring
Guns, force, violence	Power	Empowerment, inner strength, self-control
Fearless, tough guy	Identity	Unique, individual, personality
"Us" vs. "them"	Trust	Powerful, established with time, rewarding
Threats, fear based, manipulative	Respect	Earned, mutual, modeled
"No rats"	Honesty	Without judgment, safe
Conditional: car, alcohol, drugs	Friends	Supportive, reliable, caring
Conditional	Loyalty	Requires commitment and accountability
High risk, dangerous, illegal	Fun	Natural, childlike, risk taking
Earned by criminal behavior	Honor	Earned through commitment and achievement
Expectation of illegal behavior	Duty	By choice, importance of word
Obey gang rules	Responsibility	Meaningful, important, rewarding
Veterans vs. Pee Wees Older vs. younger/newer	Authority	Veterans support Pee Wees
Instant gratification	Rewards	Earned, enjoyable, worthwhile
Severe, deadly, fear based	Consequences	Just, fair, purposeful
Sex, drug use, weapons use, probation, jail, fights, suspension	Rituals/Rites of Passage	Students become teachers, mentors; they graduate, go to college, have careers

and fear before, becomes a value that is earned, mutual, and modeled; *power*, which was acquired by guns, force, and violence, becomes an outward sign of inner strength, self-control, and personal empowerment; *friends*, once a product of the ability to provide a car, drugs, alcohol, and money, become people who are supportive, reliable, and caring.

Tools and Practice Examples

How One High School Developed a Gang Intervention Program

The gang and racial tension had built up to an all-time high in this urban high school. There were daily incidents of violence and threats of violence on the campus. The environment was disruptive, and both students and staff felt unsafe. When the administration asked for faculty advice, the initial and natural responses were suppressive: "stricter policies; more police; more campus security; suspension from school." The school's social worker understood that most of the conflict was not perpetrated by personal disputes among the individuals involved but rather by gang loyalties and activities at the school. This appeared to be an opportune time for the social worker to introduce gang mediation strategies to the administration. However, when the social worker proposed multiparty gang mediation, there was great hesitation and doubt that such an intervention would have any effect. Given the resistance, the social worker offered to use mediation to help resolve individual disputes. A week later, the assistant principal called the social worker to deal with a dispute between two students who were members of rival gangs. When the mediation was held, it became evident that there were many others involved. The immediate disputants were free to speak for themselves but, according to gang culture, were not allowed to speak for others involved. Thus, a number of other (student) members of the two gangs were called into the session as they were identified, and a mutual agreement for peace was reached. No student needed to be suspended, no probation officers had to be called, and, in the end, the session was a multiparty gang mediation process. This success helped the school administration to consider more favorably the idea of such an intervention.

Later in the year, a huge rival gang fight occurred on the campus, and many students were suspended. Once again the social worker suggested intervening with a multiparty gang mediation, informing administrators that although the fight was over and the participants suspended, the problem had not been resolved. In fact, the suspension time only allowed for the rivals to plan revenge, and rumors were surfacing about the use of weapons. The administration was not comfortable having such an intervention take place on campus, so the social worker offered to intervene off campus. When this was agreeable to school administration, the social worker collaborated with an organization in the community, one that worked with gang-involved youth and was familiar with the disputants, and received permission to conduct the mediation at its facility.

A date and time was set with the disputing gangs, and each member was contacted individually to ask for his participation. The disputants were anxious, yet eager to resolve the problem. Many had probation agreements and a lot to lose, including school credits, their freedom, family relationships, and, in the worst-case scenario, their lives.

The rivals met at an office where they were first searched for weapons and then invited in for a pizza dinner. After pizza, the disputants sat at a business table where they were provided with pencil, pad, and water. The mediation was conducted by comediators with other gang intervention specialists present for safety. The disputants agreed to follow mediation rules and mutually decided to speak in Spanish during the mediation. After nearly 3 hours, a peace agreement was reached, and all participants signed.

When the youth returned to school, they found the social worker's office. Because of the rapport built during the mediation process, the students began dropping by and disclosing information about other conflicts in their personal lives. It quickly became evident to the social worker and to her young visitors that their common bond was that they were all dealing with complex and overwhelming life circumstances. They required an outlet other than the maladaptive ways that they were using to manage their problems. The social worker suggested a support group to help the young men with future gang, personal, family, and school problems. The young men agreed, and the onetime rivals participated in a support group that was inevitably the birth of the school's gang prevention and intervention program. The program grew and is still in place at the high school today, containing all the components for a comprehensive program that are described in this chapter.

Resources

Brain Gym International: http://www.braingym.org

National Youth Gang Center: http://www.iir.com/nygc/publications.htm

Key Points to Remember

Given the trends in school gang activity, intervention and prevention should not be ignored. Research indicates that intervention services for gang-involved youth can be effective if they incorporate measures identified in this chapter. Initiating a comprehensive gang intervention program requires an extensive assessment of the school and community, support from administration and staff, outreach to community agencies, coordination with the juvenile justice system, and collaboration with community partners. When initiating a comprehensive program is not possible, concentrate on implementing a support group. Other components of the program can be added to this foundation. Practitioners are in a position to profoundly affect the school by redefining the way it approaches working with gang-involved youth. Youth will respond positively to the effort to support and reconnect them to the school community and culture. This outcome can perpetuate a culture in which youth are no longer viewed as gangsters but as strong individuals who can contribute positively to their community.

References

Chapter 1

Astor, R. A., Benbenishty, R., & Meyer, H. A. (2004). Monitoring and mapping student victimization in schools. *Theory into Practice, 43*(1), 39–49.

Astor, R. A., & Meyer, H. (1999). Where girls and women won't go: Female students', teachers', and social workers' views of school safety. *Social Work in Education, 21,* 201–219.

Astor, R. A., Meyer, H., & Behre, W. J. (1999). Unowned places and times: Maps and interviews about violence in high schools. *American Educational Research Journal, 36,* 3–42.

Astor, R. A., Meyer, H. A., & Pitner, R. O. (2001). Elementary and middle school students' perceptions of safety: An examination of violence-prone school subcontexts. *The Elementary School Journal, 101,* 511–528.

Battistich, V., Schaps, E., Watson, M., & Solomon, D. (1996). Prevention effects of the child development project: Early findings from an ongoing multi-site demonstration trial. *Journal of Adolescent Research, 11,* 12–35.

Battistich, V., Schaps, E., Watson, M., Solomon, D., & Lewis, C. (2000). Effects of the child development project on students' drug use and other problem behaviors. *Journal of Primary Prevention, 21,* 75–99.

Battistich, V., Solomon, D., Watson, M., & Schaps, E. (1997). Caring school communities. *Educational Psychologist, 32,* 137–151.

Conduct Problems Prevention Research Group. (1992). Initial impact of the Fast Track Prevention Trial for conduct problems: I. The high-risk sample. *Journal of Consulting and Clinical Psychology, 67,* 631–647.

Conduct Problems Prevention Research Group. (2002). The implementation of the Fast Track program: An example of a large-scale prevention science efficacy trial. *Journal of Abnormal Child Psychology, 30,* 1–17.

Developmental Studies Center. (1995). *Child development project.* Retrieved May 18, 2004, from http://www.ed.gov/pubs/EPTW/eptw5/eptw5a.html

Developmental Studies Center. (1998, April). *Some basics of the Child Development Project.* Paper presented at the AERA conference, San Diego. Retrieved May 23, 2004, from http://waarden.goliath.nl/studie/concepten/cdp/basics.html

Developmental Studies Center. (2004). *Comprehensive program: The Child Development Project.* Retrieved May 27, 2004, from http://www.devstu.org/cdp/imp_prof_devt.html

Greenberg, M. T., & Kusché, C. A. (1998). Preventive interventions for school-age deaf children: The PATHS curriculum. *Journal of Deaf Studies and Deaf Education, 3*(1), 49–63.

Greenberg, M. T., Kusché, C. A., Cook, E. T., & Quamma, J. P. (1995). Promoting emotional competence in school-age children: The effects of the PATHS curriculum.

Emotions in developmental psychopathology [Special issue], *Development and Psychopathology, 7*(1), 117–136.

Greenberg, M. T., Kusché, C., & Mihalic, S. F. (1998). *Blueprints for violence prevention, Book 10: Promoting alternative thinking strategies (PATHS).* Boulder, CO: Center for the Study and Prevention of Violence.

Northwest Regional Educational Laboratory. (1998). *The catalog of school reform models.* Retrieved May 23, 2004, from http://www.nwrel.org/scpd/catalog/ModelDetails.asp?ModelID=6

Olweus, D. (1993). *Bullying at school: What we know and what we can do.* Malden, MA: Blackwell Publishers.

Olweus, D., Limber, S., & Mihalic, S. F. (1999). *Blueprints for violence prevention, Book 9: Bullying prevention program.* Boulder, CO: Center for the Study and Prevention of Violence.

Solomon, D., Watson, M., Battistich, V., Schaps, E., & Delucchi, K. (1996). Creating classrooms that students experience as communities. *American Journal of Community Psychology, 24,* 719–748.

Chapter 2

Buvinic, M., & Morrison, A. R. (2000). Living in a more violent world. *Foreign Policy, 118,* 58–72.

Embry, D. D. (2002). The Good Behavior Game: A best practice candidate as a universal behavioral vaccine. *Clinical Child and Family Psychology Review, 5,* 273–297.

Erickson, C. L., Mattaini, M. A., & McGuire, M. S. (2004). Constructing nonviolent cultures in schools: The state of the science. *Children and Schools, 26,* 102–116.

Flannery, D. J., Vazsonyi, A. T., Liau, A. K., Guo, S., Powell, K. E., Atha, H., et al. (2003). Initial behavior outcomes for the PeaceBuilders universal school-based violence prevention program. *Developmental Psychology, 39,* 292–308.

Flay, B. R., Allred, C. G., & Ordway, N. (2001). Effects of the Positive Action program on achievement and discipline: Two matched-control comparisons. *Prevention Science, 2,* 71–89.

Garbarino, J., & deLara, E. (2002). *And words can hurt forever.* New York: Free Press.

Josephson Institute on Ethics (2001). *2000 report card: Violence and substance abuse.* Available at www.josephsoninstitute.org

Kretzmann, J. P., & McKnight, J. L. (1993). *Building communities from the inside out: A path toward finding and mobilizing a community's assets.* Chicago: ACTA Publications.

Mattaini, M. A. (with the PEACE POWER Working Group). (2001). *Peace Power for adolescents: Strategies for a culture of nonviolence.* Washington, DC: NASW Press. Additional information available at www.bfsr.org/PEACEPOWER.html.

Mayer, G. R. (2001). Antisocial behavior: Its causes and prevention within our schools. *Education and Treatment of Children, 24,* 414–429.

Metzler, C. W., Biglan, A., Rusby, J. C., & Sprague, J. R. (2001). Evaluation of a comprehensive behavior management program to improve school-wide positive behavior support. *Education and Treatment of Children, 24,* 448–479.

Sprague, J., Walker, H., Golly, A., White, K., Myers, D., & Shannon, T. (2001). Translating research into effective practice: The effects of a universal staff and student intervention on indicators of discipline and school safety. *Education and Treatment of Children, 24,* 495–511.

Strickland, J., Erickson, C. L, & Mattaini, M. A. (unpublished manuscript). *Social validity of the PEACE POWER strategy for youth violence prevention.* Available from mattaini@uic.edu

U.S. Surgeon General. (2001). *Youth violence: A report of the surgeon general.* Washington, DC: Department of Health and Human Services.

Chapter 3

Associated Press. (2004, May 9). Two charged in drive-by shooting at MD school. *News and Observer,* p. A8.

Astor, R. A., Benbenishty, R., & Meyer, H. A. (2004). Monitoring and mapping student victimization in schools. *Theory Into Practice, 43,* 39–49.

Astor, R. A., Meyer, H. A., & Pitner, R. (1999). Mapping school violence with students, teachers, and administrators. In L. Davis (Ed.), *Working with African American males: A guide to practice* (pp. 129–144). Thousand Oaks, CA: Sage.

Astor, R. A., Vargas, L. A., Pitner, R. O., & Meyer, H. A. (1999). School violence: Research, theory, and practice. In J. M. Jenson & M. O. Howard (Eds.), *Youth violence: Current research and recent practice innovations* (pp. 139–172). Springfield, VA: Sheridan.

Bowen, G. L., Bowen, N. K., & Richman, J. M. (1998). *Students in peril: Crime and violence in neighborhoods and schools.* Chapel Hill: University of North Carolina, Jordan Institute for Families, School of Social Work.

Bowen, G. L., Bowen, N. K., Richman, J. M., & Woolley, M. E. (2002). Reducing school violence: A social capacity framework. In L. A. Rapp-Paglicca, A. R. Roberts, & J. S. Wodarski (Eds.), *Handbook of violence* (pp. 303–325). Hoboken, NJ: Wiley.

Bowen, G. L., Powers, J. D., Woolley, M. E., & Bowen, N. K. (2004). School violence. In L. A. Rapp-Paglicci, C. N. Dulmus, & J. S. Wodarski (Eds.), *Handbook of preventive interventions for children and adolescents* (pp. 338–358). New York: John Wiley & Sons.

Bowen, G. L., Richman, J. M., & Bowen, N. K. (2002). The School Success Profile: A results management approach to assessment and intervention planning. In A. R. Roberts & G. J. Greene (Eds.), *Social workers' desk reference* (pp. 787–793). New York: Oxford University Press.

Cantor, D., & Wright, M. M. (2002). *School crime patterns: A national profile of U.S. public schools using rates of crime reported by police.* Rockville, MD: Westat.

Dwyer, K., Osher, D., & Warger, C. (1998). *Early warning, timely response: A guide to safe schools.* Washington, DC: U.S. Department of Education.

Eamon, M. K., & Altshuler, S. J. (2004). Can we predict disruptive school behavior? *Children and Schools, 26,* 23–37.

Erickson, C. L., Mattaini, M. A., & McGuire, M. S. (2004). Constructing nonviolent cultures in schools: The state of the science. *Children and Schools, 26,* 102–116.

Fraser, M. W. (2004). The ecology of childhood: A multisystems perspective. In M. W. Fraser (Ed.), *Risk and resilience in childhood: An ecological perspective* (pp. 1–12). Washington, DC: NASW Press.

Hawkins, J. D., Herrenkohl, T., Farrington, D. P., Brewer, D., Catalano, R. F., & Harachi, T. (1998). A review of predictors of youth violence. In R. Loeber & D. P. Farrington (Eds.), *Serious and violent juvenile offenders* (pp. 106–146). Thousand Oaks, CA: Sage.

Nash, J. K., & Bowen, G. L. (2002). Defining and estimating risk and protection: An illustration from the School Success Profile. *Child and Adolescent Social Work Journal, 19,* 247–261.

Orthner, D. K., & Bowen, G. L. (2004). Strengthening practice through Results Management. In A. R. Roberts & K. R. Yeager (Eds.), *Evidence-based practice manual: Research and outcome measures in health and human services* (pp. 897–904). New York: Oxford University Press.

Raines, J. C. (2004). Evidence-based practice in school social work: A process in perspective. *Children and Schools, 26,* 71–85.

Richman, J. M., Bowen, G. L., & Woolley, M. E. (2004). School failure: An eco-interactional developmental perspective. In M. W. Fraser (Ed.), *Risk and resilience in childhood: An ecological perspective* (2nd ed., pp. 133–160). Washington, DC: National Association of Social Workers.

Rousseau, C. (2004, May 9). Graduates honor those slain in '98. *News and Observer,* p. A8.

Sprague, J., & Walker, H. (2000). Early identification and intervention for youth with antisocial and violent behavior. *Exceptional Children, 66,* 367–379.

Vossekuil, B., Reddy, M., Fein, R., Borum, R., & Modzeleski, W. (2000). *USSS safe school initiative: An interim report of the prevention of targeted violence in schools.* Washington, DC: U.S. Secret Service, National Threat Assessment Center.

Chapter 4

Banks, R. (1997). *Bullying in schools.* ERIC Digest. Champaign, IL: ERIC Clearinghouse on Elementary and Early Childhood Education.

Bowen, N. K. (1999). A role for school social workers in promoting success through school–family partnerships. *Social Work in Education, 21,* 34–47.

Coloroso, B. (2003). *The bully, the bullied, and the bystander.* New York: HarperResource.

Cowie, H., & Sharp, S. (1996). *Peer counselling in schools: A time to listen.* London: David Fulton.

Coy, D. R. (2001). *Bullying.* ERIC/CASS Digest. Greensboro, NC: ERIC Clearinghouse on Counseling and Student Services.

Fraser, M. W., Richman, J. M., & Galinsky, M. J. (1999). Risk, protection, and resilience: Toward a conceptual framework for social work practice. *Social Work Research, 23,* 131–143.

Haymes, E., Howe, E., & Peck, L. (2003). Whole school violence prevention program: A university–public school collaboration. *Children and Schools, 25,* 121–127.

Haynie, D. L., Nansel, T., Eitel, P., Crump, A. D., Saylor, K., Yu, K., et al. (2001). Bullies, victims, and bully/victims: Distinct groups of at-risk youth. *Journal of Early Adolescence, 21*(1), 29–49.

Nansel, T. R., Overpeck, M., Pilla, R. S., Ruan, W. J., Simons-Morton, S., & Scheidt, S. (2001). Bully behaviors among U.S. youth: Prevalence and association with psychosocial adjustment. *Journal of the American Medical Association, 285,* 2094–2100

Olweus, D. (1993). *Bullying at school: What we know and what we can do.* Cambridge, MA: Blackwell.

Rigby, K. (2000). Effects of peer victimisation in schools and perceived social support on adolescent well-being. *Journal of Adolescence 23,* 57–68.

Rigby, K. (2002). *A meta-evaluation of methods and approaches to reducing bullying in pre-schools and in early primary school in Australia.* Canberra, Australia: Commonwealth Attorney General's Department.

Smith, P. K., Ananiadou, K., & Cowie, H. (2003). Interventions to reduce school bullying. *Canadian Journal of Psychiatry, 48,* 591–599.

Young, S., & Holdorf, G. (2003). Using solution focused brief therapy in individual referrals for bullying. *Educational Psychology in Practice, 19*(4), 271–282.

Chapter 5

Abell, N., & Hudson, W. W. (2000). Pragmatic applications of single-case and groups designs in social work practice evaluation and research. In P. Allen-Meares & C. Garvin (Eds.), *The handbook of social work direct practice* (pp. 535–550). Thousand Oaks, CA: Sage.

Bernal, G., & Scharrón-Del-Río, M. R. (2001). Are empirically supported treatments valid for ethnic minorities? Toward an alternative approach for treatment research. *Cultural Diversity and Ethnic Minority, 7,* 328–342.

DeVoe, J. F., Peter, K., Kaufman, P., Ruddy, S. A., Miller, A. K., Planty, M., et al. *Indicators of school crime and safety: 2003* (NCES 2004–004/NCJ 201257). Washington, DC: U.S. Departments of Education and Justice. Retrieved April 1, 2004, from http://nces.ed.gov/pubs2004/2004004.pdf

Dishion, T. J., McCord, J., & Poulin, F. (1999). When interventions harm: Peer groups and problem behavior. *American Psychologist, 54,* 755–764.

Dodge, K. A., & Pettit, G. S. (2003). A biopsychosocial model of the development of chronic conduct problems in adolescence. *Developmental Psychology, 39,* 349–371.

Flannery, D. J., Liau, A. K., Powell, K. E., Vesterdal, W., Vazsonyi, A. T., Guo, S., et al. (2003). Initial behavior outcomes for the PeaceBuilders universal school-based violence prevention program. *Developmental Psychology, 39,* 292–308.

Fraser, M. W., & Galinsky, M. J. (2004). Risk and resilience in childhood: Toward an evidence-based model of practice. In M. W. Fraser (Ed.), *Risk and resilience in childhood: An ecological perspective* (2nd ed., pp. 385–402). Washington, DC: NASW Press.

Fraser, M. W., Kirby, L. D., & Smokowski, P. R. (2004). Risk and resilience in childhood. In M.W. Fraser (Ed.), *Risk and resilience in childhood: An ecological perspective* (2nd ed., pp. 13–66). Washington, DC: NASW Press.

Gambrill, E. (2003). Evidence-based practice: Sea change of the emperor's new clothes? *Journal of Social Work Education, 39,* 3–23.

Greenberg, M. T., Weissberg, R. P., O'Brien, M. U., Zins, J. E., Fredericks, L., Resnik, H., et al. (2003). Enhancing school-based prevention and youth development through coordinated social, emotional, and academic learning. *American Psychologist, 58,* 466–474.

Mrazek, P. J., & Haggerty, R. J. (1994). *Reducing risks for mental disorders: Frontiers for preventive intervention research.* Washington, DC: National Academy Press.

Rones, M., & Hoagwood, K. (2000). School-based mental health services: A research review. *Clinical Child and Family Psychology Review, 3,* 223–240.

Small, M., & Tetrick, K. (2001). School violence: An overview. *Juvenile Justice, 8*(1), 3–12. Washington, DC: U.S. Department of Justice, Office of Juvenile Justice and Delinquency Prevention. Retrieved April 1, 2004, from http://www.ncjrs.org/pdffiles1/ojjdp/188158.pdf

Williams, J. H., Ayers, C., Van Dorn, R., & Arthur, M. (2004). Risk and protective factors in the development of delinquency and conduct disorder. In: M. W. Fraser (Ed.), *Risk and resilience in childhood: An ecological perspective* (2nd ed., pp. 209–249). Washington, DC: NASW Press.

Zins, J. E., Bloodworth, M. R., Weissberg., R. P., & Walberg, H. J. (2004). The scientific base linking social and emotional learning to school success. In J. Zins, R. Weissberg, M. Wang, & H. Walberg (Eds.), *Building academic success on social and emotional learning: What does the research say?* (pp. 3–22). New York: Teachers College Press.

Chapter 6

Bastian, L., & Taylor, B. (1991). *School crime: A national crime victimization survey report.* Washington, DC: Government Printing Office.

Batton, J. (2003). Cost-benefit analysis of CRE programs in Ohio. *Conflict Resolution Quarterly, 21*(1), 131–133.

Burrell, N., Zirbel, C., & Allen, M. (2003). Evaluating peer mediation outcomes in educational settings: A meta-analytic review. *Conflict Resolution Quarterly, 21*(1), 7–26.

Dudley, B., Johnson, D., & Johnson, R. (1996). Conflict-resolution training and middle school students' integrative negotiation behavior. *Journal of Applied Social Psychology, 26*(22), 2038–2052.

DuRant, R., Treiber, F., Getts, A., & McCloud, K. (1996). Comparison of two violence prevention curricula for middle school adolescents. *Journal of Adolescent Health, 19*(2), 111–117.

Dusenbury, L., Falco, M., Lake, A., Brannigan, R., & Bosworth, K. (1997). Nine critical elements of promising violence prevention programs. *Journal of School Health, 76*(10), 409–414.

Johnson, D., & Johnson, R. (1995). Why violence prevention programs don't work and what does. *Educational Leadership, 52*(5), 63–68.

Johnson, D., Johnson, R., & Dudley, B. (1992). Effects of peer mediation training on elementary school students. *Mediation Quarterly, 10*(1), 89–99.

Johnson, D., Johnson, R., Dudley, B., Mitchell, J., & Fredrickson, J. (1997). The impact of conflict resolution on middle school students. *Journal of Social Psychology, 137*(1) 11–21.

Johnson, D., Johnson, R., Dudley, B., Ward, M., & Magnuson, D. (1995). The impact of peer mediation training on the management of school and home conflicts. *American Educational Research Journal, 32*(4), 829–844.

Opotow, S. (1989). *The risk of violence: Peer conflicts in the lives of adolescents.* Paper presented at the annual meeting of the American Psychological Association, New Orleans.

Paschall, M., & Flewelling, R. (1997). Measuring intermediate outcomes of violence prevention programs targeting African-American male youth: An exploratory assessment of the psychometric properties of six psychosocial measures. *Health Education Research, 12*(1), 117–128.

Stevahn, L., Johnson, D., Johnson, R., Green, K., & Laginski, A. (1997). Effects on high school students of conflict resolution training integrated into English literature. *Journal of Social Psychology, 137*(3), 302–315.

Stevahn, L., Johnson, D., Johnson, R., & Laginski, A. (1996). Effects on high school students of integrating conflict resolution and peer mediation training into an academic unit. *Mediation Quarterly, 14*(1), 21–36.

Woody, D. (2001). A comprehensive school-based conflict resolution model. *Children and Schools, 23*(2), 115–123.

Chapter 7

Blum, R. W., McNeely, C. A., & Rinehart, P. M. (2002). *Improving the odds: The untapped power of schools to improve the health of teens.* Minneapolis: University of Minnesota, Center for Adolescent Health and Development.

Collaborative for Academics, Social and Emotional Learning. (2003). *Safe and sound: An educational leader's guide to evidence-based social and emotional learning programs.* Chicago: Author.

Elias, M. J., & Tobias, S. E. (1996). *Social problem solving: Interventions in the schools.* New York: Guilford.

Elias, M. J., Zins, J. E., Weissberg, R. P., Frey, K. S., Greenberg, M. T., Haynes, N. M., et al. (1997). *Promoting social and emotional learning: Guidelines for educators.* Alexandria, VA: Association for Supervision and Curriculum Development.

Frey, A., & George-Nichols, N. (2003). Intervention practices for students with emotional and behavioral disorders: Using research to inform school social work practice. *Children and Schools, 25*(2), 97-104.

Gagne, R. M. (1965). *The conditions of learning.* New York: Holt, Reinhart, & Winston.

Goleman, D. (1995). *Emotional intelligence: Why it can matter more than IQ.* New York: Bantam.

Ingersoll, R. M. (2001). *Teacher turnover, teacher shortages, and the organization of schools.* (Document R-01-1). University of Washington, Center for the Study of Teaching and Policy.

National Research Council. (2000). *How people learn: Brain, mind, experience, and school.* Washington, DC: National Academy Press.

Osterman, K. F. (2000). Students' need for belonging in the school community. *Review of Educational Research, 70,* 323-367.

Rose, L. C., & Gallup, A. M. (2003). The 35th annual PDK/Gallup poll of the public's attitudes toward the public schools. *Phi Delta Kappan, 5*(1), 41-52.

Ryan, K., & Cooper, J. M. (2000). *Those who can, teach* (9th ed.). Boston: Houghton Mifflin.

Salovey, P., & Sluyter, D. J. (Eds.). (1997). *Emotional development and emotional intelligence: Educational implications.* New York: Basic Books.

Zins, J. E., Weissberg, R. P., Wang, M. L., & Walberg, H. J. (Eds.). (2004). *Building academic success on social and emotional learning: What does the research say?* New York: Teachers College Press.

Chapter 8

American Academy of Pediatrics. (2001). Alcohol use and abuse: A pediatric concern. *Pediatrics, 108,* 185–189.

American Association of University Women. (2001). *Hostile hallways: Bullying, teasing, and sexual harassment in schools.* Washington, DC: Author.

American Association of University Women. (2004). *Harassment-free hallways: How to stop sexual harassment in school.* Washington, DC: Author.

Arata, C. M. (2002). Child sexual abuse and sexual revictimization. *Clinical Psychology: Science and Practice, 9*(2), 135–164.

Bennice, J., & Resick, P. (2002). A review of treatment and outcome of post-trauma sequelae in sexual assault survivors. In J. Petrak & B. Hedge (Eds.), *The trauma of sexual assault: Treatment, prevention, and practice.* West Sussex, UK: John Wiley & Sons.

Calhoun, K. S., & Atkeson, B. M. (1991). *Treatment of rape victims.* New York: Pergamon.

Dishion, T. J., Patterson, G. R., & Griesler, P. C. (1994). Peer adaptations in the development of antisocial behavior: A confluence model. In L. R. Huessmann (Ed.), *Aggressive behavior: Current perspectives.* New York: Plenum.

Filipas, H. H., & Ullman, S. E. (2001). Social reactions to sexual assault victims from various support sources. *Violence and Victims, 16*(6), 673–692.

Fineran, S., & Bennett, L. (1998). Teenage peer sexual harassment: Implications for social work practice in education. *Social Work, 43*(1), 55–63.

Fineran, S., & Bennett, L. (1999). Gender and power issues of peer sexual harassment among teenagers. *Journal of Interpersonal Violence, 14*(6), 626–641.

Fontes, L. A. (1995). *Sexual abuse in nine North American cultures.* Thousand Oaks, CA: Sage.

Frazier, P. (2003). Perceived control and distress following sexual assault: A longitudinal test of a new model. *Journal of Personality and Social Psychology, 84*(6), 1257–1269.

Gidycz, C. A., & Koss, M. P. (1991). Predictors of long-term sexual assault trauma among a national sample of victimized college women. *Violence and Victims, 6,* 175–190.

Koss, M. P., Bailey, J. A., Yuan, N. P., Herrera, V., & Lichter, E. L. (2003). Depression and PTSD in survivors of male violence: Research and training initiatives to facilitate recovery. *Psychology of Women Quarterly, 27,* 130–142.

Koss, M. P., Figueredo, A. J., & Prince, R. J. (2002). Cognitive mediation of rape's mental, physical, and social health impact: Test of four models in cross-sectional data. *Journal of Consulting and Clinical Psychology, 4,* 926–941.

Koss, M. P., & Harvey, M. R. (1991). *The rape victim: Clinical and community interventions.* Thousand Oaks, CA: Sage.

Northwest Womens Law Center. (1994). *Sexual harassment in employment and education.* Seattle: Author.

Office of Civil Rights. (1997). *Sexual harassment guidance.* Washington, DC: Author, Department of Education.

Osterman, J. E., Barbiaz, J., & Johnson, P. (2001). Emergency interventions for rape victims. *Emergency Psychiatry, 52,* 733–740.

Pellegrini, A. D. (2001). A longitudinal study of heterosexual relationships, aggression, and sexual harassment during the transition from primary school through middle school. *Journal of Applied Developmental Psychology, 21*(2), 119–133.

Petrak, J. (2002). The psychological impact of sexual assault. In J. Petrak & B. Hedge (Eds.), *The trauma of sexual assault: Treatment, prevention, and practice.* West Sussex, England: John Wiley & Sons.

Resnick, H., Acierno, R., Holmes, M., Dammeyer, M., & Kilpatrick, D. (2000). Emergency evaluation and intervention with female victims of rape and other violence. *Journal of Clinical Psychology, 56*(10), 1317–1333.

Ruch, L. O., Amedeo, S. R., Leon, J. J., & Gartrell, J. W. (1991). Repeated sexual victimization and trauma change during the acute phase of the sexual assault trauma syndrome. *Women and Health, 17,* 1–19.

Safe Schools Coalition. (1999). *They don't even know me: Understanding anti-gay harassment and violence in schools.* Seattle: Safe Schools Coalition of Washington State.

Stein, N. (1993). *Secrets in public: Sexual harassment in our schools.* Wellesley College Center for Research on Women.

Stein, N. (1999). *Classrooms and courtrooms: Facing sexual harassment in K-12 schools.* New York: Teachers College Press.

Tjaden, P., & Thoennes, N. (1998). *Prevalence, incidence, and consequences of violence against women: Findings from the National Violence Against Women Survey.* Washington, DC: National Institute of Justice.

Ullman, S. (1996). Social reactions, coping strategies, and self-blame attributions in adjustment to sexual assault. *Psychology of Women Quarterly, 20,* 505–526.

Ullman, S. (1999). Social support and recovery from sexual assault: A review. *Aggression and Violent Behavior, 4,* 343–359.

Vicary, J., Klingaman, L. R., & Harkness, W. L. (1995). Risk factors associated with date rape and sexual assault of adolescent girls. *Journal of Adolescence, 18,* 289–306.

Wolfe, D. A., Wurkele, C., Reitzel-Jaffe, D., & Lefebvre, L. (1998). Factors associated with abusive relationships among maltreated and nonmaltreated youth. *Development and Psychopathology, 10,* 61–85.

Zoellner, L. A., Goodwin, M. L., & Foa, E. B. (2000). PTSD severity and health perceptions in female victims of sexual assault. *Journal of Traumatic Stress, 13,* 635–649.

Chapter 9

Ames, C. (1993). How school-to-home communications influence parent beliefs and perceptions. *Equity and choice, 9*(3), 44–49.

Ames, C. (1995). Teachers' school-to-home communications and parent involvement: The role of parent perceptions and beliefs (Tech. Rep. No. 28). East Lansing: Michigan State University, Center on Families, Communities, Schools, and Children's Learning.

Coleman, M. (1991). Planning for the changing nature of family life in schools for young children. *Young Children, 46*(4), 15–20.

Coleman, M. (1997a). Challenges to family involvement. *Childhood Education, 73*(3), 144–148.

Coleman, M. (1997b). Families and schools: In search of common ground. *Young Children, 52*(5), 14–21.

Evans, I., Okifuji, A., Engler, Bromley, K., & Tishelman, A. (1993). Home–school communication in the treatment of childhood behavior problems. *Child and Family Behavior Therapy, 15*(2), 37–60.

Fantuzzo, J., Davis, G., & Ginsburg, M. (1995). Effects of parent involvement in isolation or in combination with peer tutoring on student self concept and mathematics achievement. *Journal of Educational Psychology, 87*(2), 272–281.

Grimmett, S., & McCoy, M. (1980). Effects of parental communication on reading performance of third grade children. *Reading Teacher, 34*(3), 303–308.

Heller, L., & Fantuzzo, J. (1993). Reciprocal peer tutoring and parent partnership: Does parent involvement make a difference? *School Psychology Review, 22*(3), 517–534.

Hoberecht, R. (1999). The relationship between teacher/parent perception of communication and practices for more parent involvement at a public school. *Dissertation Abstracts International, 60* (1A). (UMI No. 95013–046)

Hughes, M., Oakes, K., Lenzo, C., & Carpas, J. (2001). *The elementary teacher's guide to conferences and open houses.* Greensboro, NC: Carson-Dellosa.

Ialongo, N., Poduska, J., Werthamer, L., & Kellam, S. (2001). The distal impact of two first grade preventive interventions on conduct problems and disorder in early adolescence. *Journal of Emotional and Behavioral Disorders, 9*(3), 140–160.

Keyes, C. (2002). A way of thinking about parent/teacher partnerships for teachers. *International Journal of Early Years Education, 10*(3), 177–191.

Penney, S., & Wilgosh, L. (2000). Fostering parent–teacher relationships when children are gifted. *Gifted Education International, 14*(3), 217–229.

Rolnick, L. (1998). The study of parent–teacher communication: The social/cognitive and efficacy bases of teachers' communicative strategies. *Dissertation Abstracts International, 58* (9A). (UMI No. 95005–039)

Stiffman, A., Orme, J., Evans, D., Feldman, R., & Keeney, P. (1984). A brief measure of children's behavior problems: The Behavior Rating Index for Children. *Measurement and Evaluation in Counseling and Development, 17*(2), 83–90.

Thorkildsen, R., & Stein, M. (1998). Is parental involvement related to student achievement? Exploring the evidence. *Phi Research Bulletin, 22.* Phi Delta Kappa Center for Education, Development, and Research.

Werthamer-Larsson, L., Kellam, S., & Wheeler, L. (1991). Effect of first grade classroom environment on shy behavior, aggressive behaviors, and concentration problems. *American Journal of Community Psychology, 19*(4), 585–602.

Chapter 10

American Association of University Women. (2001). *Hostile hallways: Bullying, teasing, and sexual harassment in school.* Washington, DC: Author.

Banyard, V., Plante, E. G., & Moynihan, M. M. (2004). Bystander education: Bringing a broader community perspective to sexual violence prevention. *Journal of Community Psychology, 32,* 61–79.

Berkowitz, A. D. (2002). Fostering men's responsibility for preventing sexual assault. In P. Schewe (Ed.), *Preventing violence in relationships: Interventions across the life span* (pp. 163–196). Washington, DC: American Psychological Association.

Foshee, V., Bauman, K. E., Greene, W. F., Koch, G. G., Linder, G. F., & MacDougall, J. E. (2000). The Safe Dates program: One-year follow-up results. *American Journal of Public Health, 90,* 1619–1622.

Hanson, K. A., & Gidycz, C. A. (1993). Evaluation of a sexual assault prevention program. *Journal of Consulting and Clinical Psychology, 61*(6), 1046–1052.

Heppner, M. J., Humphrey, C. F., Hillenbrand-Gunn, T. L., & DeBord, K. A. (1995). The differential effects of rape prevention programming on attitudes, behavior, and knowledge. *Journal of Counseling Psychology, 42*(4), 508–518.

Heppner, M. J., Neville, H. A., Smith, K., Kivlighan, D. M., & Gershuny, B. S. (1999). Examining immediate and long-term efficacy of rape prevention programming with racially diverse college men. *Journal of Counseling Psychology, 46*(1), 16–26.

Lonsway, K. A. (1996). Preventing acquaintance rape through education: What do we know? *Psychology of Women Quarterly, 20,* 229–265.

Marx, B. P., Calhoun, K. S., Wilson, A. E., & Meyerson, L. A. (2001). Sexual revictimization prevention: An outcome evaluation. *Journal of Consulting and Clinical Psychology, 69*(1), 25–32.

Norris, J., Nurius, P. S., & Dimeff, L. (1996). Through her eyes: Factors affecting women's perception of and resistance to acquaintance sexual aggression. *Psychology of Women Quarterly, 20,* 123–145.

Nurius, P. S. (2000). Women's perception of risk for acquaintance sexual assault: A social cognitive assessment. *Aggression and Violent Behavior, 5,* 63–78.

Nurius, P. S., Norris, J., Macy, R. J., & Huang, B. (2004). Women's situational coping with acquaintance sexual assault: Applying an appraisal-based model. *Violence Against Women, 10,* 450–478.

Nurius, P. S., Norris, J., Young, D. S., Graham, T. L., & Gaylord, J. (2000). Interpreting and defensively responding to threat: Examining appraisals and coping with acquaintance sexual violence. *Violence and Victims, 15,* 187–208.

Olweus, D. (1994). Bullying at school: Long-term outcomes for the victims and an effective school-based intervention program. In L. R. Huessmann (Ed.), *Aggressive behavior: Current perspectives* (pp. 97–130). New York: Plenum.

Rozee, P. D., & Koss, M. P. (2001). Rape: A century of resistance. *Psychology of Women Quarterly, 25,* 295–311.

Sanchez, E., Robertson, T. R., Lewis, C. M., Rosenbluth, B., Bohman, T., & Casey, D. M. (2001). Preventing bullying and harassment in elementary schools: The Expect Respect model. In R. A. Geffner, M. Loring, & C. Young (Eds.), *Bullying behavior: Current issues, research, and interventions* (pp. 157–180). New York: Hayworth.

Schewe, P. A. (2002). Guidelines for developing rape prevention and risk reduction interventions. In P. Schewe (Ed.), *Preventing violence in relationships: Interventions across the life span* (pp. 163–196). Washington, DC: American Psychological Association.

Stein, N. (1999). *Classrooms and courtrooms: Facing sexual harassment in K-12 schools.* New York: Teachers College Press.

Ullman, S. E. (2002). Rape avoidance: Self-protection strategies for women. In P. Schewe (Ed.), *Preventing violence in relationships: Interventions across the life span* (pp. 137–162). Washington, DC: American Psychological Association.

Chapter 11

Avery-Leaf, S., & Cascardi, M. (2002). Dating violence education in schools: Prevention and early intervention strategies. In P. A. Schewe (Ed.), *Preventing violence in relationships: Interventions across the life span*. Washington, DC: American Psychological Association.

Bandura, A. (1977). *Social learning theory*. Englewood Cliffs, NJ: Prentice Hall.

Banister, E. M., Jakubec, S. L., & Stein, J. A. (2003). "Like, what am I supposed to do?" Adolescent girls' health concerns in their dating relationships. *Canadian Journal of Nursing Research, 35*(2), 16–33.

Banister, E. M., & Schreiber, R. (2001). Young women's health concerns: Revealing paradox. *Health Care for Women International, 22*(7), 633–648.

Bergman, L. (1992). Dating violence among high school students. *Social Work, 37*(1), 21–27.

Bethke, T. M., & DeJoy, D. M. (1993). An experimental study of factors influencing the acceptability of dating violence. *Journal of Interpersonal Violence, 8*, 36–51.

Black, B. (2004). Evaluation of single-gender and mixed-gender dating violence and sexual assault prevention programs. Unpublished raw data.

Black, B. M., & Weisz, A. N. (2003). Dating violence: Help-seeking behaviors of African American middle schoolers. *Violence Against Women, 9*(2), 187–206.

Callahan, M. R., Tolman, R. M., & Saunders, D. G. (2003). Adolescent dating violence victimization and psychological well-being. *Journal of Adolescent Research, 18*(6), 664–681.

Carlson, B. E. (1990). Adolescent observers of marital violence. *Journal of Family Violence, 5*, 285–299.

Cascardi, M., Avery-Leaf, S., O'Leary, D., & Slep, A. M. S. (1999). Factor structure and convergent validity of the Conflict Tactics Scale in high school students. *Psychological Assessment, 11*(4), 546–555.

Center for Prevention and Study of Violence. (n.d.). *Blueprints for violence prevention: Overview of multi-systemic therapy*. Retrieved May 31, 2000, from http://www.colorado.edu/cspv/blueprints/model/ten_Multisys.htm

Davies, J., Lyon, E., & Monti-Catania, D. (1998). *Safety planning with battered women: Complex lives/difficult choices*. Thousand Oaks, CA: Sage.

Davis, D. L. (2004). Group intervention with abusive male adolescents. In P. G. Jaffe, L. L. Baker, & A. J. Cunningham (Eds.), *Protecting children from domestic violence: Strategies for community intervention* (pp. 49–67). New York: Guilford.

Durlak, J. A. (1997). *Successful prevention programs for children and adolescents*. New York: Plenum.

Foshee, V. A., Bauman, K. E., Arriaga, X. B., Helms, R. W., Koch, G. G., Linder, G. F., et al. (1998). An evaluation of Safe Dates, an adolescent dating violence prevention program. *American Journal of Public Health, 88*(1), 45–50.

Foshee, V. A., Linder, G. F., Bauman, K. E., Langwick, S. A., Ximena, B. A., & Heath, J. L. (1996). The Safe Dates project: Theoretical basis, evaluation design, and selected baseline findings. *American Journal of Preventive Medicine, 12*(5), 39–47.

Hansen, M., & Goldenberg, I. (1993). Conjoint therapy with violent couples: Some valid considerations. In M. Hansen & N. Harway (Eds.), *Battering and family therapy* (pp. 69–92). Newbury Park, CA: Sage.

Henton, M. J., Cate, R., Koval, J., Lloyd, S., & Christopher, S. (1983). Romance and violence in dating relationships. *Journal of Family Issues 4*(3), 467–482.

Hilton, N. Z., Harris, G. T., Rice, M. E., Krans, T. S., & Lavigne, S. E. (1998). Antiviolence education in high schools: Implementation and evaluation. *Journal of Interpersonal Violence 13,* 726–742.

Hovland, C. I., Janis, I. L., & Kelley, H. H. (1953). *Communication and persuasion.* New Haven, CN: Yale University Press.

Insko, C. A. (1967). *Theories of attitude change.* New York: Appleton-Century-Crofts.

Jaffe, P. G., Sudermann, M., Reitzel, D., & Killip, S. M. (1992). An evaluation of a secondary school primary prevention program on violence in intimate relationships. *Violence and Victims, 7,* 129–146.

Jaffe, P. G., Wolfe, D., Crooks, C., Hughes, R., & Baker, L. L. (2004). The fourth R: Developing healthy relationships through school-based interventions. In P. G. Jaffe, L. L. Baker, & A. J. Cunningham (Eds.), *Protecting children from domestic violence: Strategies for community intervention* (pp. 200–218). New York: Guilford.

James, W. H., West, C., Deters, K. E., & Armijo, E. (2000). Youth dating violence. *Adolescence, 35*(139), 455–465.

Jezl, D., Molidor, C., & Wright, T. (1996). Physical, sexual, and psychological abuse in high school dating relationships: Prevalence rates and self-esteem issues. *Child and Adolescent Social Work Journal, 13,* 69–87.

Lavoie, F., Vezina, L., Piche, C., & Boivin, M. (1995). Evaluation of a prevention program for violence in teen dating relationships. *Journal of Interpersonal Violence, 10*(4), 516–524.

Levesque, R. J. R. (1997). Evolving beyond evolutionary psychology: A look at family violence. In N. L. Segal, G. E. Weisfeld, & C. C. Weisfeld (Eds.), *Uniting psychology and biology: Integrative perspectives on human development* (pp. 507–513). Washington, DC: American Psychological Association.

Levy, B. (1999). Support groups: Empowerment for young women abused in dating relationships. In B. Levy (Ed.), *Dating violence: Young women in danger* (pp. 232–239). Seattle: Seal.

Malik, S., Sorenson, S., & Aneshensel, C. (1997). Community and dating violence among adolescents: Perpetration and victimization. *Journal of Adolescent Health, 21,* 291–302.

MEE Productions. (1996). *In search of love: "Dating violence among urban youths."* Philadelphia: Center for Human Advancement.

Molidor, C., & Tolman, R. M. (1998). Gender and contextual factors in adolescent dating violence. *Violence Against Women, 4*(2), 180–194.

O'Keefe, M. (1997). Predictors of dating violence among high school students. *Journal of Interpersonal Violence, 12*(4), 546–568.

O'Keefe, M., & Treister, L. (1998). Victims of dating violence among high school students: Are predictors different for males and females? *Violence Against Women,* 4(2), 195–223.

Peacock, D., & Rothman, E. (2001). Working with young men who batter: Current strategies and new directions. National Resource Center on Domestic Violence. Retrieved May 19, 2004, from http://www.vawnet.org/DomesticViolence/ Research/VAWnetDocs/AR_juvperp.php

Prothrow-Stith, D. (1991). *Deadly consequences.* New York: Harper Perennial.

Rosenbluth, B., & Bradford-Garcia, R. (2002). *Expect Respect: A support group curriculum for safe and healthy relationships* (3rd ed.). Austin, TX: Safe Place.

Schewe, P. A. (2000). *Report of results of the STAR Project to the Illinois Violence Prevention Authority.* Retrieved May 14, 2004, from http://tigger.uic.edu/~schewepa/ MPApres.htm

Schewe, P. A. (2003). *The teen dating violence prevention project: Best practices for school-based TDV prevention programming.* Unpublished report.

Silverman, J. G., Raj, A., Mucci, L. A., & Hathaway, J. (2001). Dating violence against adolescent girls and associated substance use, unhealthy weight control, sexual risk behavior, pregnancy, and suicidality. *Journal of American Medical Association,* 286(5), 1–18.

Skuja, K., & Halford, W. K. (2004). Repeating the errors of our parents? Parental violence in men's family of origin and conflict management in dating couples. *Journal of Interpersonal Violence,* 19(6), 623–638.

Sudermann, M., Jaffe, P. G., & Hastings, E. (1995). Violence prevention programs in secondary (high) schools. In E. Peled, P. G. Jaffe, & J. L. Edleson (Eds.), *Ending the cycle of violence: Community responses to children of battered women* (pp. 232–254). Thousand Oaks, CA: Sage.

Sugarman, D. G., & Hotaling, G. T. (1989). Dating violence: Prevalence, context, and risk markers. In M. A. Pirog-Good & J. E. Stets (Eds.), *Violence in dating relationships* (pp. 3–32). New York: Praeger.

Vezina, L., Lavoie, F., & Piche, C. (1995). Adolescent boys and girls: Their attitudes on dating violence. Fourth International Family Violence Research Conference.

Weisz, A. N., & Black, B. M. (n.d.). *Relationships should not hurt: Programs that reach out to youth to reduce dating violence and sexual assault.* Manuscript in preparation.

Weisz, A. N., & Black, B. M. (2001). Evaluating a sexual assault and dating violence prevention program for urban youth. *Social Work Research,* 25, 89–100.

Wolfe, D. A., Wekerle, C., Scott, K., Straatman, A. L., Grasley, C., & Reitzel-Jaffe, D. (2003). Dating violence prevention with at-risk youth: A controlled outcome evaluation. *Journal of Consulting and Clinical Psychology,* 71(2), 279–291.

Chapter 12

Chandler, K. A., Chapman, C. D., Rand, M. R., & Taylor, B. M. (1998). *Students' reports of school crime: 1989 and 1995.* Washington, DC: U.S. Department of Education, Office of Educational Research and Improvement, National Center for Education Statistics, and U.S. Department of Justice, Office of Justice Programs, Bureau of Justice Statistics.

Goldstein, A. P. (1998). *The peace curriculum: Expanded aggression replacement training.* Erie, CO: Research Press, Center for Safe Schools and Communities.

Gottfredson, G. D., & Gottfredson, D. C. (1999, July 29). *Survey of school-based gang prevention and intervention programs: Preliminary findings.* Paper presented at the National Youth Gang Symposium, Las Vegas, NV.

Howell, J. C., & Lynch, J. P. (2000). *Youth gangs in schools.* Washington, DC: U.S. Department of Justice, Office of Justice Programs, Office of Juvenile Justice and Delinquency Prevention.

Police Executive Research Forum. (1999). *Addressing community gang problems: A model for problem solving.* Washington, DC: U.S. Department of Justice, Office of Justice Programs, Bureau of Justice Assistance.

Index

Note: Page numbers in *italics* refer to boxes, figures, and tables

AAA (Assess, Acknowledge, Act)
model, 121
ABCD (Affective-Behavioral-Cognitive-Dynamic), 16
Active listening, 88–89
Aggravated assault, 62
Aggression Replacement Training, 148
Aggressive behavior, 61–69
background research on, 61–65
and bullying, 9, 56
interventions
selective, 61–66, *63–64*
key points, 69
and sexual assault or harassment, 102
tools, *63–64*, 66–69
Alternative schools
and peer conflict resolution
strategies, 72–80
American Association of University
Women (AAUW), 104
Antibullying policies, 9, 53, 103
Anti-gay putdowns, 97
Anxiety disorders
and sexual assault or harassment, 98

Behavior Rating Index for Children
(BRIC, Stiffman), 112
Boot camps, 27
Brain Gym International, 150, 155
Bullying at School (Olweus), 39
Bullying prevention
background research on, 52
interventions, 52–57
life skills training groups, 53–54,
57–59
school staff training, 52–53
student awareness, 53
working with bullies, 54–57
working with victims, 54–56
key points, 60

practice examples, 57–59
resources, 59–60
and sexual assault or harassment, 102
and violence prevention programs,
4, 10
Bullying Prevention Program (BPP),
4, 9–10, 28, 55
Bystander skill-building, 122

Campbell Collaboration (CC), *63*, 64
Center for the Study and Prevention of
Violence (Univ. of Colorado), *64*
Child Development Project (CDP),
5, 10–14, *12*
Class meetings, 87–89
Classroom conflict resolution
strategies, 83–95
and social and emotional learning (SEL)
background research on, 84–86
interventions, 86
key pooints, 94–95
practice examples, 86–92, *90,
91, 93*
resources, 94
Collaborative for Academic, Social, and
Emotional Learning (CASEL),
62, *63*, 84
Communication skills
and peer conflict resolution
strategies, 79–80, *81*
CommunityBuilders, 28
Co-occurring disorders
of aggressive behavior, 61
of substance abuse
aggressive behavior, 62

Dating violence prevention, 127–139
background research on, 127–130,
129–130
key points, 139

173

Praise for Sisonke Msimang
and *Always Another Country*

'Few of us have felt the grinding force of history as consciously or as constantly as Sisonke Msimang. Her story is a timely insight into a life in which the gap between the great world and the private realm is vanishingly narrow and it bears hard lessons about how fragile our hopes and dreams can be.' **Tim Winton**

'Msimang pours herself into these pages with a voice that is molten steel; her radiant warmth and humour sit alongside her fearlessness in naming and refusing injustice. Msimang is a masterful memoirist, a gifted writer, and she comes bearing a message that is as urgent and timely as it is eternal.' **Sarah Krasnostein**

'It is rare to hear from such a voice as Sisonke's— powerful, accomplished, unabashed and brave. This is a gripping and important memoir that is also self-aware and funny, revealing the depths of a country we've mostly only seen through a colonial perspective.' **Alice Pung**

'Msimang is a talented and passionate writer, one possessed of an acerbic intelligence ... This memoir is also full of warmth and humour.' *Saturday Paper*

'[An] eloquent memoir of home, belonging and race politics.' *Big Issue*

'An excellent blend of both the personal and political ... a bold memoir ... a tale that will sustain itself for generations.' *Books + Publishing*

Sisonke Msimang is a South African writer. Her first book, *Always Another Country: A Memoir of Exile and Home*, was shortlisted for the Alan Paton Award for Non-fiction. Sisonke's work has appeared in the *Sydney Morning Herald*, *Foreign Policy*, the *Guardian*, the *New York Times* and *Al Jazeera*. Sisonke divides her time between Johannesburg and Perth.

The Resurrection of Winnie Mandela

SISONKE MSIMANG

TEXT PUBLISHING MELBOURNE AUSTRALIA

The Text Publishing Company acknowledges the Traditional Owners of the country on which we work, the Wurundjeri people of the Kulin Nation, and pays respect to their Elders past and present.

textpublishing.com.au

The Text Publishing Company
Wurundjeri Country, Level 6, Royal Bank Chambers, 287 Collins Street, Melbourne Victoria 3000 Australia

Originally published in South Africa by Jonathan Ball Publishers, Johannesburg and Cape Town, 2018
This edition published by The Text Publishing Company, 2019
Reprinted 2023

Book design by Imogen Stubbs
Cover photograph: Winnie Mandela at the commemoration service for ANC member Ben Moloise, Johannesburg © Paul Weinberg/South Photos/Africa Media Online
Typeset by J&M Typesetting

Printed and bound in Australia by Griffin Press, an accredited ISO/NZS 14001:2004 Environmental Management System printer

ISBN: 9781925773675 (paperback)
ISBN: 9781925774467 (ebook)

A catalogue record for this book is available from the National Library of Australia

The paper this book is printed on is certified against the Forest Stewardship Council® Standards. Griffin Press holds chain of custody certification SCS-COC-001185. FSC® promotes environmentally responsible, socially beneficial and economically viable management of the world's forests.

To Angela and Stan and Wally—the stalwarts.

Contents

Introduction
Unforgettable

I was not going to bask
in his shadow and be known as Mandela's wife.

—Winnie Mandela

Like many migrants, I live a bifurcated existence. Perth is six hours ahead of my home country, South Africa, so one eye is always on the clock as I try to figure out if anyone will be awake yet in Johannesburg for a quick chat. If you look at my Twitter timeline, you can tell how homesick I'm feeling—when I'm low, I immerse myself in South African politics. I'm constantly online, making jokes and trading memes only a South African could understand and ranting about people too far away to make any difference to my life.

I miss the drama of South African politics, the life-and-death nature of it all. In Australia the prime minister might change frequently, but the democratic system has a built-in stability. Politicians are a distraction here, often an unwelcome irritation. In South Africa, on the other hand, our leaders have the power to hurt us—we're wounded by their betrayals. The difference is visceral. Because of our history, we don't know how to do politics any other way—it's a national obsession.

In early April 2018, I was scrolling through Twitter, catching up on the news of the day, feeling lonesome and far away from home, when I saw it: *#RIPWinnieMandela*. It was hashtagged, which meant it was not a rumour: the hashtag is the online world's version of a confirmed report.

It was fitting that I would hear the news this way—on social media. Winnie Mandela was a profoundly modern woman. Her defiance and rage, her beauty and radical chic, her cool and cutting humour made her an icon to generations of South Africans. One of the fiercest critics of the apartheid regime, she led her people in a struggle for justice. She was the mother of our nation, her name and face known across the country. Her achievements are all the more significant when you are aware of where she came from. She was born into a complicated and violent history. Her family was poor. She should not have made it out of the village, let alone to Johannesburg—and yet she was for many years perhaps one of the most recognisable African women in the world.

In the week that followed her death, Nelson Mandela

dominated every column written about her. In death, as in life, he loomed larger than her—but there was more at play than his incredible fame. The South African media characterised Winnie as a murderous thug. They referred to her as the 'mugger of the nation', and Nelson as a saint. Much of the international coverage focused on her marriage to Mandela and the scandals that had marked her middle age. There was only passing mention of the part she had played in the struggle for liberation, and only fleeting reference to the terrible sacrifices she had made. Her contribution seemed to have been forgotten.

The erasure of Winnie Mandela felt all too familiar. Women are written out of history all the time. And yet I had grown up knowing that she was a force. I had witnessed the respect she commanded, not just as Nelson Mandela's wife but as a formidable speaker and freedom fighter in her own right.

A spontaneous counter-campaign sprang up in response. Younger women wrote Ma Winnie a new song, raising their voices in respectful—in some instances even reverential—homages to her life. I was one of many feminists who had come of age in the post-apartheid era who added their voices to the chorus. We argued for her to be treated with more respect and pushed for her story to be told in all its complexity and power.

She had meant so much to South African women, her experiences, her hurts and grievances echoing our own.

Like so many others, she was denied a life with the man she loved. Her husband was in prison, not down the mines or working abroad, but when women saw her photos or heard her speak at rallies, they knew she understood how it felt to be alone. Like them, Winnie had to live apart from her children, too. She knew the pain of the millions of black South African women who were domestic workers in white people's homes and had to leave their children with relatives in rural areas.

Winnie was every woman. This was why her articulate rage, her belligerence and her persistence were so potent. She found a way to voice all the anger South African women felt. When she pushed a police officer, or lashed out sarcastically at the prime minister, she was doing so on our behalf. She spoke to white men in authority the way others wanted to but couldn't, for fear of losing their jobs, getting beaten or arrested. Winnie said what she wanted and suffered the consequences, but she remained unbowed. Often—because of her public stature—she got away with things that would have earned anyone else a harsh rebuke.

We adored her for having the guts to do what we could not do, to say the things we could not say. We cheered when she said, 'I am a living symbol of whatever is happening in the country. I am a living symbol of the white man's fear.' This is why she became such a powerful symbol of resistance for black women across South Africa, and ultimately black women across the African diaspora.

Many of the new generation of more radical men saw Winnie as an icon too. She did radical well, dressing the part, her fist always in the air. There are countless clips on YouTube of Winnie Mandela giving the black power sign. She'd roar 'Amandla!' at the crowd—*Power!*—and listen with satisfaction as the crowd roared back 'Awethu!'—*It's ours!* She was fearless, and she made others forget their fears too, inspiring insurrection. Right after her husband was sent to prison, Winnie was quoted in the media saying, 'They think because they have put my husband on an island that he will be forgotten. They are wrong. The harder they try to silence him, the louder I will become.' She had been loud, and so when she needed us to defend her we were loud too, singing her praises.

I cannot pretend otherwise: I am interested in redeeming Ma Winnie. But acknowledging her role in the fight for freedom, and the violence done to her, is impossible without acknowledging her own violence against others— the kidnappings, beatings and murders carried out on her orders. This book is an attempt to grapple with her complexity, to write into her contradictions rather than shy away from them. This is a generosity seldom accorded women. Women are supposed to be neat and clean and yet Winnie's story is messy and not straightforward. She heals and she wounds; she is staunchly loyal and yet she is an adulterer. Much like the country for which she fought, Winnie was both dazzling and confounding.

When the world relegates her to her ex-husband's shadow, it is also relegating South African women's stories to the nation's shadows. When it denies her story, it denies the stories of countless women. I want to bring her back into view, and in so doing, I want to bring us all back into the picture, to tell a bigger, richer and far more inclusive story. In the end, I don't care whether you love her or hate her, but I want you to know that she lived and she fought— that Winnie Madikizela-Mandela was here.

Mbizana

I had grown up walking tall in my home. I had been taught by
my mother and my father that I must walk tall. I am me; I am
black; I must be proud of my blackness ... I am going to be
who my father taught me to be. I am going to walk tall.

—Winnie Mandela

You, Winifred Nomzamo Zanyiwe Madikizela, are born in
a small place. Your life, however, is large—as large as the
open sky. It is a life spread wide—as wide as the wings of
the eagles that soar above the Mzamba River, which flows
to the sea through the lush hills of Mbizana from the exact
place where you were born.

The land on which you crawl as an infant is old, as old
as the bones of the daughters and sons of Sibiside, the
patriarch of the Mbo people. Sibiside led his small clan
from the shores of the Great Lakes in East Africa, down,
down, down, all the way south, until finally they arrived in

Pondoland. Sibiside and his people must have stood on a cliff, overlooking the Wild Coast with its crashing waves and its crushing winds. He would have cast his eyes out across the sky and then down, in from the horizon, all the way in, taking in the same shoreline your own eyes will scan countless times. Sibiside and your ancestors arrived long before white men. They had no way of knowing that the land they surveyed would one day serve as theatre to two centuries of blood and hate and vengeance. It is in this tough land, cold in the winters and hot in the summers, that you learn to be tough yourself.

You live in a small compound in a small clutch of homesteads called Mbizana. White men find it difficult to place two consonants together and so they call it Bizana. They erect signs and put this anglicised word on maps. It comes to be known officially as Bizana, stripped of its original meaning—izimbizana, the place of clay pots.

At the centre of the homestead are two modern houses with corrugated-iron roofs. They are surrounded by ten or so rondavels built with traditional materials—polished mud and immaculately woven thatch. Inside each hut there are women and children—part of the Madikizela clan. It is your father's kraal—his enclosure—and so there are aunts and cousins and siblings but no other men. His brothers have their own homesteads to look after and their own wives and children to feed. You take orders from everyone who is older than you and in turn you boss around the young ones. You live the early part of your life in this way: fetching water, scrubbing pots and lighting fires, then sitting in a circle with the rest of the kids to eat dinner every night.

Your grandmother on your father's side presides over the compound. Gogo is regal—tall and sturdy, like a queen—with long straight lines scarred into her cheeks. She remembers the way life was before her country was invaded by 'those strange people who gave her children strange names that she could not pronounce and never did'.

Her son—your father—is known as Columbus, which is not the name your grandmother gave him. Your mother's name is Gertrude, and this too is a name your grandmother will never use. Instead she calls your parents Kokani and Nomathamsanqa—the African names they were given when they were born.

Your grandmother is cleverer and larger and older than anyone you know. She is much smarter than the few men who live in the compound. She rules with an iron fist. She is black black black, like the shadows of the trees, and she scoffs at your mother, who has some European ancestry and therefore has very fair skin and light eyes. Mama reminds Gogo of the white invaders who made her life miserable when they challenged the authority of her husband—a well-respected Mpondo leader in his day. History is just a stone's throw from her memories.

Gogo loves you in spite of the European blood that courses through your mother's veins and inevitably flows through yours. She is thankful that your mother has given her so many grandchildren. You are flesh of her flesh, blood of her blood, so she moulds you as best she can to be an African woman, proud of her people and her heritage.

But Gogo is not the only one whose wisdom guides you. Your parents are uncommon folk, even though they live a perfectly ordinary life—and unlike your grandmother, they can read and write. In the year of your birth, 1936, only twelve per cent of black South Africans knew how to read. Columbus and Gertrude are part of a new breed, members of a pioneering group of African schoolteachers. You attend the school your father built and of which he's the principal. Your mother also teaches at the school.

On Sundays your parents worship a big god. Your mother in particular is a religious fanatic. You believe God is cruel because God takes away your little sister when you are only seven. When you are eight, your mother locks you in a room and forces you to pray out loud. She asks God every day for a son because all the children she bears are girls—one after the other it is girls—until finally your lone brother arrives right at the end, the last child of ten. This makes you want to 'prove to her that a girl is just as good as a son'. You can run fast as the wind, and you jut your chin out stubbornly when the boys challenge you to a stick fight.

The people of the Eastern Cape—your people—are well known for their ferocity and determination. From your very first heartbeat you have lived at the intersection of everything ancient in the water and the land and the sea and the sky and the trees and all that is yet to be. You have one foot in the old ways and the other in the new. You are mud and you are brick and you are thatch, and, yes, you are also steel. You have been raised with the same fighting spirit as the warriors who fought the Kaffir Wars.

When you are an African born in a small place, you are assumed to be ignorant. You are assumed to have no history at all, and no perspective of your own. Nothing could be further from the truth. History matters very much to your people. The knowledge of who begat whom, where the streams began and the rivers ended, who started which fire and who had the wisdom to put it out—all of this history is embedded in your songs and your prayers, so that history is a living and breathing part of you. History pulses in and through you—and like most Africans of your generation, you are aware not just of its truths, but also of its lies and deceits.

When your people have survived genocide, you know all too well the power of myth. You understand from a young age that history is remade to satisfy the vanity and suit the interests of the settlers.

The first lie the whites tell is that the land was empty when they arrived. This is the mother lie—the one from which all others emanate. They proclaimed your country *terra nullius*, 'nobody's land', in spite of all the evidence to the contrary, and still somehow the myth endures, many years later. It never occurs to you to believe either this nonsense or the bigger lie, which is that when whites arrived they brought with them civilisation. Your father, who is a proud rural man, teaches you otherwise.

He teaches you—and all the children who sit in the modest school he built with his own hands in that small place on the periphery of everything that matters—an alternative history. He doesn't just teach: he helps you to understand that sometimes what is taught as fact is simply fiction—the product of cultural ego and chauvinism and, yes, blatant unimaginative racism.

The biggest gift Columbus Madikizela bestows upon you is the blessing of the counter-narrative. He teaches you the wisdom of questioning the words of those in authority. You understand that you are one in a long line of people who have been dealt an injustice merely because of your skin colour. He teaches you to believe in yourself—to be angry about the injustice, rather than resenting the colour of your skin.

It is your father who teaches you about the Kaffir Wars.

***

The Kaffir Wars are the longest-running military action in the history of Africa, lasting a hundred years. Between 1789 and 1889, your people fight nine wars against European settlers. The first three are fought against Boer frontiersmen, descendants of Dutch settlers who established a supply station at Cape Town in 1652. The Boers spread inland, to the east, where they encounter the Xhosa. The Xhosa own large numbers of cattle and other livestock and live in highly organised, tightly structured societies, often in villages and towns with populations of ten thousand or more. The Boers try to claim the Xhosa's land for themselves and steal their cattle. When the Xhosa take their cattle back, the Boers accuse them of theft.

That is not what the history books say, but one of the many things your father teaches you is that you should not trust the words white men write—even if those words are in books. Columbus reads to you from these books because as a school teacher he has no choice. Then he puts the textbook aside and tells you, 'Now, this is what the book says, but the truth is these white people invaded our country and stole the land from our grandfathers. The clashes between white and black were originally the result of cattle thefts. The whites took the cattle and the blacks would go and fetch them back.'

The conflict intensifies when the British arrive in the early nineteenth century, seeking to colonise the Eastern Cape. A fourth war is fought, then a fifth. It is the sixth war, and the death of King Hintsa, that your people can never forget, despite all the wars that come after it. Tales of Hintsa's murder and mutilation were still in the mouths of the elders when Gogo was born. It is one of the most important stories your father tells, involving black kings and white soldiers and a desecrated royal corpse. Recounted in your father's voice, this war comes to life, animating your sense of pride and injury.

This story begins in 1820, when the British decide to address burgeoning social unrest at home by exporting their poor and hungry to Africa, where Britain has a toehold at the tip of the continent. Advertisements in *The Times* describe the Cape as having the finest soil and climate in the world, as well as 'all the luxuries of life'. Ships set sail loaded with thousands of men and women, all of them expecting a land of milk and honey. These new settlers have no idea that the plots earmarked for their use by Lord Charles Somerset, governor of the Cape, lie smack in the middle of a war zone.

In its wisdom, the Cape colony has decided that the new immigrants will be settled in the 'neutral zone' between territory the British have claimed in the west and that of the Xhosa in the east. It is land that the Xhosa have only recently been driven from—land on which they have lived and hunted and grazed their cattle for centuries, and which they wish to take back.

Maqoma is a Xhosa ruler already legendary for his courage and intellect. He is king of the Rharhabe, one of the Xhosa's two main royal houses. His father, King Ngqika, had been fearful of the British, and as a result conceded significant territory to them. Maqoma is similarly wary of the British, but—having witnessed their unjust behaviour—he is determined to stand up to them. In 1822, just two years after the arrival of the new settlers, Maqoma establishes his own kingdom in the heart of the so-called neutral zone. In anger, the colonists repeatedly raid Maqoma's kingdom, taking cattle and sometimes women and children. Maqoma and his brothers stage counter raids, but by 1829 the colonists have managed to expel him.

Maqoma retreats north, but he remains angry and defiant. The situation escalates in 1834, when a group of British men evict Maqoma from his newly established royal house. He is reluctant to wage a full war, as his people and stocks are depleted from the almost constant battles of the previous few years. Still, the offence is significant—and humiliating. Maqoma has no choice. He organises a group of princes, including his brothers, all of whom command their own followers. Together, they mount a series of attacks on the settlers in the neutral zone. The white farmers allege that thousands upon thousands of blacks take part in these attacks. This is patently untrue—for all their courage, Maqoma and his men have been severely tested by ongoing wars, and they simply don't have the numbers or the capacity to inflict the kind of damage the settlers are claiming. It is clear, however, that the attacks have shaken the settlers.

Africans who have grown up on the wrong side of history know all too well the powers of exaggeration possessed by Europeans tasked with documenting the past, and these farmers are no exception. Their inflated reports inflame the colonial administration, which responds with disproportionate violence. Cape Town sends a large number of troops to the area, hoping once and for all to put an end to these frontier wars. The mission is seen as so important that the governor himself, Benjamin D'Urban, visits the area to take stock of the situation. He is joined by Harry Smith, a senior military commander just arrived from Britain. Both men are hardliners who have no interest in negotiations or concessions. They agree it is imperative that they crush African dissent and they are prepared to use excessive force. Indeed, by the end of their campaign they will—by their own records—have killed an estimated four thousand Xhosa and stolen more than fifty thousand head of cattle.

In the meantime, D'Urban and Smith's plan gives them an opportunity to deal with Hintsa, king of the Gcaleka Xhosa. It does not matter that Hintsa rules a different royal house, or that he has nothing to do with the conflict at hand. Nor does it matter that Hintsa has made it known to all that he wishes to avoid disputes both with other African groups and with the settlers, desiring only to keep his people safe and retain the land and cattle he already controls. What matters is that King Hintsa occupies territory the British have been eyeing for some time now. Removing Hintsa—a widely respected and cool-headed leader—would allow the British to push the frontier much further north and to the east.

In April 1835, Smith and D'Urban launch a surprise attack, one company going after Maqoma and his men, while another—under the command of Smith himself—heads straight for Hintsa's palace. They accuse Hintsa of masterminding Maqoma's attacks on the settlers. The king denies any involvement, citing his policy of neutrality. They accuse him of lying. His neutrality, they say, is a pretence.

They force King Hintsa to sign a document promising to pay twenty thousand head of cattle in exchange for those the Rharhabe 'stole' in raids the year before, ostensibly under Hintsa's orders. They also insist that he pay them one thousand horses. Once again, Hintsa declares his innocence, but the settlers are not interested in his protestations. Under duress, he signs the document. Still they are unsatisfied. Smith and his soldiers kidnap Hintsa and put him on a horse. They leave Gcaleka territory and head back to join the party searching for Maqoma and his brothers on Rharhabe land.

They want the king to tell 'his' people to cease hostilities. They want him to announce to the Rharhabe—a people over whom he has no control—that the entire territory between the Keiskamma and the Great Kei rivers will henceforth be ruled by another monarch—King William IV, who lives far away in England. They inform them that the area will henceforth be named Queen Adelaide Province, after the white monarch's wife. Although Hintsa knows nothing of the royal house of England, D'Urban and Smith want him to tell the Rharhabe that they are now British subjects.

It is unclear whether the British are completely ignorant of Xhosa politics, failing to understand Hintsa's relationship to other Xhosa leaders, or if this is a cynical exercise intended to provoke internal conflict among the different Xhosa houses. Regardless of the colonisers' motives, the kidnapped king knows that he cannot tell a house other than his own what to do. Issuing a decree of this nature would result in a war between the houses. Neither can Hintsa afford to pay the debt the British have forced on him.

As the party nears Rharhabe territory, the issue of the cattle weighs heavily on Hintsa. Handing over twenty thousand cattle to the British will make it impossible for his people to feed themselves. He turns to Smith and asks, 'What have the cattle done that you want them? Why must I see my subjects deprived of them?'

'That you know far better than I do,' Smith responds sharply. Hintsa understands finally that there is no reasoning with his captors.

He decides to escape and spurs on his horse. The guardsmen give chase and shoot. He is badly wounded. With his strength ebbing away, the king watches as a young soldier named George Southey points his gun at him. Southey is one of the children of the settlers who arrived in 1820, and throughout their journey he has served as interpreter for the king because he speaks isiXhosa.

Smith, watching from atop his own steed, gives the order. Hintsa asks Southey, in their shared tongue, not to shoot. Southey pulls the trigger, shooting him in the head.

The king is dead. The troops quickly strip him his regalia, stealing the beads and brass and finery he is wearing. They cut off Hintsa's ears and try to pull the teeth from his mouth. They leave his body on the veldt to be found by animals, or by his subjects. The message is clear: a king of savages deserves no more respect than a dog.

Three egregious sins have been committed, not just against the king but against those he represents. First, the king is dead—murdered despite his explicit desire for peace. Second, his body has been mutilated, although he did nothing to deserve such disrespect. And third, he has been left to the elements, and his people denied the opportunity to bid his soul farewell in the customary way.

The affront, to Hintsa's nation and the nations of all those who live on this battlefield of colonisation, is so profound that it alters forever the terms on which the invaders are met by darker-skinned people wherever in Africa they come across them.

...

You are born into this history, but it is not until you are nine years old that you discover that blackness and powerlessness sit on the same stool. It is 1945, and the latest war between the European powers has just ended. Your father has followed the war closely, siding with the Allies. When it ends, there is jubilation. There are signs advertising a celebration in town. Mama is sick—she is always sick—so you convince your father to allow you to go to town for the festivities.

You are without either parent that evening when you arrive in the tiny town centre. A little gang, you are all in a good mood. You soon discover that the town hall is only open to whites. Today's events are only for them. Your collective excitement turns to bitter dismay as you realise that the sole reason you cannot participate is that you happen to be black.

You and your sisters stand on the pavement. You watch from the street as the white merrymakers inside the town hall cheer. They see the little black urchins outside and they throw sweets onto the streets. You have to pick them up from the dirt.

You are humiliated. Across the world a war was fought to save Jews from the death chambers and put an end to the ambitions of a maniac who had started a race war. Yet here you stand, black children who have been robbed of their joy by the racism of whites.

You stand there on the pavement and you learn through your humiliation that life must hold more for you. The vastness of all that lies before you—and the full understanding of how clever and yet how constrained your father is—hits you hard. You now see the world more clearly, and your father's humiliation, too, but you are proud of him, proud of his mind.

The memory of this day stays with you for the rest of your life.

Soon after this your mother dies. You learn that your family is very poor. Your mother's illness has drained your father's pockets, every penny spent on doctors' fees all over the district. You wash your father's khakis—his baggy trousers so full of holes—and iron them each night. You shed secret tears when your classmates tease you about your shabbily dressed father.

Like all girls, you learn during the long, hard months ahead that you cannot be done without. You become indispensable around the house. You have to nurse your three-month-old brother. For six months you stop going to school. Instead, you stay at home to work in the fields, milk cows and look after the family's sheep and goats. Your father cannot even afford to hire a herd boy, as even the poorest of families often do. In the end you go back to school, but it's a miracle that you pass Standard 6.

...

In 1948, when you are twelve years old, the whites fully commit to the establishment of an apartheid state. The National Party comes to power on a wave of hate.

Apartheid codifies practices that have been in place for decades, creating an official system of laws and policies that claims to have its basis in the 'science' of race and renders black people economically and politically subordinate to white people. White South Africans live in a parliamentary democracy and can fully participate in a political system that operates for their benefit. Black South Africans are disenfranchised by the same system, with no right to vote.

The apartheid system operates on two levels. What is known as 'petty apartheid' includes segregating public facilities like beaches and water fountains and maintaining separate entrances for white and black people at shops and post offices and banks and so on. 'Grand apartheid' refers to a series of overarching structural measures that determine where black people and white people can live and work. Grand apartheid creates physical barriers between black and white South Africans, based on a complex but crude system of racial stratification. Over time the National Party government develops schools for the various race groups— one school system for whites, another for 'Africans', another for 'coloureds', and yet another for Indians. Apartheid also legislates separate housing and neighbourhoods for each of these race groups.

The overarching objective of the Nats is to ensure that black people remain in rural areas, in marginal zones with low agricultural potential. The foundation for this was laid in 1913 with the passage of the Native Land Act, which set aside 7.5 per cent of the land in South Africa for Africans, and decreed that no African would be allowed to purchase land outside their tribal lands. Whites—who represented less than 10 per cent of the population at the time of the 1913 Act, were to own 90 per cent of the land—by law.

The apartheid regime that comes into power in 1948 builds on the injustices of the 1913 Land Act. It begins to forcibly remove black people who live in areas that are designated 'white'—often in communities that have occupied these places for many generations. All of this is done to further entrench the migrant labour system that has been in operation since gold and diamonds were discovered in the late 1800s.

Given the demographics of the country and the needs of the mining and agricultural sectors of the economy, the implementation of this vision requires significant planning and regulation. Controlling the movement of black people in and out of cities where their labour is vital, and onto commercial farms that require their skills to plant and harvest enough food to feed the nation, becomes the full-time job of thousands of bureaucrats across the country. These bureaucrats grant and withhold permission for fathers to visit their families at Christmas and for wives to travel to cities to search for their husbands. By the time apartheid officially ends in 1994, there are countless stories of passes granted or denied. The decision of a faceless man in a white shirt and grey trousers sitting at a desk in Pretoria will mean everything to a family in mourning or a couple wishing to celebrate together.

In its quest to imagine South Africa as a country of white men, the National Party government invents the ludicrous concept of Bantustans. It would be funny if it had not caused such misery. They quite literally set about creating a real-life dystopia. Bantustans are places where 'Bantus' live. 'Bantu' is a bastardisation of the word abantu, which means 'people' in various local languages, and is used by the settlers as a derogatory term for black people. Each Bantustan is drawn up following pseudo-cultural lines. The racist ideology that leads to the creation of the Bantustans is that living in a communal environment—albeit on marginal land that cannot be used for agriculture and is located far from any other economic activity—is good for black people, because they are an inferior race, ill-suited to modernity and urban life. In its wisdom, the apartheid state decides that people ought to be living in traditional societies governed by chiefs. (The notable exception to this is that black people are allowed to leave their cosy Bantustans to work for white people in mines, on farms and as domestic workers, gardeners, and as menial labourers in poorly paid urban jobs that white people are unprepared to do themselves.) All of these changes—the schools, the separate entrances, the laws—are put in place to create a white society in which black people only exist as workers or servants.

You watch from your small corner of the world, in Mbizana, as these rules regulating who Africans are and where they can and cannot go begin to exert a force far greater than nature.

***

You attend school at Shawbury Native High School. For the first time, you wear shoes—they are part of the school uniform. You help the younger students. Nomawethu Mbere, one of your classmates at Shawbury, remembers, 'We had these debating clubs and the way she disciplined the students and kept them together was remarkable. She had very good marks and she loved sports; she was very good at netball. She used to win trophies at the sports festival in Umtata.'

You are a golden girl from the beginning. You are a born leader, so moving to Johannesburg, where everyone with dreams and ambitions lives, is only a matter of time. You began your journey away from your small village the day you learned how to read.

When your mother died, you understood in some part of yourself that you would never escape poverty if you did not leave this place. Though you love your father, and you respect his mind, you know that you cannot be sentenced to a life of choicelessness. So, like thousands of girls across the country, brown women with big dreams, you craft your own destiny through your own quiet determination.

You build on Gogo's pride, and her disdain for whites. Her pride tells you there is no shame in being African.

You build on your father's intellect. His lessons tell you there is another way to understand history.

You draw from Hintsa's story. He speaks to you from the past, imploring you to be defiant.

It surprises no one when you are accepted at Jan Hofmeyr School of Social Work. It is 1953 and you are seventeen years old—a country girl going to Joburg. You leave your home town robust and strong and ready, knowing the horizon will 'never become narrow and provincial' if you follow your instincts.

Johannesburg

How soon country people forget. When they fall in love with
a city it is forever, and it is like forever. As though there never
was a time when they didn't love it. The minute they arrive
at the train station or get off the ferry and glimpse the wide
streets and the wasteful lamps lighting them, they know they
are born for it. There, in a city, they are not so much new as
themselves: their stronger, riskier selves.

—Toni Morrison, *Jazz*

The city is large and busy and it stinks, but the women smell
beautiful. They are perfumed and powdered and a little bit
blurry from the beer they sometimes drink. The women you
meet here in Johannesburg are all learning to be something
new. The city seeps into you and makes you a new kind of
woman too.

You are innocent and young—you call yourself a country
bumpkin. But you are not. The education you have had, and
your natural authority and your father's lessons and your
mother's death—have made you worldly. You fit here—you
simply become more of who you have always been.

Johannesburg in the 1950s is like New York and Chicago and Paris rolled into one. Here, black people love and labour and are in the midst of creating an entirely new set of identities, split between the countryside, where many of them have their roots, and the city, where all of them have their feet. They are here because of the gold and diamonds, and because they have few other choices.

...

Johannesburg is born because of gold. There is no naturally occurring body of water anywhere near the city and so it exists for only one reason: because of the precious metal that lies deep beneath its surface. In 1886, just as the Kaffir Wars are ending, a city emerges atop the furnace-hot underground metropolis of tunnels and warrens, springing up and sprawling out across the rolling grasslands of the Highveldt. New buildings rise where gold deposits have lain deep in the earth for millennia, and the settlers—who have by this time defeated the Khoisan and the Xhosa and the Zulu and all the other great nations they encountered from the Cape all the way up to the great Limpopo River— secure a gleaming future for themselves. Mining creates a viable industrial economy. Struggling settler farmers take their chances, leaving their farms and arriving in Johannesburg in droves to seek their fortunes.

Over the next few decades Johannesburg calls into existence a new type of black citizen too—a sort of urban native, one whose identity is forged in the city's beer halls and mining compounds and social clubs as much as it is in the ancient customs and initiation rites of the hills and valleys. These new South Africans are increasingly cosmopolitan, their world a melting pot of languages and cultures from across the country—indeed from the entire region, including Mozambique and Zambia and Lesotho. Like all great modern cities, Johannesburg is exciting because it is home to people from so many different places.

In the early years the city grows quickly and unevenly. It is dirty and crowded and full of rogues and bandits of all social classes and all races. It is full of men. In the late 1800s and the early 1900s the ratio of white men to white women is two to one, and among black people the imbalance is even starker, with ten African men for every African woman within the city limits. In the compounds, where men live when they are not underground, there are twenty-four black men for every black woman. The imbalance has some fairly predictable outcomes. One is that sex work is ubiquitous. There are brothels all over the city, and as many as one in ten women is a sex worker. The women come from everywhere—as far as Europe and as close as nearby villages now swept up in the mining boom.

In the 1930s the city begins to change. It is no longer driven purely by the labour of men. Women begin to arrive in larger numbers, pushed by growing poverty in rural areas. There aren't many options for them in formal employment.

Some black women serve as domestic workers in the homes of whites. Others bring their traditional skills with them, creating a lively informal economy by brewing beer and cooking and selling food to the hungry and homesick men who live in the mining compounds. Their industriousness drives business in shebeens and social clubs, where men come seeking companionship and camaraderie, where they eat the food that reminds them of home and listen to the new music that is evolving in the shacks and backyards of Johannesburg.

The women set up their homes in chaotically mixed neighbourhoods like Sophiatown—the home of black culture and music, where in the 1950s writers and thinkers and musicians will congregate, people like Bloke Modisane and Can Themba, Hugh Masekela and Miriam Makeba. The women who make Sophiatown home find a way to brew beer and make music and love their men and raise their children.

The authorities don't know what to do about the presence of black women in Johannesburg. They aren't sure whether to regard them as a threat or a stabilising force. On the one hand, they are often the wives or companions of men living in the grey zones like Sophiatown, or in compounds. These men might otherwise be lonely and restless. The women are also seen as an antidote to the 'homosexual problem' that administrators have wrung their hands about since the establishment of single-sex dormitories at the turn of the century. On the other hand, they challenge the social order the apartheid machine is so desperately trying to impose on the city. African men are only in Johannesburg to provide labour. Allowing their wives and lovers into the city removes the pretence that these men are only temporary residents.

African men are units of labour—a key ingredient in the apartheid system. They have already been forced to carry identity documents for years, documents that tie them to a particular address and stop them moving freely from country to city or vice versa, but African women are not subject to the same stringent laws. Women are supposed to stay in rural areas—technically, there is nothing for them to do in the cities—but the authorities largely leave them alone. Under traditional law they are considered minors, subordinate to their fathers or husbands, rather than persons in their own right. Colonial laws have done little to challenge this state of affairs; where a law refers to 'natives', it usually means men, and is rarely concerned with women and their conduct. While there is a 'need' for a small group of African women to serve as domestic labour for the city's white families, there really isn't any justification for developing a large-scale pass system directed at African women. This will change as over time as the policies of apartheid make life increasingly miserable for rural Africans and domestic labour more affordable for white households. Initially, though, no attempt is made to control the movement of African women to the city. Their presence there isn't exactly legal, but it isn't exactly illegal either.

This state of limbo is both a blessing and a curse. It allows black women to be free in ways that white women are not—to escape European moral sanction—while at the same time liberating them from the strictures experienced by rural women living within traditional patriarchal structures. They often live alone, free of men and therefore independent. Yet because they often engage in illegal activities to survive—activities like brewing traditional beer and selling food without the proper licences—they are criminalised. In this sense, many African women in the city walk the fine line between the freedom that comes with not being important and the scrutiny that falls upon those who are deemed to be undesirables in the eyes of the law.

It is not only black men and women who flood into the city. Poor whites also make their way to the City of Gold, alongside an influx of European migrants fresh off the boat. They all compete for jobs and space. It does not take long, in these circumstances, for anxiety to set in about white poverty. In the 1930s, hewing closely to the racialised politics of colonialism and white settler society, working-class and poor whites who live in Johannesburg begin to organise, campaigning for labour protection.

In the meantime, the wealth from gold builds the fortunes of a handful of white patriarchs, among them

George Albu, who arrived from Germany with his brother Leopold in 1876; Sir Abe Bailey, a close friend and associate of Cecil John Rhodes; and Barney Barnato, whose fierce rivalry with Rhodes is the stuff of legend. These Randlords build large mansions in neighbourhoods like Houghton, with its breathtaking views of the city, and Observatory, where the wide streets lined with jacarandas and homes set back on large plots recall British manor houses.

Their wealth and the opulence of their lives are in stark contrast to the squalor of the mining hostels and working-class compounds where poor whites live. The difference between the lives of the new urban poor and the gold barons is impossible to ignore. From the very beginning, inequality defines the city.

But if white poverty is a real problem, black poverty is an even bigger problem. As is the case everywhere else in the country, the most extreme poverty and exploitation are reserved for black people. Whites are on top and blacks— the losers in the wars of dispossession, forced away from their agrarian lives and into the city—are right at the bottom. And not only figuratively: black men toil in mines that are more treacherous than any in the world. South African gold is particularly hard to reach, and to this day South Africa's mines remain some of the deepest and most dangerous on the planet.

Over time, the millionaires who own the companies that dig the gold collude to reduce competition for labour and the costs associated with deep-level digging. The millionaires develop a brutally efficient system of recruitment, compensation and accommodation. Pretoria is the political and administrative capital, but Johannesburg and Kimberley run the country. The millionaires tell the bureaucrats which laws they want passed to facilitate the digging. In this sense, apartheid is born underground long before the National Party comes to power in 1948. It is birthed in the tunnels beneath the city. Johannesburg gives birth to the extreme form of racist capitalism that will come to define the South African political and economic landscape.

The economy starts to mature, solidifying until black people's subordinate status within it is virtually set in stone. Johannesburg now exists to satisfy the needs and desires of wealthy whites. Soon the whole society is organised around and depends upon the provision of cheap black labour. In the late 1940s and early 1950s, the new apartheid government is settling into power. Dozens of new laws are written to ensure the races stay firmly apart. What had not yet been stolen through the long and bloody process of colonisation is now taken by legislative means.

In 1949 the Prohibition of Mixed Marriages Act is passed. The following year, an Office of Racial Classification is established. The bureaucrats of the apartheid state realise that South Africans must be aware of their racial classification in order to comply with the act, so a formal system is devised, dividing humans into four 'races': black, white, coloured and Indian. In a display of the absurdity of it all, the 'coloured' category (loosely speaking, mixed-race people) is later expanded to include the subcategories of 'Cape coloured', Malay, Griqua and Chinese.

Several criteria are established to differentiate between white and coloured people. These include characteristics of the person's head hair and other body hair, their skin colour and facial features, the area in which the person lives, their friends and acquaintances, and their eating and drinking habits.

By the early 1950s, the regime has started to focus on the movement of black people within urban areas, and not just on controlling the movement of black people to and from cities. By 1951, one-fifth of the population of African women is living in urban areas. The Natives Abolition of Passes and Coordination of Documents Act is passed the following year. Under this law, the many documents African men have until now been required to carry are replaced by a single passbook, colloquially known as the dompas, which literally means 'dumb pass' in Afrikaans. Naturally the word dumb refers to the 'natives' rather than the racist system.

The passbook contains information about the carrier's identity, employment, place of legal residence and, most importantly, permission to be in a particular urban area. The 1952 act foreshadows changes to come, stipulating that

African women will also be required to carry passbooks at an unspecified date in the future.

...

You arrive in Johannesburg in 1953, hot on the heels of these changes. Africans in the city are in a state of agitation. There are many minds and hearts engaged in the resistance. Demonstrations are rocking the city under the banner of the Defiance campaign. The campaign is the first large-scale multiracial political mobilisation against apartheid laws. More than eight thousand people will be jailed for failing to carry passes, violating curfew and entering locations and public facilities designated 'whites only'. The entire point of the campaign is to clog up the system in order to demonstrate how silly the pass laws are—how petty. Every arrest plays into the protesters' hands. The campaign has been orchestrated by the African National Congress—a leading political organisation with a long history in the fight against racism in South Africa—and a young lawyer, Nelson Mandela, head of the ANC's Youth League, is the campaign's national organiser.

While the so-called natives are angry and increasingly organised, the white authorities are in no mood for dissent. They fear that showing any weakness will jeopardise their white-supremacist project. There are many, many blacks in the country and they could rise up at any moment. The bureaucrats and their political masters are convinced that the harder they hold the line, the less likely it is that the blacks will revolt. Many of those arrested, including Nelson Mandela, are charged with treason.

You are studying at the Jan Hofmeyr School of Social Work. The school's motto is 'Know thyself', and Mandela is its patron—that same young lawyer who organised the Defiance campaign, and whose name is becoming increasingly prominent. It will be some time before you meet him.

The school attracts the brightest young minds, drawing its students from across the African continent. Its alumni include well-known women's rights activist Ellen Kuzwayo; Gibson Kente, who will go on to win numerous awards for his plays; Joshua Nkomo, the future vice president of Zimbabwe, and Eduardo Mondlane, who will lead a revolution in Mozambique. The halls are a hotbed of political activity and intellectual thought, and there is no doubt in your mind that it will provide you with a firm foundation as an activist.

Within months of arriving in Johannesburg, you have a circle of friends who are intelligent, confident and outgoing. Many of them are future leaders, women and men whose names will ring though history.

Adelaide Tsukudu becomes one of your first friends in Johannesburg. She takes you under her wing. One day she will be Adelaide Tambo, and she and her husband will flee north to Zambia, then on to London. Oliver Tambo will run the ANC as its president for almost thirty years, while Nelson waits on Robben Island.

Ruth Mompati will go into exile in Zambia and serve as a senior figure in the ANC, eventually becoming an ambassador and a parliamentarian.

Ruth First will be killed, the target of a parcel bomb, while living in exile in Mozambique.

Albertina Sisulu's husband Walter will be sentenced to life on Robben Island with Nelson. Albertina herself will be imprisoned and detained. She will also be 'banned' for eighteen years—longer than any other person in South Africa's history. A banned person is forced to resign any offices they may hold and confined to their home. They are prohibited from meeting with more than one other person at a time, with the exception of family members, and cannot speak or write for a public audience. A banned person cannot even be quoted by others in print. The aim is to erase a person's public existence—to render them mute. Most of your friends will find themselves banned at one stage or another.

Florence Matomela and Frances Baard and Kate Molale and Helen Joseph and Adelaide Joseph and Hilda Bernstein—these giants also become your friends. Already many people across the country know their names and in time they will all become legends. You take your place easily among them.

The hostel where you live in Jeppe Street houses ordinary

workers, and most of them belong to the ANC. You are only seventeen, but your new friends take you to meetings at the Johannesburg Trades Hall, and afterwards, as you walk home, you talk about politics, and about the leaders and their strategies. You talk with them about whether the Defiance campaign will work, and discuss the next moves the racist regime will make. The language they speak is political. It is clear and unequivocal, and soon you speak it too—as fluently as your mother tongue.

Johannesburg affirms your innate belief that women can do anything they want to. You have always known women are strong—you grew up taking this for granted. You fought with the boys in the fields. You have always known that women are clever, too—you got top marks in school. But now you realise there is a world of ideas in which women must involve themselves.

In 1955 you finish your studies and become the first black social worker in the country qualified to work within the health system, linking outpatients and their families with the resources they need. You begin your practical work at Baragwanath Hospital, where you meet Dr Nthatho Motlana, a giant of the medical profession and a man who will be like an uncle to you. You work under his guidance during your clinical practice. You are only nineteen years old, but you make an impression. He admires your gusto and heart, but he is concerned for you. 'She worries so much about people,' he says, 'much more than about herself.'

Nelson

The day Nelson comes out of prison, we must go and complete the second part of our ceremony. I still have the wedding cake, the part of the cake we were supposed to have taken to his place. It is ... in my house in Orlando, waiting for him.

—Winnie Mandela

First you only hear the name. Everywhere you go, his name is on people's lips. In the meetings you go to with your friends, they talk about him. He is part of the leadership of the ANC, and the ANC is the representative of the aspirations of the people. Sometimes in *Drum* and in *Bantu World* there are photos of him. He is dashing—tall and somewhat stern.

A friend has been assaulted by the police and you accompany her to court for moral support. You sit in the public gallery so that you can have a good view of the proceedings. The place is crowded and busy, but despite all the noise and clamour it is impossible to ignore her lawyer. He has a commanding presence—'towering, imposing … actually quite awesome'. From the very beginning, Nelson has this effect on you. You never tell him that you saw him first—that you watched him as he worked, as he argued. You never tell him that he left you feeling awestruck.

You finally meet one afternoon in 1955, when you are with Adelaide and Oliver. He comes across to greet them, and as he does you look at one another. You smile and allow yourself to be introduced as 'Winnie from Bizana'. The attraction is instant and immediate.

He gets your telephone number easily enough and soon he calls to invite you to lunch. He takes you to an Indian place, and you sit there, 'a little country bumpkin from Pondoland'. You are almost in tears because of the hot, hot curry. He notices and gives you a glass of water.

You become an item very quickly and because he is Nelson and it never occurs to him that you might not be interested in him, and because you are Winnie and you probably decided when you saw him in the courthouse that day, long before he saw you, that you liked him.

You are attracted to Nelson because he is attracted to politics. Some ordinary man with ordinary views who does not care about the state of the world and the condition of the people would not be good enough for you. A man who has never read a book and cannot tease you about your own convictions would not be good enough for you. Politics grounds you—it provides you with a home in the big city. You meet Nelson because of your politics: you are a debater and a participant in a moment of dramatic change. You do not become political because of him—you are drawn to him because of his politics. You say this time and again, and Nelson knows this about you.

Others refuse to understand it, but you are not some ingenue looking for a man. They gossip about the fact that he is eighteen years older than you, as though you are incapable of making your own decisions and determining for yourself whom you will love and under what conditions. You choose Nelson just as much as he chooses you. You have much to learn, and Nelson will teach you many things, but he will learn from you too.

He is still married to his first wife, Evelyn, who is a cousin to Albertina Sisulu, and they have four children. Evelyn is not in the picture, though. Whatever transpired between them took place before you arrived on the scene. He lavishes on you the sort of attention only a single man can give.

After that first date the relationship moves quickly. Nelson sends a car when he knows you will be finishing work. Even when he doesn't have time to see you, he makes sure someone is there with a message or some sort of arrangement that lets you know he is thinking of you. After some time a routine develops. There is a car waiting for you after work every day. It takes you back to the hostel, and in this way you know Nelson is thinking about you. Sometimes he arranges for you just to come and watch him—in the gym, sweating, or at a meeting, speaking.

Nelson has a way of showing how intelligent he is without making it a big deal. He makes you laugh. He teases you often. And he has these little stories that are amusing but always make a larger point, like the one about the old white lady with the broken-down car. Nelson helps her to push-start her car and in thanks she offers him five cents. Nelson refuses the money and the white woman gets angry. She jumps out of her car with her hands on her hips and says, 'Look at this kaffir! He wants twenty-five cents! Well, you won't get it from me!'

The question of marriage comes up, at his instigation, but he is ever so cool about it. He does not bother with getting on his knee and proposing. You like this about him. You are both unconventional in this way. You do not ask about Evelyn—if he is asking about marriage, you know it must mean he is no longer married. One day as he is driving, he says, 'You know, there is a woman, a dressmaker, you must go and see her, she is going to make your wedding gown. How many bridesmaids would you like to have?' By this time you're madly in love with him, as he is with you. It is such a mutual feeling and understanding that the two of you don't have to talk about it.

You marry in 1958. Nelson is known as a shameless flirt and a womaniser. People still whisper about his wife,

Evelyn. There are also rumours that he has been involved romantically with Lilian Ngoyi, the formidable president of the African National Congress Women's League, whom you admire very much for her outspoken nature and her ability to mesmerise a crowd. And there is talk of an affair with his secretary, Ruth Mompati. You ignore all of this because you have no serious competition. He loves you, some say, even more than you love him.

If Nelson's reputation with women worries your father, he never says a word to you about it. Instead, the humble and mighty Columbus—the one who taught you to ask questions and be sceptical—is extremely proud of your choice. Nelson has been charged with treason for his role in the Defiance campaign and could face a long time in jail, but nonetheless your father is proud. You are also unfazed by Nelson's legal predicament. You and Nelson carry on your romance as though nothing in the world could ever go wrong.

Your love story is beautiful. It is so beautiful that it is easy to forget that Nelson has been banned and is not allowed to leave the boundaries of the city. He has to ask permission to travel to the Eastern Cape—to Mbizana—for his own wedding. The authorities give him just four days. The ceremony is rushed, and there is no time to do everything tradition requires. You have to dash back without even completing the gift-giving rites that are part of the Xhosa marriage ceremony.

Your daughters Zenani and Zindziswa are born—Zeni in 1959 and Zindzi in 1960. In 1961, Nelson is acquitted of treason. He still faces restrictions, and is not allowed to leave the country, but he is finally able to be fully at home, without onerous bail conditions and without having to spend most of his time preparing court papers and plotting legal arguments. For a short time you let yourself believe this might be the beginning of a normal family life. You will not be permitted to indulge this daydream. Indeed, you know in your own heart that there can never be an ordinary life for you and Nelson as long as apartheid exists.

One morning you are washing Nelson's shirt and you find a slip of paper in the pocket. He has paid rent in advance for a period of six months on the tiny Orlando house in which your family lives alongside hundreds of other African families packed like sardines into small, dusty brown yards. You wonder why he has done this, but you don't have to wonder for long.

That afternoon a car comes to fetch him. He doesn't tell you that he is about to leave. He never says he is going underground and that you may not see him for a while. He simply asks you to pack a suitcase for him. The house is full of people, and you are not really sure where he is going or why. By the time you are done packing, and before you can even hand him the suitcase, Nelson is gone. He is in the car and it is driving off and just like that Nelson enters into the life of an outlaw.

You love him, so you are generous instead of angry when you describe his departure. You simply say, 'I think he found it too hard to tell me. With all that power and strength he exudes, he is so soft inside.'

He becomes the talk of the town. Every political figure in the country is talking about him, every newspaper and radio station too. Nelson is officially on the run. Your husband the lawyer and activist is now a fugitive.

Every once in a while he pops up here or there, but he is wanted by the police, so he can never be anywhere for too long. You miss him terribly, but just when the ache is beginning to feel unbearable, he appears. He sends for you, or he shows up in disguise, pretending to be a chauffeur and beaming out at you with that devilish smile from under a driver's cap.

You learn to 'wait for that sacred knock in the early hours of the morning'. Sometimes you get a knock and it is not him. It is someone else, who tells you to follow them. You get in your car and you follow this person, then you switch cars, then you switch again, and sometimes you change cars ten times and Nelson is at the end, in a hide-out, and the two of you can be alone with no disturbances. Most of the time the hide-outs are in family homes, in the quiet places where white people live. Each time you arrive at one of these places, it is obvious that arrangements have been made for the family who live there to stay away while you are there together.

After a few months you hear that Nelson has left the country. He slips across the border like a bandit—like a man on a suicide mission, or deranged by dreams of peace. Perhaps they are the same thing. He is growing more and more militant, and so he goes to Egypt to learn the art of war. He travels to Ethiopia as well, meeting with troops and drawing inspiration from those who take up armed struggle in their quest for freedom. He is no longer convinced that the ANC's strategy of nonviolence—borrowed from Gandhi—is effective. He proposes that the ANC establish a military wing—Umkhonto we Sizwe, meaning 'the spear of the nation', usually known as MK.

Six months later, in July 1962, he returns. There is a new audacity about him. He is not reckless, but perhaps he has a sense of invincibility. He says later he always knew that arrest was a possibility, but that even freedom fighters practise denial.

The next month he is captured, near Howick, on the road leading south from Johannesburg to Durban. The authorities try him, and the most wanted man in South Africa is sentenced to five years in prison, for inciting violence and for leaving the country illegally.

In July 1963, while he is still in prison, a raid is carried out on a farm in Rivonia, on the outskirts of Johannesburg. The police find evidence of the ANC's plans to wage guerrilla warfare. Along with nine others, Nelson is charged with sabotage and conspiracy to overthrow the government. His co-defendants are Walter Sisulu, Govan Mbeki, Ahmed Kathrada, Raymond Mhlaba, Denis Goldberg, Elias Motsoaledi, Rusty Bernstein, Andrew Mlangeni and James Kantor.

Before the Rivonia trial begins, Nelson is released on bail so he can prepare for it. He and his comrades will be tried for 199 acts of sabotage. At the trial Nelson stands up and admits to sabotage. He is riveting, his performance haunting, and his voice breaks the hearts of many people around the world. He says, 'I did not plan it in a spirit of recklessness, nor because I have any love of violence. I planned it as result of a calm and sober assessment of the political situation that had arisen after many years of tyranny, exploitation and oppression of my people by the whites.'

On 12 June 1964, Nelson and his co-accused are sentenced to life imprisonment. On the day of the sentencing, you travel to the Palace of Justice in Pretoria with your girls and hold them tightly while they wave their father goodbye. You squeeze them so you have something to grasp, even if it is fat little thighs and squishy tummies. You hold on and you wonder how you will breathe without him.

By this time you are a subject of interest to the Security Branch. You are the wife of the most famous black terrorist in the country, and throughout the trial you have spoken eloquently in his defence. So in this moment of loss, when the idea that you may never again see your husband as a free man threatens to pull you down, in the midst of the singing and the tears and the noise, someone grabs you by the arm. You turn to see a member of the Security Branch. He shouts above the crowd, 'Remember your permit! You must be back in Johannesburg by twelve o'clock.' By now you have also been banned, and so you cannot stay in Pretoria past a certain hour. Even if your husband has just been sentenced to life in prison, the petty rules are the petty rules. You look at this small, silly white man and, without saying a word, you kick him. Then you turn back and look for Nelson's face in the crowd.

This will happen again and again over the course of the next few decades: a cop will try to exert his power and you will refuse to give him the satisfaction. You will never back down against an officer of the racist apartheid state. Every single time you encounter a policeman in every year that is to come, you will treat him with the contempt he deserves.

Nelson has this way of knowing what is coming. When you see him just before they ship him off to Robben Island, he gives you a sad, formal little speech. You can tell he has thought deeply about it and wants you to feel better than you are feeling, as far as that's possible given the circumstances. Years and years stretch out ahead of you both. He says, 'You are young, and life without a husband is full of all kinds of insults. I expect you to live up to my expectations.'

There is so much meaning in these words. What he doesn't say also hangs heavily in the room. He is older, and if life will be full of insults for you, it will be full of sadness for him. These two truths meet one another in that moment of saying goodbye. Nelson has a way of articulating all the feelings in the world, of thinking of you when really he should be thinking of himself.

As for his expectations, you are well aware that he is talking about your role as the head of the house and as the bearer of his name. He is placing a heavy crown on your head, but you are firm in your belief that you can carry it.

The first six months without him are the hardest. The loneliness is worse than fear—worse than the most wretchedly painful illness you can imagine. You yearn for Nelson, thinking always of that love which you cannot enjoy. In that dreadful period when you have to accept that he is gone, and will not turn up in a funny outfit or knock on the door in the middle of the night, you begin to feel like the most unmarried married woman in the world.

Nelson is allowed only one thirty-minute visit a year. When you see him there is no physical contact allowed— just your fingers on thick glass and his hand up as though to touch yours. It will be years before you can feel his skin again. There are always guards listening. Afterwards you try not to forget a thing he said and to remember how he looked.

His absence is a gaping wound and his love is the only

salve. His love lifts you and anchors you. Your love does the same for him. Nelson gives you courage. You have always been a leader, and a brave sort of woman—long before you met Nelson you were this way. But knowing him and loving him have made you need him. You were strong before you met him but now, quite suddenly, you are afraid. The warmth of his love is no longer there. You miss him and you mourn the time you have not yet spent together.

The same is true for Nelson. Inside that jail cell, your husband is heartbroken. The risks he took as he established an underground army and hid explosives never seemed to frighten him. Now, though, you know he is struggling. You know he misses you desperately.

The officials in the censorship bureau read all your letters to Nelson. They black out certain sections—especially where you discuss some of your legal challenges. Sometimes they withhold the letters altogether. Still, you can see that the words that get through to him matter. They matter to him as much as his words matter to you. You pour your heart and soul into your letters. You know the censors will read them and that they may snigger and laugh at the feelings you share, but you do not care. Your letters are the only way Nelson can know what is in your heart, so you write yourself into them as fully as you can. You write so he can remember how clear and funny and outrageous you are. You write to remind him of your fine mind and the depths of your heart. 'I find living in hope the most wonderful thing,' you write to him. 'I have grown to love you more than I ever did before … Nothing can be as valuable as being part and parcel of the formation of the history of a country.'

He memorises all your letters—it is the only way to ensure they are not destroyed. Knowing this, you tell him the truth as only you can tell it, because you know it will inspire him, and that it will make him fall in love with you a little bit more. You know this is what he needs to survive. He needs your love to accompany him, just as you need his to remind you that you are not alone—that your sacrifices are shared.

This is the most profound solidarity there is: to fall in love, and then, in the service of freedom, to be prevented from fulfilling that love.

Prison

I cannot pretend that today I wouldn't gladly go and water
that tree of liberation with my own blood if it means the
children I am bringing up under these conditions will
not lead my kind of life.

—Winnie Mandela

With the leadership of the ANC either imprisoned or in
exile, you become enemy number one. The state has no one
to look at but you, so they begin to harass you in earnest.

The scrutiny and disruption compound all the difficulties
of missing Nelson, and loving him and needing him. It is
not enough that Nelson is in prison—the racists want to
make your life and the life of his children impossible.

You have been a banned person since 1962, but in 1965
they turn up the heat. You are no longer allowed to leave the
neighbourhood of Orlando West. You lose every job you are
able to secure. You know all the questions by heart, but the

last question is always 'What about political commitment?' It ends the same way every time: 'Sorry, you qualify for the job, but your political views don't make it possible.'

Every school the girls attend, the principal and teachers are warned. Soon enough the girls are no longer welcome and you must look for a new place for them. Eventually, in desperation, you place them in a school for mixed-race children—a 'coloured' school. Officers of the notorious Security Branch visit the school one day and detain the principal. Finally, in 1967, you decide the girls must leave the country. They are only seven and eight, but the pressure is too much. They are enrolled at a boarding school in Swaziland—close enough to visit but far enough to be beyond the reach of the regime.

You spend most of your time in detention—in and out, going around and around. You begin to understand that you will have to live like this. You will have to accept, for instance, being awoken at night in your home, and having the cramped premises searched. You learn how to respond to raids, how to behave when you hear that midnight knock, when those blinding torches shine simultaneously through every window of your house before the door is kicked open. You know what it all means:

> It means the exclusive right the security branch
> has to read each and every letter in the house.
> It means paging through each and every book
> on your shelves, lifting carpets, looking under

beds, lifting sleeping children from mattresses
and looking under the sheets. It means tasting
your sugar, your mealie meal and every spice on
your kitchen shelf. Unpacking all your clothing
and going through each pocket.

In 1969, five years after Nelson was sent to Robben Island,
the Security Branch raids multiple homes. In the early
hours of 12 May, the police arrive at your house. You are
awake at the time, reading a biography of Trotsky. You
hear them coming and you hide the book, along with some
documents, in the stove. You know full well that books
such as this one are banned: they are 'communist material'.

The kids, who are visiting from Swaziland at the time,
are fast asleep. The police break down the door and begin
shouting. They take down Nelson's suitcases and cause a
mess, and they make a terrible noise. The girls wake up,
frightened. This is the last time they will see you for a long
time, because the police arrest you and take you with them
in their car, dragging you away from your children as they
scream and cling to your skirt. The girls have no idea where
you are going and neither do you.

You are driven to Pretoria Central Prison. You are held
indefinitely under the Terrorism Act, which allows anyone
suspected of involvement in terrorism—which is defined
in the broadest terms possible—to be held for two months
without trial. This is one of many laws drafted by the
apartheid regime to deal with the activism that has persisted

in the aftermath of Nelson's imprisonment. You are one of twenty-one people snatched from their homes that night. All of you are activists, and so, by virtue of your affiliation with banned organisations, and your possession of banned literature—the works of communists and the like—you are all considered terrorists.

The girls know nothing of any of this. They only know their father is in prison and now you are gone too. They only know that you have been taken in the middle of the dark and terrifying night.

So begins a new hell—one that will last seventeen months.

You are kept alone in a cell with a bright light that is never turned off, and you learn things you never previously had reason to learn. You learn, for instance, that the first thing you do when you're put in a cell is make a calendar, because you lose track of the days in solitary confinement, especially when you're living in permanent blinding light.

Within the first few days you have to contend with more than just the incessant light. You are interrogated, and of course you are assaulted too.

Your cell is next to the assault chamber. Prisoners are lashed with a cane, and sometimes they are beaten with a hosepipe. All day long, the women who are beaten in the torture chamber by the guards with the strong arms scream out in pain.

Your daily routine is full of nothing. You begin your

day by rinsing out your mouth and washing your hands and face. There is no toilet, so you urinate in the bucket provided. Then you roll up your blankets. Then you clean the cell. You never stop being meticulous. Some days you shine the floor.

You read the graffiti on the wall. Then you talk to the ants. Then you walk for miles and miles, round and round, backwards and forwards, in a desperate attempt to kill the empty long lonely minutes, hours, days, weeks, which drag by at a snail's pace, gnawing at your soul, corroding it, leaving it torn and battered.

For the first two hundred days—more than six months— you have no formal interaction with anyone other than your interrogators. This is just the first stint in prison, although you do not know this yet.

In February 1970 you and your co-accused appear in court. The attorney-general himself shows up and essentially admits that the state doesn't have a case—that it never did, and that it never had any reason to detain you.

You have no way of comprehending this. You cannot be angry because the news is such a relief, and yet you cannot be happy because the time behind bars has been such a waste. The judge says you can all leave, and you imagine seeing your girls again.

But it is not to be. As soon as you arrive back at the prison, the security police re-arrest you all. They say you have all violated the terms of your detention by writing letters. You ask, in your sarcastic way, whether letters are acts of terrorism, but no one is laughing except you and you never receive a proper response. You and your fellow accused are getting yet another taste of the blatant injustice of the system. The very Terrorism Act that you are said to have violated does not meet any international standards of justice. It has been written as a pretext to arrest anyone who disagrees with the regime. You have developed a grim sense of humour. Injustice no longer surprises or scares you. As they go through the farcical procedure of charging you again, one of the prison officials tells you that you will remain in custody for at least eight years.

You are interrogated for five days and six nights. One of the interrogators threatens that you will be 'broken completely, shattered … finished'. You are deprived of sleep and accused of being a whore. This is a taunt you will hear time and again over the years. Because you are a woman, and a beautiful one at that, the police—and later your own comrades—will sexualise you. As soon as Nelson is imprisoned, the idea that you are unfaithful to him looms large in the imagination of your enemies.

The prison officials taunt you with baseless accusations: 'The bloody bitch has sucked the saliva of all the white communists, look at her!'

One of them accuses you of cheating on Nelson with a white activist—a man named Denis Goldberg. He mocks you, saying, 'I should have taken tape recordings of your lovemaking and played them for your husband.'

Dear Denis, who was convicted alongside Nelson and is in jail even as these men brutalise you, does not deserve to be accused of this filth.

'Winnie would seduce the Pope if she wanted to use him politically,' another says.

'If I had a wife like you, I'd do exactly what Nelson has done and go and seek protection in prison. He ran away from you. What kind of woman holds meetings up till four o'clock in the morning with other people's husbands?'

You hold your tongue. Whether or not the comrades you meet with are other people's husbands is neither here nor there. You are a political operative and so you meet with other political operatives. You meet with lawyers—who happen to be men—who are involved in Nelson's case. You meet with journalists—who happen to be men—to share information. You attend meetings late at night and read documents produced by fellow 'terrorists'—some of whom are men. But you are a young, beautiful woman who is no longer protected by her handsome, fearsome husband, and so these police officers can call you a whore.

On the fifth night of their torture you start having fainting spells—long blackouts—that you find 'very relieving'. It is the first time you realise that 'nature has a fantastic way of providing for excess exhaustion of the body'.

After the interrogation, you are released back into the cells. You still have no idea how long you will be detained.

But here you are. Daily life becomes a battleground; every day is war. One way to make sense of it is to begin to fight for small things. You want reading material and time to exercise, and you want proper food and clean blankets.

You also want the charges against you clarified. Every time a magistrate comes to inspect the conditions under which the prisoners are held, you make it a point to ask him questions. 'What are the charges?' you keep asking. You know you are entitled to this information by law. Your questions irritate the prison authorities. This pleases you. You push and push and push to irritate and irritate and irritate. One day the authorities tell you, 'We shall decide when to charge you. You must stop at once telling the magistrate every time that you want to be charged.'

You move from irritation to impertinence. You show the utmost contempt for your guards, and this angers them perhaps more than if you were simply full of rage. You decide to fully inhabit their view of you. You will become everything they hate. So you amplify the persona of the sort of clever black person these sorts of racists detest. The more they push you, the more you spit contempt at them. You burn with superiority.

At the same time, you pay an incredibly high price for this resistance and this rage. You struggle to sleep, and when you do, you have nightmares and wake up screaming. The blackouts grow worse. You become very thin. If you stand up suddenly, you fall.

When you think about your girls, you talk to them out loud. You have imaginary conversations with them. You have always had such control over your feelings, but now you have none. The tears come constantly. You cry and cry and cry, almost hysterically, whenever you think about the last time you saw them.

You bang your head against the wall. Over and over. The frustration and sadness overwhelm you. You become obsessed with understanding the story of your life. You play it in your mind again and again—all the events that have unfolded in your life. You cry, thinking about losing your mother all those years ago in Mbizana. You cry when you remember the shabbiness of your father's clothes. Inside her cell, the dangerous terrorist, wife of the mighty Mandela, becomes a child again. Everything is tainted with sadness. You are trapped in the past, in that small rural place with the river and the cattle and the crashing waves. Instead of the happy memories there is only bleakness. You are a sad girl. You are not Winnie Mandela—you are a black child trapped in poverty, taken back to desolation, humiliated and trapped like Hintsa, that long-dead king, and your captors refuse to recognise that you are royalty.

You worry and worry and worry, and when you remember you are not a child but a woman, and a mother, and Nelson Mandela's wife, you become convinced that somehow this is all your fault—that you have to save everyone else who was detained with you. You feel strongly that it is you the authorities are after. The others are just collateral damage. This is true, of course—but only partially so. The others are brave warriors too. They are adults who have chosen to fight for their rights—just like you and Nelson. Still, this strong sense of responsibility haunts you. In time it will consume you. As the decades spool out, you will at times be blind to the contributions of others, and you will sometimes forget that you are not the only one who is suffering.

You decide to commit suicide, but in a gradual way that will not shame Nelson and the girls. You do not want your death to be interpreted as an act of cowardice. So your plan is to make it all look like a natural death. You want to die in a way that will highlight the cruelty of the regime and the absurdity of the Terrorism Act.

Your plan is very clear. You want Nelson and the girls to know you loved them even in your final hours. To get that message to them you need to land yourself in the prison hospital so you can figure out a way to contact your lawyer. You stop taking the medicines for your heart condition and for the blackouts. You stop eating, and only drink black coffee. You no longer try to sleep. You just stare ahead all night, your eyes wide open, thinking about your suicide plan. You tell yourself your death will 'stir up world opinion and touch the conscience of your fellow South Africans'.

Each bout of chest pain and each blackout lasts longer; certain parts of your body jerk and twitch. You stand apart from yourself and watch this all happen, feeling strangely happy within yourself.

Finally, and mainly because you have lost so much weight, you are hospitalised urgently. The prison staff clear the hospital of other patients. You are such a threat that your solitary confinement must continue even when you are gravely ill. You do not mind, however, because the stay in hospital allows you to hear news of the outside world. You get a look at the newspapers—at the *Star*, which tells of protests by students at the University of the Witwatersrand, who want to know why you are still in detention. The press is asking questions too, and the minister of justice has issued a statement saying that you should either be released or charged.

You are not dissuaded from your suicide plan, but your mental anguish abates somewhat. You never for a moment believed you were not precious and valuable: your plan had nothing to do with a diminished sense of self-worth, and everything to do with the cause. You write this plainly and clearly in your journal. You know that one day, when the journal is found, it will redeem you and show you for who you are—a brave soldier, and a woman who cares more about justice than her own happiness.

In hospital you also manage to smuggle a note out. You have thought so deeply about the children and Nelson—about how you want them to be proud of you. The goodbye note shows them all of this.

The doctors who examine you know nothing of your plan. They are trying to save your life. They tell you that your heart is working against unimaginable odds. You no longer think of it as *your* heart, though, just as you do not see your body as your own any more. All of this flesh and all these bones belong to someone else. There is a woman named Winnie who used to be alive; she still operates the body but no longer really exists. Before this detention and before the solitary confinement she was a mother and a wife. Now she is only a freedom fighter—a woman who will soon be a martyr.

They send you to a psychiatrist. They think you are losing your mind. The psychiatrist asks you a series of ridiculous questions, and his nurse joins him in this interrogation masquerading as a display of concern. They might almost be funny, these questions, if they were not so deeply insulting. These two idiots with their nonsensical questions remind you once again that anger is the appropriate response to your situation.

Absurdly, they ask how they can help you to solve your problems. Your response is precisely what they deserve. You say, 'My problems are solitary confinement, and the political problems I have do not belong to a psychiatrist's diary. In fact, the person who needs your interview is the one who subjects human beings to solitary confinement for over a year.'

They do not seem to be put off by your tone or your

responses. They clearly have no shame, or they simply have no way of understanding the woman who sits in front of them. Some whites can only perceive black people in a single dimension. They cannot understand black people who behave in ways that challenge the limits of their racist imaginations.

'Do you feel you are chosen by God for the role you are playing amongst your people—the leadership role? Do you hear God's voice sometimes telling you to lead your people?' the psychiatrist asks.

'If you have no more questions to ask, I suggest we put an end to this interview,' you say. 'I deeply resent the indirect insult on my national pride and my husband's. Would you ask Vorster's wife the same question if the situation was reversed?'

Even here, in this stupid little office, where inconsequential whites hold all the power and you are on the brink of starving yourself to death, you know very well that you are a mighty human being. Your acid tongue spits and your intellect smoulders and you see yourself as though from a distance. You watch yourself grow and you want to smile, because you are proud of the audacity—isibind, your people call it—that animates you. You have the gall to compare yourself to the prime minister's wife—Mrs BJ Vorster herself, in all her white Calvinist femininity. Worse yet, you have just, by implication, compared your husband—a mere native in the eyes of these two—to the prime minister of

South Africa. This is a brilliant manoeuvre—the kind of intellectual one-upmanship that makes you legendary.

The low-level bureaucrats do not appear to know what to say or do. You are sleep-deprived and half-mad from torture and yet still you have the temerity to assert that you belong in the prime minister's official residence in leafy Pretoria. Your words are more than just shocking to these two prison health officials—they are transgressive.

***

You do not die in prison. Somehow, the connection you feel to the outside world when you go to hospital assists your recovery. You take on battles over food and prison conditions. You persist, and once again become the leader Nelson told you he expected you to be before he was sent to the island. You rediscover the woman you were before you met him. You find your self-belief, become assured, determined, implacable.

Finally, on 14 September 1970, 491 days after you were first arrested, you stand trial under the Terrorism Act. You are free to go home and this time there is no catch.

Your children are brought from Swaziland and you are finally reunited with them. The next day you wake up early and go to the court to apply to visit Nelson on Robben Island. Permission is granted for five days later, and in the meantime you race to see your father, who is waiting for you in Mbizana.

When you return to Johannesburg, you learn that you cannot go and see your husband. On 18 September, just days after your release, the authorities renewed your banning order and you are not permitted to leave Orlando.

You must see Nelson. You are desperate to look into his eyes and tell him how you are and hear his news. You know he is worried about your silence, and you wonder what they might have told him on that devilish island. You contact your lawyers, and eventually, on 3 November, you travel from Johannesburg to Cape Town and then take the ferry across the water to the island.

Like earlier visits, this one is emotional and painful. Once again, you are so close and yet you cannot touch him. You sit down. Nelson looks at you and you look back. There is heavy glass between you, but you both raise your hands and can almost imagine how the other's fingers feel. The window is blurry, so you can't see his perfect mouth, his wide forehead, and you have no way of knowing how many new grey hairs he has.

Time is short and you have much to discuss—the house and legal matters and the children and their schooling, and who needs to attend university, and who is well and who is sick and who has died. You will try to sneak in some politics, knowing the guards will interrupt you because that it their job—not simply to guard but to listen and ensure nothing of import is discussed. So you sit talking with an urgency and a desperation that are obvious to anyone watching. You talk about matters both mundane and important, with your hearts breaking and mending at the same time. You burn Nelson's smile into your mind, as you do with his letters. This will carry you—at least for a while.

•••

When you are a freedom fighter, and especially one who is a woman, it can be hard to stop fighting. The minute you relax, someone will point and say it is because you are soft.

No one can accuse you of this. The 1970s are a difficult decade. You are banned and detained and banned and detained and remanded to court and then released in an endless cycle. Your lawyers are on call at all times. In 1974 you commemorate ten years without your husband, and it becomes obvious that your primary offence is no longer the fact that you are Nelson Mandela's wife—it is that you are who you are. You, Winnie, are a problem.

After all these years you are no longer quite the same. You were always impatient, always proud and easily angered. But now there is something even tougher in you. Something that is beyond reasoning—a bitterness that will not dissolve. You ascribe this quality to what happened to you in detention. You say:

> Now, if the man I'm dealing with appeared carrying a gun—in defence of my principles, I know I would fire. That is what they have taught me. I could never have achieved that alone. You

learn to test the quality of your ideals when they
do that to you, year in and year out, they actually
make a politician out of you. So the measures
they impose on us really build us.

In 1976, the Soweto uprising signals a new era in the fight
against apartheid. This time it is the children who stage
the revolution—not a group of educated but renegade
lawyers. When the apartheid regime decides to introduce
Afrikaans as the medium of instruction at all black schools,
the children rebel. Afrikaans is a hated language—the
embodiment of the white nationalism that has wrought
misery on the lives of black people in South Africa. Besides,
there is only one country in the world where Afrikaans is
spoken: South Africa. The youth rightly see this new policy
as an attempt to consign them to irrelevance. Children who
are not taught in English will be cut off from the world,
incapable of forging an international future. They take to
the streets, and for months the country burns. The regime
cracks down hard and many of the student leaders flee the
country. They go into exile to join the army Nelson created
before he went to jail. They leave to take instructions from
Oliver Tambo in Zambia.

The regime recognises your power and your appeal. They
know how much the students respect you. They are aware
that you have been working with them on the streets of
Soweto, and that if ever there was a moment when your
electric eyes and high-voltage speeches might spark flames,

it is now. And so, as soon as the protests begin, they arrest you. They lock you up for three months. Ha! You wear it like a badge of honour. Nothing can hurt you any longer.

Or so you think.

Banished

Exile here means being in prison at your own expense.
—Winnie Mandela

In May 1977, you are informed that you have been banished to a tiny rural town called Brandfort, about 350 kilometres south-east of Johannesburg.

Islands are ideal for banishment. The British, for example, liked to banish their enemies to Saint Helena, an island nearly two thousand kilometres from the west coast of Africa. In 1890, they banished the Zulu king Dinizulu to Saint Helena, as they had done many years earlier with Napoleon. Dinizulu spent seven years in exile. And of course between 1900 and 1901, during the bitter Anglo–Boer War, over six thousand Boers were sent there. But while Saint Helena may have been a favourite spot for the British, they dispatched troublesome leaders to other places too. King Prempeh, the deposed leader of the Ashanti people in West Africa, was sent to the Seychelles in 1900.

The island with which you are best acquainted, though, is Robben Island in Table Bay. Nelson may be the island's most famous prisoner now, but other great leaders have been sentenced to life there before him. Autshumato, leader of the Gorinhaikonas, who lived on the shores of the Cape, was sent there in 1658, not by the British but by the Dutchman Jan van Riebeeck, after Autshumato had taken back cattle the Dutch had stolen from him. Not one to be held against his own will, Autshumato stole a boat and escaped, the only person in history ever to have managed this feat.

It is ironic, then, that you are kept on a flat piece of land in the middle of a country that is burning with rebellion. The house where you live in Brandfort is not even a metaphorical island—it is not on a plot of land so large or a farm so remote that it may as well be in the middle of an ocean. Instead, the small three-roomed house sits alongside a row of others that look exactly the same.

The apartheid regime, in its wisdom, has sentenced you to live in a place where your charisma and intellect will have a lasting effect on the local community. You are surrounded by the very people whose rage will ultimately bring the racist regime to its knees.

Your tiny house is in a township that locals call

Phathakahle ('handle with care'). It is one of almost a thousand houses, 'little greyish yellow boxes, one exactly like the other in monotonous rows'. If we zoom up and out from your house we see a street full of houses that are too small to hold the dreams of those who live in them. It is easy to imagine that the houses in Phathakahle are uniformly filled with plastic-covered couches too big for the rooms into which they have been wedged. On the walls are framed pictures with captions that say 'Black is Beautiful' and photographs of loved ones and certificates and diplomas. There are albums crammed with memories that sit in cabinets bought on credit. In the kitchens are cupboards, too bare sometimes, but there is laughter in those houses, and other signs that life has not been extinguished, that indeed life in Phathakahle is being lived as fully as is possible.

The conditions in which you live are desolate and bare, but no more so than the conditions in which your neighbours live—people who have committed no crime and are not serving any penal sentence. Your banishment is thus a metaphor: it speaks to the banishment of all black South Africans, your sentence a mere reflection of the collective condition of black people. Being in Brandfort is, for you, a constant reminder of the sickness of your society—a reminder that your country itself is a virtual prison, that even in your own country you can never be free. Anyone living outside prison walls is simply in a bigger prison.

Only the apartheid government could banish someone to a place where others live not as prisoners but as ordinary black subjects. You think to yourself—not for the first time—that racists, in addition to being cruel, are stupid. Their aversion to black people, their inability to see black people as fully human, makes them blind to logic. They have sent a fiery, charming, intelligent woman, a leader of the ANC and a seasoned fighter, to a place full of poor and oppressed black people. They think Winnie Mandela will serve out her sentence in silence, and that the community around her will, like stones, remain mute and unaffected by her presence.

This is not how it works. Life in Brandfort is hard, but you feel a strong sense of responsibility. You have always been committed to the cause—your cause, your people, your politics—and you have always expected a lot of yourself. You are aware too that in your capacity as Nelson's wife, your people expect your courage to be unwavering, and your resistance to be unflinching. You are an ambassador of sorts—an exiled dignitary living in her own home.

When you are banished, you are not permitted to interact with others in groups. Only one person is allowed in the house with you at once. You never take any of this seriously—how many people are in the house and at what times, when you are to travel and under what conditions. It is all white noise, as far as you are concerned.

The worst thing when you were in detention was not

knowing where your children were—not seeing them and not being able to love them close up. So when they banish you to Brandfort, you take Zindzi, now aged sixteen, with you. She is your baby, and being close to her keeps you safe. She is not there all the time—sometimes she is at boarding school in Swaziland, or staying with friends—but she's there frequently enough to let you be okay.

Although you continue to espouse the philosophies and ideas of the ANC, you are also influenced by the growing black consciousness movement and the fiery rhetoric of Steve Biko. He is in some ways a kindred spirit—angry and unapologetic and proud.

Like other youngsters of his generation, Biko is adept at communicating his belief that black people can and should exist beyond the limits imposed by the racist regime. Biko sees black consciousness as an idea more potent than any political party. He has learned from the crackdown on Nelson and the others who went to Robben Island that the apartheid regime needs organisational targets. In promoting black consciousness, Biko argues that the regime cannot target a movement that grows in the minds and hearts of the people. Proud and angry black people will act on their own to attack the regime, and this will, he says, be far more effective.

Biko is surefooted and speaks quickly—the sort of brash young man who will not shut up, the kind of darkie who provokes white men to punch him in the face.

Six months after you arrive in Brandfort, Biko is killed in detention. He dies in a cell similar to those in which you have been held.

His death is both shocking and entirely unsurprising. There is an inevitability about the short arc of his life. Biko's death sparks international outrage, and he becomes a martyr.

In the aftermath, the country changes. Even here in dusty, sleepy Brandfort, the mood turns, becoming angrier. The young people who roam the streets in their torn t-shirts have a recklessness about them.

You take up your role as an ambassador with aplomb. Biko may be dead but Mandela is still alive—and so long as he is, hope remains. So you learn to speak seSotho, which is the local language here—so different from the Xhosa you grew up speaking. You smile at the neighbours and wave at the children passing by.

Inevitably, as time goes on, these same children start 'spontaneously raising their little fists in the universal Black Power sign'. During the day nobody speaks to you, but at night the parents come over and they express their solidarity. It is evident they know all about Nelson and the ANC, and that the spirit of Biko lives in them. Like the people of Soweto, they understand that the government and its laws are the source of their misery.

With this sort of encouragement, you slowly begin to build a life. You start a creche for the little ones who so desperately need a good meal, and activities to keep them busy. For the older ones—the ones just entering awkward adolescence and broody teenage years—you plan homework clubs and sports matches to get them off the streets and out of trouble. You arrange training for the women who teach at the creche, and you use your expertise as a social worker to address the malnutrition so evident in all the children in the community. Your yard is a hive of activity, and you continue to mobilise and educate as though nothing is stopping you.

In 1981, as the expiry of your banishment order draws near, you once again find yourself caring what the regime might do. You do not like to be in this position—it gives the racists too much power. Still, you hope against hope that the order will not be renewed, so you can go back to Soweto, back to the centre of things, back to the heart of the struggle to liberate the country.

A few days before, your friend and aide in Brandfort, Matthews 'MK' Malefane, meets with senior police officers to prepare: a ministerial delegation is to visit your home, accompanied by the chief of police. He will later recall:

> I cooked the best lunch ever from the best mutton and beef cuts and wors from our local butchery. The ministerial delegation finally arrived and we engaged in very pleasant chit-chat about what an inspiration Mama Winnie was, and why can't we find peace living together, and so on. They

> thoroughly enjoyed and profusely thanked us for
> the lunch, then they all stood and left without
> a word.

When the visitors leave, Matthews follows them out. They hand him an envelope, which he takes back inside for you, Winnie, to open. They have extended your banning order.

'I shall never forget the deep pain and disappointment on her face, but stoically and with resolute strength she recovered her composure and signed the document,' Matthews later says. 'I took it out and handed it back to the delegation, who with bowed heads filed out through the gate to their vehicles and sped off.'

***

Looking at this scene from a distance of four decades, it is hard not to want to weep. You are a woman who has learned to live without hope. You have carefully steeled yourself against personal expectations because too often your private wishes have come to nought. Still, you can't help yourself. Hope is inherent in living. To give up on hope is to give up on the future; it is to give up on the idea that Nelson will one day emerge from prison; it is to give up on the ability of your people to triumph. And how could a freedom fighter ever give up on that?

This is the question at the heart of your struggles. How can you fight so hard for justice—an act that requires nothing but hope—while protecting your heart from hope's vagaries? You understand intimately the pain at the centre of this paradox: hope will save your people, but if you have too much of it, hope will kill your soul.

In time you will learn to be propelled by anger or hatred or stubbornness instead. When you are tempted to believe in the goodness of all humanity you remind yourself how much the racist regime would like to see you dead. This gives you a strange sort of power. You are not guided by soft ideas about love and kindness. You are driven by a desire to defeat injustice.

You are driven, more and more, by the need to avenge the crimes committed against you. They were once generic— the same crimes committed against all black people—but the many wounds you have suffered since Nelson was jailed have been personal. Just as a family whose child is murdered may seek both justice and revenge in a jail sentence, you want apartheid to end both because it is immoral and because its architects have wronged you and your family. It is deeply personal.

I picture you standing in that little three-roomed house, about to sign the paper that extends your banishment, and I know that there are hundreds of women just like you, standing still and breathing deeply, at that very same moment, in almost every government-erected block of concrete across South Africa. Like you, they have learned to hold in the pain, to recover their composure and lift their heads high in order to face their children and the world.

I look at you all standing so strong, with such a heavy burden on your souls.

•••

In the wake of the Soweto uprising and Steve Biko's murder, a new generation of activists has begun to make their mark. While you have been in Brandfort, a new movement has been born—one that works hand in hand with your banned party, the ANC. In black communities across the country many small organisations have sprung up. They gather under the banner of the United Democratic Front. Created in 1983, the UDF is a coalition of over four hundred civic, church, students' and workers' organisations, and its goal is the establishment of a non-racial, united South Africa.

The current prime minister, PW Botha, is a hardliner, totally committed to maintaining apartheid, but by the mid-1980s he is under pressure from the international community, which increasingly treats South Africa as a pariah state. The murders of black activists in detention, the continued incarceration of Nelson, the constant harassment of the black population—all of these have the Nats on the back foot. Still they refuse to address the fundamental problem, which is that their society is explicitly founded on a racist premise.

They attempt to play around the edges, introducing a new constitution. It makes no attempt to guarantee equal rights to the citizens of South Africa, instead creating three separately elected chambers of parliament: one for each of the 'races', except Africans. Africans remain non-citizens, because they have been issued 'passports' by the Bantustans. These travel documents—like the Bantustans—are not recognised by any country in the world except South Africa Naturally this 'new' constitution, which merely entrenches white supremacy, sparks outrage in the general population, further mobilising anti-apartheid activists.

In the face of such insults, marching and singing and appealing to the conscience of the regime seem patently outmoded. The times call for something new.

***

By 1985 South Africa is burning. A state of emergency has been declared, and the already significant powers of the apartheid regime have been further extended. The country is effectively at war. Indeed, the white army is embroiled in a bitter war against liberation movements fighting for black independence in Angola and Mozambique. The apartheid regime is fearful that freedom for these people will threaten white supremacy in South Africa. They anticipate that newly independent black states will harbour and support ANC revolutionaries, and they are not incorrect in this assumption. They are fighting within South Africa's borders too. Hardened young soldiers have been deployed in the black townships—the segregated black areas that have mushroomed on the fringes of every city.

In September, someone petrol-bombs the tiny house in Brandfort. You refuse to live there after this. You decamp to Soweto, in defiance of your banishment. The authorities are not sure how to respond. In close consultation with Nelson, your lawyer petitions the Supreme Court, requesting that the order be lifted. Your team argues that banishment constitutes unreasonable punishment. It has been eight long years. You are no longer a young woman—though you are still strong. At fifty, you are more comfortable in your rage than you have ever been before.

The banishment order is lifted, but now you are informed that you are banned from entering Soweto. This is ridiculous, of course. It demonstrates how much the government fears you. It does not want you anywhere near Soweto, where the masses love you and where you command great respect and wield great power in spite of your long absence.

They are also aware that you only have one home—the Orlando house in the middle of Soweto that you decorated so lovingly when you married Nelson. Perhaps they are hoping you will go back to Mbizana. They are mistaken if they think you will ever capitulate.

You hear about the ban on your entry to Soweto just before you see Nelson in the Cape. He is no longer on the island—he has been moved to Pollsmoor Prison because the authorities, concerned about mutual radicalisation, are trying to separate him from some of the younger political leaders imprisoned during the crackdowns of the late 1970s.

When you return you go straight to Soweto instead of heading back to Brandfort. You do so in broad daylight, in open defiance of the new order. You are tired of obeying the rules of an illegitimate regime.

You get in the car with Zondwa—Zindzi's brand-new baby boy. He is your first grandchild. You cradle him in your arms and sit in the back seat and you decide that you are going home. The car pulls onto the road, headed for Soweto.

Your journey is covered by the international media. The *New York Times* reports that you are 'tailed by plainclothes officers in six cars, and further carloads of journalists', and that when you cross 'the city boundary', the police cars pull ahead and edge you off the highway. By the time they pull you over, you are in fighting fettle.

The police say you are under arrest; they 'don't want to use force', they say.

You ask one of the officers to remove his hand from your shoulder; you tell them not to touch you: 'Don't do what you have done before,' you say.

Finally, when Zondwa starts crying, you tell the cops sternly and without a hint of defeat, 'I am coming of my own accord. Don't drag me out of the car.'

The regime has no hold on you. You refuse to be humiliated by another delegation of cowardly white men. You think of that white envelope, of the rushed departure of those state officials who couldn't face telling you the truth. You swallow the lump in your throat.

You have freed yourself. The authorities do not persist in their campaign to prevent you from moving back to Soweto. You are home.

Ungovernable

Together, hand in hand, with our sticks and our matches, with
our necklaces, we shall liberate this country.

—Winnie Mandela

By 1985 there is broad consensus among those fighting the
racist regime that the end is close. The ANC has called
on South Africans to render the country ungovernable.
Reading the mood of the people and hearing reports of
cadres working on the ground, the ANC embarks on a
strategy to paralyse the apartheid regime by creating chaos.
It is evident to all those following political developments
that the regime will be brought to its knees by the masses,
rather than by the strategists in Lusaka.

That year, the annual January statement delivered by
Oliver Tambo is especially fiery. As the ANC celebrates its

seventy-third birthday, he suggests that the time is ripe to 'build up the popular armed forces, to transform the armed actions we have thus far carried out into a people's war'.

In April the ANC issues a statement titled 'The Future Is Within Our Grasp', which forms the basis of a pamphlet distributed widely within South Africa. It is also read out repeatedly on Radio Freedom, the voice of the party and its military wing:

> Ambushes must be prepared for policemen and soldiers ... with the aim of capturing weapons from them. Our people must also manufacture homemade bombs and petrol bombs with material that can be locally obtained. In addition, our people must also buy weapons where possible ... Our people must begin to identify collaborators and enemy agents and deal with them. Those collaborators who are serving in the community councils must be dealt with. Informers, policemen, special branch police and army personnel living and working amongst our people must be eliminated.

In June the ANC leaders meet in Kabwe, a town outside Lusaka, for their annual conference. They make two strategic decisions. The first is that the movement will include soft targets such as vocal government supporters, farmers in border areas, state witnesses and police informers. This is against the Geneva Convention and draws criticism from the ANC's supporters in the human-rights arena. Still, the stakes are high, and so the rules must be relaxed: moral rectitude has a time and a place.

More importantly, Tambo suggests that the establishment of people's courts, self-defence units and street committees is the key to fighting the people's war. For the first time, the leadership is acknowledging that people on the ground are taking matters into their own hands. The movement produces and distributes guides to revolutionary conduct, instructing the people on the proper way to deal with enemies and informers:

> For serious crimes against the people, even more seriousness and dignity is required. And where the death sentence is decided upon, ways should be found not endangering the court. To carry it out, appropriate structures should be used, and the forms should serve as a deterrent while not exceeding the limits of revolutionary decency.

In September, Radio Freedom issues another call to action, this time targeting white civilians:

> We must attack them at their homes and holiday resorts just as we have been attacking black boot-lickers at their homes. This must now happen to their white colleagues. All along it has only been black mothers who have been mourning. Now the time has come that all of us must mourn. White families must also wear black costumes.

The broadcast explains that MK's actions at the time 'are a continuation of petrol-bomb attacks, the necklaces against the sellouts and puppets in the townships, the grenade and stone-throwing attacks that are being carried out daily by oppressed workers and youths … against the heavily armed troops and police'.

The reference to necklaces is sinister. By this time the practice of 'necklacing' has begun to emerge in many different townships. The necklace is a mob-justice punishment in which a tyre is hung around the neck and across the shoulders of a suspected informer or spy, and set alight. Necklacing is always a public act. It is a gruesome spectacle designed to instil fear.

The identification of so-called collaborators and spies is often controlled by white police officers and security branch officers. Still, the perpetrators and the victims of necklacing are always black. It is no surprise, then, that the act itself comes to be seen as an example of black people's barbarity—precisely the kind of violence white people fear from black people. It does not matter that necklacing is the consequence of organised white violence that is hidden from view. It doesn't matter that soldiers shoot black children who throw stones, or that 'interrogators' throw black activists out of high-rise buildings. News coverage of burning bodies held aloft while black crowds sing and chant in glee plays into the hands of the apartheid regime. There are few white people who can watch these scenes without asking, 'If they can do this to their own, what more will they do to us when they get the chance?'

The ANC's own records show that it does not condemn the violence against fellow black people that has begun to grip the townships. In fact, this notion of dealing with informers effectively comes up frequently in ANC documents of this era. At the very least, it is clear that the party is signalling that it understands the masses' practice of necklacing 'sellouts and puppets'. By not condemning the act, the ANC plays a delicate and dangerous game, feeding the atmosphere of recklessness and amping up the flamboyantly violent rhetoric of the moment.

Indeed, even in foreign capitals like London and Paris, where it might pay to be less outspoken on these matters, the ANC does not hold back. On 10 October, the official ANC representative to the United States says publicly in a media interview, 'We want to make the death of a collaborator so grotesque that people will never think of it.'

The UDF is slightly more circumspect. With its people on the ground, and an organic sense of what people are feeling and thinking at street level, it sounds a note of caution. In a report produced that the time, the UDF notes that while it has brought about 'the flowering of organisations throughout the country … in the same period we have seen relatively spontaneous mass mobilisation sweep the country like wildfire. The relationship between the processes of mobilisation and organisation is a very complex and dynamic one. One thing is clear, however: the process of mobilisation has far outstripped that of organisation.'

This is an admission that the movement has lost control. The UDF recognises that people are angry, and the structures to contain and manage that anger cannot be built fast enough.

•••

At some point during the course of this year, in a township called Thumahole outside a small town called Parys, not far from Brandfort, a ten-year-old boy nicknamed called Stompie is arrested for breaking into a bottle store. Stompie's full name is James Moeketsi Seipei and he will become a crucial part of your story. You do not know him yet, but like so many of the boys of that era, Stompie sees little difference between the defiance required to steal and the rebelliousness necessary to engage in political activism. He is one of the little soldiers who will soon form the people's army.

Heeding the UDF and ANC call to rebellion, Stompie frequently finds himself in trouble. By age eleven he is on his way to becoming a full-blown comrade. He has a mind like a steel trap: he has memorised the Freedom Charter and can rattle it off on demand.

He has learned—by watching—how to throw stones and raise hell. He is a fixture on the scene, a sort of spokesperson, semi-famous as a child outlaw.

•••

Over the course of 1986, the question of necklacing assumes a greater political significance. Indeed, the whole issue of vigilante violence and what the media and the government refer to as 'black-on-black violence' becomes a thorn in the side of both the ANC and the UDF. Necklacing has come to epitomise the grisly nature of township combat, and it is distracting the attention of local and international media from the apartheid regime's continuing crimes.

As the violence spins out of control and it becomes apparent that there is no way to put the genie back in the bottle, key leaders within the movement begin to equivocate. Unfortunately, the ANC and the UDF are caught in a bind. If they condemn necklacing and vigilantism, they risk losing their mass support base. If they do not, they risk losing the moral high ground, raising questions among internal constituencies such as churches and external supporters such as global human-rights organisations.

Finally, in March 1986, Radio Freedom broadcasts an endorsement of the sort of violence that is now causing widespread concern within the movement. It is unclear who has drafted the statement, but its import is obvious. It boasts of the effectiveness of the masses' use of 'Molotov cocktails and necklaces, stones and knives'.

···

In April, at a rally just outside Johannesburg, you say, 'We work in the white man's kitchen. We bring up the white man's children. We would have killed them at any time we wanted to. Together, hand in hand, with our sticks and our matches, with our necklaces, we shall liberate this country.'

Your remarks about necklaces are much like those of others, and you say little in your speech that has not already been broadcast on Radio Freedom. Still, within the ranks of the UDF and the ANC there are whispers of disapproval, and it causes shock waves in the media, where your comments are seized upon with horror. The once-revered wife of Nelson Mandela has shown her true colours: she has endorsed the unconscionable use of a barbarous tactic.

You are Winnie Mandela, and this means the ANC cannot simply permit you to say what you think. It is one thing to rage in Brandfort and to give interviews to the media in which you rail against the racist regime. It is another altogether to say, with cameras trained on you, that you endorse necklacing—and yet you have done so, and you refuse to show remorse.

The consternation with which your statement is met reflects a growing concern about your conduct since you returned from banishment. You are too independent, they say. You refuse to communicate properly with ANC leaders, they say. You are imperious. And there are whispers about money—about prizes that have been awarded in Nelson Mandela's name.

Initially, the ANC leadership makes no attempt to silence you. How can they? You will not listen anyway, and they know it. Besides, they have no moral authority to sanction you when they themselves are so confused about their stance on violence, and indeed when senior leaders continue to endorse necklacing. In the absence of a clear policy on this brutal form of punishment, the movement would be hypocritical to openly reprimand you.

In fact, a few months after your speech at the rally, ANC secretary-general Alfred Nzo is quoted in London's *Sunday Times* as saying that collaborators with the enemy 'have to be eliminated', and that whatever the people use to eliminate those collaborators is their decision. 'If they decide to use necklacing,' he says, 'we support it.'

***

As the revolutionary rhetoric fires up, Stompie is beginning to earn some local notoriety. He is the leader of a group of children engaged in a series of running battles with the cops. When the police come looking for him, people never seem to have seen him, but they say they know of him. One of the men who knocks on his mother's door trying to find him says, 'We don't know—is he a child or is he a person? Why do you let him go into politics?'

But 'getting into politics' is not really a matter of a choice when you are a black person in South Africa. And Stompie is both a child and a person. When he is detained in July 1986—just a few months after your necklacing speech—Stompie is not treated like a child. The apartheid regime is incapable of seeing black children for what they are. At the age of twelve Stompie becomes the youngest political detainee ever. This begins a difficult period for him as he cycles through various prisons. In less than a year, Stompie has been incarcerated at Sasol, Leeuhof, Heilbron, Koppies and Potchefstroom prisons. You still have not met him. You know nothing of his existence. Stompie lives in the middle of nowhere, one of thousands of boys whose anger is fuelling the revolution.

***

In December 1986, ANC leader Chris Hani, with whom you are close, argues that necklacing is not a weapon of the ANC. 'It is a weapon of the masses themselves to cleanse the townships from the very disruptive and even lethal activities of the puppets and collaborators,' he says. 'We do understand our people when they use the necklace because it is an attempt to render our areas and country ungovernable, to make the enemy's access to information very difficult.'

Comrade Chris cannot bring himself to disavow the necklacers—that would be hypocrisy—so he suggests the phenomenon was not created by the ANC. He argues that necklacing is a revolutionary form of reprisal, a tool and a product developed by the masses. And he insists that it's not about 'black-on-black' violence: 'The necklace has been used against those who have been actively collaborating with the enemy,' he asserts.

In making it clear that collaborators must be dealt with, Hani is speaking out of both sides of his mouth. It is obvious now, looking back, that there is a distinction between what can be said in public and what can be done in private. Hani understands that one can only go so far when others are listening.

You do not understand this. Or perhaps you do but you do not care. Propelled by hatred of the racist regime and all those who support it, and fuelled by an understandable desire for justice and vengeance, you are incapable, at this stage in your life, of moderation.

The movement, on the other hand, is beginning to understand precisely how important moderation will be in the coming years.

Finally, in 1987, Oliver Tambo issues a statement in which the ANC says that the necklace as a form of punishment should stop. 'It has rightly or wrongly served its purpose and there is no way that people should continue with it.'

This is a far cry from condemnation, but it draws a line in the sand. From this point on the ANC is seen as having condemned necklacing. As time passes and memories fade, you will be held up as the only one who endorsed it, the exemplar of ill-discipline. It will be you alone among the leadership who once spoke out in support of necklacing.

It doesn't matter that this isn't true. It doesn't matter that, in fact, the leadership fomented revolution, incited violence and then pulled back and hedged and equivocated. This is the nature of history—the inconsistencies are smoothed over and the narrative tidied up so that there is a single, simple story that suits the interests of the victors. The archive tells us the truth, though—that you were not alone, that you were not a radical, crazed outlier. You were simply the most visible troublemaker in the crowd.

***

As the ANC finally settles on a party line, in Thumahole the young Stompie decides it is time for a change. The police are constantly harassing him, and so he decides to throw them off his trail, to go to Johannesburg for a fresh start. This decision sets him on a course that will alter his life. In Johannesburg he will meet you and you will take him into your home.

Trials and Tribulations

The famous residence at 8115 Orlando West in Soweto served
simultaneously ... as a safe house for returned MK guerrillas,
a weapons dump, a barracks for the Mandela football
squad, a prison for recalcitrants, a punishment yard in which
innumerable beatings were administered, and a transit camp
from which the executioner set forth.

—Paul Trewhela

When she visited you in Brandfort to tape the conversations
that were eventually transcribed, smuggled out of the
country and turned into the bestselling book *Part of My Soul
Went With Him*, your biographer Mary Benjamin noted that
you were 'often in the company of two young men—friends
of the family from Soweto—with a few youngsters from the
township keeping a respectful distance'. When she asked
you who they were, you smiled and said, 'My bodyguards.'

In 1986, shortly after you return from Brandfort, you
are asked to mediate a conflict among the youth of the
neighbourhood. The country is at war, so tempers are always

flaring. The young people who belong to the Orlando West branch of the Soweto Youth Congress—a civic organisation that plays an important role in the UDF—ask you to help, and within no time some of the youngsters are living with you, in the yard of the house that Nelson left so long ago. The boys stay with you because they have nowhere else to go. Many young people have dropped out of school since the Soweto uprising. Indeed, an unofficial boycott of schools continues because Afrikaans is the official medium of instruction. Without schools to attend, and with rising political militancy, the line between non-political crime and legitimate protest is porous. Black unemployment soars. Many of the boys in your yard are juvenile delinquents cum political activists who drift in and out of their own homes, or who have left townships in other parts of the country seeking work in Johannesburg.

This is how the Mandela United Football Club is born. At different points the MUFC has up to a hundred 'members', although the core group numbers about fifteen. They wear yellow and green tracksuits and look as though they are perpetually warming up for a match, but they do not play football—or not any more often than other kids in the township, anyway.

The boys quickly become like children to you. They are an extension of your activism. Despite their loyalty to you, the boys are not especially disciplined activists. They only sporadically attend meetings of local organisations, but they check in with you daily. They hang around, making trouble, looking like trouble, fixing trouble. They are peacemakers and bodyguards. They drive away the media when they get too close. They serve as a buffer between you and the crowds when you attend a rally or a funeral.

The leader of the club is Jerry Richardson. Jerry is one of those neighbourhood guys who has been around forever—since before you were banished. He likes exercising. He has a thick oily mane of chemically processed wavy hair and a finely trimmed moustache, so he looks a little bit like an African-American matinee idol. You can imagine his face on the packaging for hair creams and grooming products.

Jerry never seems busy. He is always available. He is always trailing you. He ingratiates himself with you, and anyone else of standing in the community. He is that guy: easy to send on errands, obsequious, and—like so many people in this era and in this neighbourhood—both utterly reliable and impossible to trust.

Jerry becomes the 'coach' of the club. Years later, testifying before the Truth and Reconciliation Commission (TRC), he will say that the club had 'many, many players'—specifically, five divisions, each containing fourteen players. What he does not say, but what everyone knows, is that the football club members are a ragtag collection of informers and spies and revolutionaries. They are orphans with balled-up fists, and hope and anger competing for space in their hearts.

They adore you and fear you, and you need them. You gather them around you for the kind of protection the girls cannot provide. By this time Zenani has her own life in Swaziland—she has married into the royal family there. Zindzi, on the other hand, is a constant presence. She is now a young mother and is often by your side. A woman named Xolisa Falati is also around often. She moves in with you, although there are rumours that she is a spy. No one knows where she came from or why she is suddenly so close to you. Like Jerry, she is obsequious—agreeing with everything you say, insinuating herself into every aspect of your life. Xolisa seems to know about everything Jerry says and does.

Within a year the MUFC transforms itself from a group of roguish boys into a social menace, a vortex of confusion and chaos. Its members are deeply enmeshed in community affairs and in local politics—as are you.

Your relationship with the club is strangely symbiotic—you are like an auntie, or a mother, not just to the boys but to the whole neighbourhood. Your ties to the community aren't purely political; your connections to the people around you are personal, intimate even. Sometimes, when there is conflict in a house—when a couple fights, for example—a child is sent to fetch you so that you can tell everyone to calm down. 'If you hit me again, Ma Winnie will deal with you.' If you are too busy to go, Jerry Richardson or one of the boys will go, to represent you.

On the political front, you are involved in smuggling guns and people across the border. You know many of the movement's secrets, and you shepherd some of its most important guerrilla fighters, keeping them fed, clothed and armed. There are secret missions and cars and night trips, and so much mystery and intrigue, and so many assumed names, and people who disappear and then reappear. It is hard to keep track of who is who—the faces and identities and what they need and where they are going and when they will arrive. You are a centrifugal force. Everything revolves around that small four-roomed house in Orlando.

Your book has made money, and you have used that money—your own money, money that you have earned, regardless of what others may say—to build another house. The house is large and beautiful—some say it is ostentatious. It even has a swimming pool. It is a house fit for a king and a queen, for a prime minister and his wife.

It is to this house that Nelson will return when he is released. Your belief that he will one day be free has never flagged—but until then, you will stay in the small house in Orlando in the heart of the community you have been a part of since the day you married Nelson and the revolution. You will only move into your palace when he is free—when South Africa is free.

In the meantime, life is not easy. Each day the boys in the club get into more fights. Each day you are drawn deeper into intrigue. With each new day, too, you move further away from your long-time comrades in the ANC, or perhaps they move further away from you. Some people still try to maintain contact. Sometimes one of them visits to sit with you in the house. They come to say, 'Winnie, please, there are spies around you,' or 'The boys are violent—can you not tell them to stop?'

You find yourself baffled by these visits. A war is raging, and these kind, polite women and men who think they can pray their way to liberation, or believe that mass meetings and reading groups will save them, are sorely mistaken. You can tell by their worried faces that they don't know what to say or how to behave when they are around you.

From Lusaka, Oliver Tambo writes to you. He frets about you, because he is a good man—he involves you as much as he can. You sense it is mainly out of respect for Nelson, but his attention and support mean a lot nonetheless.

•••

One day in the middle of winter, 1987, there is a fire and your house burns down. The tensions between the boys in the tracksuits and the kids at the school down the road have exploded. There are flames everywhere. There is no denying there is a crisis, and that it emanates from your home.

The leadership of the Mass Democratic Movement—an alliance between the UDF and the Congress of South African Trade Unions—jumps into action. They see the fire as evidence that the community has turned against you.

The good people of the movement form what they call the Mandela Crisis Committee, apparently reporting directly to Nelson in prison.

This is strange to you. Suddenly there is a whole committee of people, including some Nelson has never met, who are in direct communication with him? Despite all your years together, the letters and the visits, despite your never-ending campaigning on his behalf, Nelson seems uncertain about the strategies and tactics you have seen fit to use in the pursuit of freedom. You are deeply wounded by this development, by his agreeing to have these people speak to him about you.

The crisis the members of the committee seek to mediate is unclear to you. Are you the crisis? Are Nelson and Winnie Mandela in crisis? What, exactly, is the nature of the crisis? Are they worried about your safety because your house has just burned down? Is that the crisis? What could Nelson possibly do about that, sitting there in Pollsmoor Prison?

When they come with their emissaries and their pleading faces, you do not say much. You feel yourself harden. You want to tell them to go and jump. They get nowhere. The crisis deepens.

They try to warn and caution you for months. Between August and December 1988, they do their 'crisis committee' work—communicating the so-called concerns of the community to you and urging you to attend UDF and neighbourhood committee meetings. You refuse to entertain questions from people who have no clue about your underground work and no idea of the pressure you are under. They don't have any inkling of the risks you take when you smuggle guns and hide comrades and send messages. So you laugh to yourself sometimes, as you read their earnest statements, imagining what they must be telling Nelson. You think about all the secrets they will never know—all the secret missions you have supported, the guns and the money. And yet they accuse you of not being part of the little neighbourhood groups set up to mete out street justice, or to rewire the electricity? You are vital to the movement, a keeper of its most important secrets. You do not need to attend meetings—you are busy doing real work.

After the fire it becomes obvious that you will need to move into the new house. You had hoped to wait for Nelson's return, but that was only a romantic idea anyway. Now you have nowhere to go, so you move into the double-storey modern building on the edge of Diepkloof. Its high walls afford a measure of privacy that was not possible in the old place.

Hidden from view, and isolated from the community that has always been your source of support and strength, your relationship with the boys intensifies. Perhaps soon there will be a football match, something to justify the uniforms and the never-ending training sessions.

Before long Stompie appears in your yard. He has only been in Johannesburg for a short time, but he soon makes his way to Orlando, drawn to the ever-growing swirl of hardened little recruits that is the MUFC. Stompie is special, though—different from some of the others, who follow orders and take instructions without any real commitment to politics.

Although he is becoming embedded in the politics of the big city, Stompie continues to spend a lot of time in Thumahole. He goes back and forth—visiting his mother and relatives, attending rallies and getting into trouble.

In 1988 he goes home to attend a funeral—a comrade known as Master Naketi is dead, and Stompie, wise to the ways of the world, is there to say his farewells. Funerals are no longer simple send-offs; they are political events, places where grief and rage meet, where mourners make their peace with the vulnerability of the black body. Funerals are a reminder of the impermanence of life— and, in these violent times, a macabre preparation. Those who attend them know all too well that the next funeral could be their own.

Police are always present at funerals—to catch comrades, to bait them, to watch them. They arrest Stompie and he is sent away again, to Koppies. On 1 December 1988, Stompie appears in court. He stands accused of burning government vehicles.

His mother attends the hearing to support her son—her small, small boy, always in trouble. She goes back to Parys afterwards, but he doesn't. He decides to cool it in Johannesburg—Thumahole is too dangerous, in his assessment.

Six weeks later, on 6 January 1989, Stompie's body is found in an open field near your new house in Soweto.

***

Although they have been the subject of much investigation, Stompie's movements in the weeks after he sees his mother and before his death are hard to piece together. The details will never be fully known, but what is clear is that after 1 December, Stompie makes his way to the shelter at the Methodist church in Orlando.

Also known as the Methodist manse, the shelter is often used as a safe house by young boys on the streets. It is run on a part-time basis by Methodist minister Paul Verryn, a much respected and loved community member who is active in the local UDF structures.

Rumours about Stompie have been circulating for some time. People say he has been broken under police interrogation and has become a spy—there are thousands of informers and spies on the payroll of the regime, so if the rumours are true, it would not be unusual. There is a porousness and fluidity between the categories of 'activist' and 'informer' that are seldom openly discussed.

On 29 December 1988, you, Winnie, send a driver to the shelter to collect Stompie and three other boys—Kenneth Kgase, Pelo Mekgwe and Thabiso Mono. They are taken to your house. By your account, you order their removal from the shelter to protect them, because you have heard that Verryn has been molesting them. Verryn denies the allegations, and no evidence of the claims ever surfaces; the boys, too, deny the claims of abuse.

At your home, the boys are severely beaten. There will be conflicting reports about whether or not you participate in the actual violence. Some say you begin the beatings yourself—that you physically assault the boys. You will dismiss this claim as ridiculous, saying that you weren't even there when the beatings allegedly happened.

Word gets out that the kids are at your home and that they are in danger. Everybody knows the football club is vicious. Paul Verryn is summoned; envoys of the Mandela Crisis Committee are hastily organised and sent to you. 'Release the boys,' they plead.

Apparently, you refuse, insisting the boys are under your care because you don't trust Verryn. The envoys push harder, and eventually three of the boys are released. Stompie is not one of them.

At some point following the departure of the other boys, Dr Abubaker Asvat is called to your house. Dr Asvat is a pillar of the community and a longstanding friend of yours. Although he is not an ANC member, he is part of the resistance against apartheid and has often tended to victims of gunshots and torture. He examines Stompie and confirms that he has been severely beaten.

Three weeks after Stompie's body is found, on 27 January 1989, Dr Asvat is shot in his clinic in Soweto. Witnesses say there were two gunmen. Immediately, rumours swirl that you have had a hand in it. The suspicions are not isolated. Since November 1988, two neighbourhood boys who used to hang around your house as part of the football club have been missing. Lolo Sono and Siboniso Shabalala were last seen in a pick-up truck with you and others inside. Dr Asvat's death tips the scales.

In February 1989, the Mass Democratic Movement issues a public statement distancing itself from you and your actions. They say you have abused the trust and confidence you have enjoyed over the years, and that your practices have often violated the spirit and ethos of the democratic movement. 'We are not prepared to remain silent,' they say, 'where those who are violating human rights claim to be doing so in the name of the struggle against apartheid.' And then they accuse you of murder:

> We are outraged at Mrs Mandela's complicity in
> the recent abductions of Stompie. Had Stompie
> and his three colleagues not been abducted by
> Mrs Mandela's 'football team', he would have
> been alive today.

As far as you are concerned, the hypocrisy of those who read out the statement at the press conference is evident. They call themselves leaders. They hold themselves up as the standard-bearers of morality, presenting themselves as clean and unsullied while you are covered in blood. They have no idea what you do, no understanding that, for you, the revolution is not a picnic.

You cannot be expected to issue incendiary speeches and then depart, leaving the people alone to do the dirty work. You are a soldier and always have been, and this means you are not sorry and you will never be sorry. There are no apologies in war. The mealy-mouthed statement may work on the media, but it will not work on you.

You seem unmoved by Stompie's death. You seem not to know that you are seen to have gone too far, and so you have no impulse to make amends. You carry your attitude of unrepentant superiority with you everywhere you go. It protects you like a shawl.

···

That shawl of determined energy is firmly wrapped around your shoulders when Nelson is finally released in February the following year. It is a moment of bittersweet jubilation. There you are, against the backdrop of the beautiful Cape mountains, wearing a black-and-white top and a skirt. You are no longer young and today you are not stylish. You wear sensible shoes and your middle has spread, and perhaps because the last time we saw you standing next to Nelson you were that young blushing newlywed, now you look tired. You are smiling, though. Your afro is large and you could hold up the sky with that mighty fist.

The ANC men swarm around Nelson, and these are the first steps, the final mile. They usher both of you into a car and there you sit in the back seat like royalty—no, better, like the prime minister and his wife, just as you had predicted all those years ago in the hospital at Pretoria Central Prison. You are driven to the Cape Town city centre, where crowds sing and the ululation lifts the skies, and for this day there is joy.

So much goes unspoken after Nelson's release, even as the entire nation is talking about the two of you. Winnie and Nelson Mandela are the news, and everyone wants to speak to you, when what you need more than anything else is to be left alone with your husband. You need to talk and to cry and to whisper, and to make up for lost time—to pour out enough words to heal, and to mourn all those years stretched out behind you, all those years of not touching, of only looking through thick glass, of stuffing months of longing into thirty-minute visits.

You can't have the time alone that you so desperately crave—the revolution to which you are both married demands that you keep moving, and so you do. But Nelson is free, and he is in charge now. It is time for him to reassert control, to demonstrate his loyalty to you.

This is complicated by the emergence of rumours that you are having an affair with Dali Mpofu, a young lawyer who is also active in the ANC.

The court case begins a year after Nelson's release, in the midst of the negotiations that will determine South Africa's future. The country is taking steps towards a tentative peace. It is a delicate moment—so much hangs in the balance. A settlement is on its way, and you—still fighting spies and chasing informers, dragged down by wars both petty and grand—are caught unawares.

Nelson uses his lawyerly mind to corral the troops, who have swapped their camouflage uniforms for suits, as he gathers them around conference tables and talks with focus and speed. It is his turn to protect you. He does his best under the circumstances.

When the matter of Stompie Seipei begins in February 1991 at the Rand Supreme Court in downtown Johannesburg, Nelson is with you. He attends the hearing, pointedly entering by your side and then making his way to sit in the gallery.

You are represented by George Bizos, one of the most respected human-rights lawyers in the country and an old friend of Nelson's—one of the lawyers who defended him in the Rivonia trial. Dali—the young man about whom everyone is whispering—is also on the legal team. But it is George and your husband who fill the room with their authority and their dignity. They are men of a different era, men's men, with deep voices and grey hair and large reputations. They lend the room an air of sagacity and sadness. They are fighting for you out of loyalty, but it is not clear whether they believe you are innocent.

In public Nelson says he supports you, but in private it is another matter altogether. In private you have few words for one another. You are angry at him and he is angry at you. There is so much love and anger and silence between you, so much betrayal on both sides.

For fourteen weeks you attend the proceedings. Each day you hold your head high as you walk into the court.

The case revolves around the abductions of Kenny Kgase, Pelo Mekgwe and Thabiso Mono, and the abduction and murder of Stompie Seipei. Your co-accused are Jerry Richardson, Xoliswa Falati and your driver, John Morgan.

Two weeks before Pelo Mekgwe is due to testify, he disappears. The other two, Kenny Kgase and Thabiso Mono, back out, saying they are too scared to testify against you. This only adds to the sense that you are lawless, and capable of great violence.

The courtroom becomes a lonely and absurd theatre, and the trial a sordid spectacle. When Falati speaks out against you, the activists in the ANC and UDF click their tongues, wondering how such a woman could have been your confidant. Falati's testimony alternates between incoherence and rage, but still there can be no mistaking the fact that she blames you directly for Stompie's death. When Jerry Richardson speaks, the same questions arise. Why were these your closest friends? What happened to make you trust them?

There is only one answer and it is hard to acknowledge: you needed them. You were lonely. Your need fills the room. There are buckets and buckets of your need. You were so lonely, so terribly desirous of attention and admiration. The dimwits and liars in the court attest to this. You were so full of need that you organised an army of children to keep you company.

The case reveals a clear pattern of criminal behaviour by each of the accused. It is an apartheid courtroom with no moral authority, but still it is evident that crimes were committed.

That said, it is impossible to know what really happened, because the cast of unsavoury characters who testify against you offer conflicting versions. One says he saw you stab Stompie; another confesses to having murdered the boy himself. Someone says you were there; another says you were not. So many of the people involved in this affair are unreliable. Worse, many are known spies—traitors and informers. They are the kind of people who had no place in the movement in the first place.

It appears that you were surrounded by untrustworthy types, opportunists like Richardson and Falati, who were on the payroll of the racist regime and who were trying to bring you down—often using your own weaknesses—or trying to bring down people around you. The connections, the betrayals, the layers of conspiracy are confusing and complex—like a ball of wool that gets tangled into a knot time and again. It looks as though you were mired in something that was no longer the revolution, although it took place against its backdrop.

The court—a white judge named Stegmann presiding—finds you guilty on four charges of kidnapping and four of being an accessory after the fact to assault. John Morgan is found guilty of kidnapping. Xoliswa Falati—whom you will hate until the day you die, although you were once so close—is found guilty of kidnapping and of assault with intent to do grievous bodily harm. It was Falati who told you that Verryn was a sexual abuser, and her actions led directly to the kidnapping of the boys. Jerry Richardson is found guilty of murder because in his testimony he admitted to killing the boy. You will hate him forever as well because of his accusations. He told the court that although he 'finished off Stompie', you personally participated in assaulting the child with your fists and with a sjambok.

Justice Stegmann accepts your alibi—that you were not present. Still, he says, the abductions could not have been carried out without your prior approval. He points out that you failed to report the crime. He says you covered it up and continued to consort with the assailants, who remained in your home, living with you, after they had been accused by others in the community of abducting and killing Stompie.

He says this as though he and his court have some sort of jurisdiction over you. They do not. The idea that you would have approached a police station and reported any murder of any black child is nonsensical. The idea that the cops might have taken seriously a black child's life, and his death—especially a child who had Stompie's record—demonstrates the absurdity of this entire process. Stegmann is part of an illegitimate system and he simply has no right to adjudicate.

It is evident in the sentence he hands down that the judge understands the limitations of his powers. There is a political tightrope he must walk. The country outside his courtroom is inching towards freedom and his verdict could be explosive.

You are convicted of kidnapping and sentenced to six years in prison.

You appeal, of course, and new information emerges. The media never report on it, but the court finds that you probably did believe Verryn was a threat to the boys: there had been rumours circulating about Verryn long before Stompie and the others boys were abducted that December day, and you had taken them seriously. Indeed, as George Bizos later noted in his memoir, you had approached Reverend Frank Chikane, secretary of the South African Council of Churches, some months before, and Chikane had spoken to Verryn's bishop, Peter Storey, about the situation. The appeal judges set aside your six-year jail term and instead give you a fine and a suspended sentence.

So you are free to go and will not serve jail time, but there is a stain on your mighty name.

...

The court case is over, and now there is the fact of Nelson to deal with. There is the fact that he is back but that he is no longer yours; even the small part you once had is no longer yours.

He belongs to the movement, and the movement is preparing to deliver him to the world. There are things the young turks in the party need Nelson to say and do and it is best if you are not part of any of it, because they do not trust you, just as you do not trust them.

You understand that this is not only about protecting his good name. You understand that the leaders of the movement are furious at you and are no longer prepared to pretend to tolerate your insubordination, your wildness, your ill-discipline.

It pleases you that there is no more pretending. The animus between you and those who have always hated you is out in the open now. Still, it breaks your heart a little.

It is worse than that, though. Nelson knows about Dali. Then, when the Sunday papers publish a letter that you wrote to your lover in the early months after Nelson was released, the whole country knows as well. The letter details your growing estrangement from Dali; it is clear that things are not working out as you had hoped they might. You say in the letter that you have fought with Nelson over your affair, that you haven't spoken to him in five months. You reproach Dali for his lack of concern. 'You are supposed to care for me so much,' you write, '[... but] you are not bothered, because you are satisfying yourself every night with a[nother] woman.' You are infatuated, jealous; your need and your anger are obvious. You are wounded.

All of this hurts Nelson. Given his long absence, it can hardly be a surprise that you have found someone. Still, the public nature of the disclosures and the salacious tone of the newspapers are humiliating.

If the roles had been reversed and you had been imprisoned, things would have been very different. Nelson would have remarried and you would have languished forgotten on the island, and it would have been no reflection on him. Men have needs. Women sacrifice. Women are loyal. Men are men.

In any case, you are hurt too. Nelson has hurt you because he has refused to berate those who turned against you in his long absence. All the people who gossiped about you, those who issued that statement and disavowed you, are Nelson's advisers. They keep his diary and brief him. This is a betrayal that is hard to swallow. After all those years, your time in solitary, the effects on the girls, all of that, Nelson still belongs only to these ANC people.

But it is not simply about the ANC and the affair. There is something deeper at play. You now stand at different ends of the political spectrum. You no longer see eye to eye about the future. Nelson wants to compromise—he cannot see how the country will move forward without a negotiated settlement. You disagree. You cannot and will not trust the Boers. They are unrepentant, and conditions are still not ripe for talks.

Whereas Nelson was once the most militant man you knew, he has emerged from prison more moderate, tame even. Your political differences could not be starker. He has been gone all this time, so he thinks he can trust them. You know them—you have fought them in the streets—and you know he is being naive.

You part in the end, because you must, because both of you have always loved politics more than you have loved yourselves.

A year after the court case, in April 1992, a month before the second round of negotiations for a democratic South Africa, Nelson announces that the two of you will separate. Saying that the separation has been 'mutually agreed on', his statement notes:

> Comrade Nomzamo accepted the onerous burden of raising our children on her own ... She endured the persecutions heaped upon her by the government with exemplary fortitude and never wavered from her commitment to the struggle for freedom. Her tenacity reinforced my personal respect, love and growing affection. It also attracted the admiration of the world at large. My love for her remains undiminished.
>
> I shall personally never regret the life Comrade Nomzamo and I tried to share together.

Circumstances beyond our control however dictated that it should be otherwise. I part from my wife with no recriminations.

Nelson is putting aside all distractions. Like a champion runner, he is preparing mentally, getting ready to complete the final stages of the marathon that has been his life.

Your parting from Nelson signals a new chapter for the country. Nelson Mandela is redeemed because he has ended his close association with you. You are now his ex-wife, and this allows him to be elevated morally. You are no longer there to drag down his reputation.

Around the same time, Nelson is increasingly referred to in the press and among comrades by his clan name, Madiba. The name has its roots in the crags and rivers of Qunu, where he was born. He is still Mandela, of course, but he assumes the status of an elder. He wears the name like the royal cloak it is, and as he does so man melds into myth.

In the years to come, though your love for one another never fades, you will become his foil. You, Winnie, will be the dark shadow that allows Madiba to be South Africa's shining light.

Truth and Reconciliation

I am not one of those who believes that our soldiers, for
instance, should face the TRC and apologise for actions they
did during the struggle.

—Winnie Mandela

A remarkable series of negotiations take place between
1991 and 1993 to end apartheid and create a democratic
and non-racial South Africa. The birth of the new South
Africa is written in ink rather than blood, and the ANC,
with Madiba at its helm, emerges as the leading force in
these negotiations, pushing and cajoling and haranguing
a population of white people who believe they have
everything to lose by ending racist rule. White people
are fearful and reluctant, and at times black people are
impatient and angry. Yet Madiba and his colleagues never
waver. The character of the new society must be shaped

by a deep and abiding respect for human dignity. In the new South Africa, everyone will be free, and whites will be grateful to be released from the moral purgatory of apartheid. A cornerstone of the agreements is that a formal reconciliation process will take place as soon as elections have been held—the first free and fair elections in the history of the country—and a new government installed.

In May 1994, Nelson is inaugurated as the first black president of South Africa. Around the world, over a billion people watch. You are not at his side. Instead, as he takes his oath, pledging to uphold the constitution he has just helped to draft, Zenani stands by his side. You are proud, and—though you will never admit it, even to yourself—you are heartbroken.

Once the ANC is in power, a team begins to work on the legislation that will eventually become the Promotion of National Unity and Reconciliation Act of 1995. A year later, the Truth and Reconciliation Commission is created. The TRC's mandate is to investigate gross human-rights violations perpetrated between 1960 and 1994—crimes that include abductions, killings and torture. It will investigate all actors, both the state and the liberation movements, and it has the power to grant amnesty. Anyone who makes 'full disclosure of all the relevant facts relating to acts associated with a political objective committed in the course of conflicts of the past' will walk free.

The TRC is deeply controversial.

Embedded in the TRC's social DNA are three fundamental flaws. The first is that the commission treats the former enemies of the struggle as though both sides were equal actors in a conventional war. The presumption of moral equivalence offends you. The notion of equal accountability between two such unequal opponents is laughable.

The second flaw, as you see it, is that the bar for amnesty is set too low. This is because the commission is deeply invested in the idea of truth-telling as a form of justice rather than a step towards justice. Those who tell the truth about their crimes and can demonstrate they were acting on the orders of higher-ups, in service of political objectives, will be given amnesty.

The third flaw is that the commission's scope is far too narrow. Crimes committed at a broad structural level are excluded from its investigations, meaning that black South Africans are denied a public forum in which to reckon with the violations of human dignity inherent in carrying a pass or being forced to live in segregated communities. The entire racial-classification scheme was an affront to human dignity, and yet the TRC has no mandate to deal with this matter. Neither can it deal with the systemic economic crimes that make poverty such a feature of black life. Simply by virtue of being born black in South Africa, every single black person is owed reparations—but at this critical moment, the founding moment of the new republic, this crucial fact is ignored. Under the terms of the commission the case for restitution cannot be made.

In the months preceding the hearing, you indicate your scepticism of the entire process. You participate in an in-camera session away from the glare of the media, after which you say, 'When the commission treats me like a leper and its chairperson hugs our former oppressors, then I worry about what type of reconciliation we are fostering.'

It is evident the ANC and the commissioners want you to apply for amnesty. They want you to stand before the nation and say the events of the 1980s were a mistake. You have known this was coming from the moment you began to hear talk of this new forum that would supposedly heal the wounds of the past. You refuse to satisfy them; you won't legitimise this farce of a commission. You refuse to apply for amnesty.

You go a step further by insisting on a public hearing. The TRC had planned on interviewing you in private, but you decline their polite attempt to manage you. You want to show up the hypocrisy of the entire exercise. You want to demonstrate—through your posture and your statements—that you consider the commission itself a sham. You do not respect the process—not just because of the way you feel you have been targeted but because you are ideologically opposed to it. It stands as a towering example of the ways the movement has capitulated and allowed the racists to frame the agenda of the new South Africa. Sometimes you wonder whether the TRC was designed not to deal with the racists, but to deal with you.

So it is that you appear before the commission over a period of nine days, beginning on 24 November 1997. The hearings are organised in clusters. Media bosses are questioned during one set of hearings. Big business and the banks are interviewed during another. There are special hearings that look at children, and others focused on women.

It seems absurd that the well-oiled institutions run by white men are provided with a few days each to talk about how they upheld apartheid, while you, Winnie Mandela, leader of a scrappy football club, are asked to give your account over nine days. The private corporations that profited from apartheid caused untold pain to millions. They subjugated and oppressed black South Africans. Mining companies left the dead in mineshafts and abandoned men with silicosis so that they died in the arms of their loved ones in rural areas across the country. But by and large the damage done by white men in grey suits did not leave any bodies. There was no evidence. They ruined lives, but they seldom left bodies. With the football club, on the other hand—that tiny vortex of pathos that had little infrastructure and even less direction and was under your command—the bodies were easily catalogued.

The TRC investigators look back a decade, trying to find evidence of your involvement in the deaths or disappearances or torture of eighteen people linked to you and the football club. You appear at the hearing as a hostile witness, as a woman who considers herself not simply innocent but morally superior to those who have called her here. You contributed more to the struggle and sacrificed more, and now you resent them calling you to account as though you have something to be sorry about.

You wear your dark glasses and listen to a parade of witnesses peddle what you say are lies about you. You watch the commissioners with their officiousness and their questions and their procedures and processes, and disdain is written all over your face.

When you are finally called to testify, you are belligerent and testy. You insist that far from harming anyone, your instinct was to protect those children—that you *did* protect them—and you did it while fighting a just war, when many others just sat in their houses.

The tension builds and builds.

The chair of the TRC is Anglican Archbishop Desmond Tutu. He is desperate for reconciliation, looking for any sign of repentance, sniffing out forgiveness. In his haste, he forces hugs and imposes his rainbow love on everyone. He wants the country to move forward. He is in a rush. It is evident to everyone. There is something too brazen, too crude about this attempt to knit together people who stand so far apart.

This is how the hearing is reported: Tutu is a man crazed with forgiveness, blinded by it, perhaps.

On the last day of your hearing, Archbishop Tutu calls on relatives of victims and former combatants to come to approach him. He leans forward as though he is in church, praying over the faithful. 'We all stand here to recognise the pain and anguish of so many,' he says solemnly. 'We want them to know they have our very deepest sympathy for what they suffered. We hope they have it in their hearts to reach out to those who may have caused them pain, to reach out in order for our land to be healed.'

Tutu's moment is spoiled by the fact that many of those who are being asked to forgive are still very angry. The wronged parties, the families whose children encountered you when you were at your worst, have had no answers. The TRC records quote an advocate who did not wish to be named saying:

> How can there be reconciliation unless there is some acknowledgement of the violence that has been committed? ... People want to know what has happened to their families. They live with the pain of not knowing. Reconciliation is all very well, but now there is at least some doubt as to whether Madikizela-Mandela is telling the truth or not. I think the moment chosen for this reconciliation, when she was not answering questions satisfactorily, was completely inappropriate.

The spectacle is difficult to watch. It speaks to all that is wrong about forced apologies and forced forgiveness. It is noble but perhaps in some ways counterproductive to insist on resolving matters of the heart and soul to a schedule, on some sort of externally mandated timeframe. 'Sorry' means something when it is heartfelt—otherwise it is only a word. Sometimes, used too quickly, it is a 'get out of jail free' card for the wrongdoer—an insult that goes straight to the heart.

Archbishop Tutu has an impossible task. The man of God cannot make love appear where there is none, nor can he conjure contrition out of thin air. His tears and hopes cannot take the victims' pain away, nor the hurt their families still feel.

Finally, when his attempts to pray and love and cajole you and the victims into some sort of reconciliation fail, Tutu is forced to change tack. He asks you to apologise to the families of Stompie and Lolo and Siboniso. He wants you to admit that things went horribly wrong.

He tries to flatter you into an admission. 'You are a great person,' he says, 'and you do not know how your greatness would be enhanced if you said, "Sorry, things went wrong for me."'

You consult your lawyer. This deliberate act of leaning towards him is pointed: you are building into your apology a sense that it is not spontaneous; whatever comes out of your mouth following your brief remarks to your lawyer will be based on his guidance, rather than any sense of moral obligation.

So what comes next is tinged with bitterness. It is a concession, yes, but it is far from an apology. You say:

> I will take this opportunity to say to the family
> of Dr Asvat, how deeply sorry I am. To Stompie's
> mother, how deeply sorry I am. I have said so to
> her a few years back, when the heat was very hot.
> I am saying it is true, things went horribly wrong.
> I fully agree with that, and for that part of those
> painful years when things went horribly wrong
> and we were aware of the fact that there were
> factors that led to that, for that I am deeply sorry.

Your 'sorry' means very little, because you don't want it to. You aren't sorry—you have simply been forced to say it in order to move the process along. You are only attending so your disdain will be clear to everyone involved.

Long after the hearing is over, you remain angry and bitter about it. You will never stop being angry about it. Years later, just before your death, you will remember how furious Tutu made you. You will say:

> I was the one person who kept the fires burning
> when everybody was petrified. I didn't blame
> them, because those dark forces of apartheid
> were killing our people like flies. I didn't blame
> them when sometimes I would shoot that fist
> alone, and they were too petrified—put me on
> trial before the TRC and a Desmond Tutu sits
> there judging me. Judging me!

Some think you have not been judged harshly enough. Some feel you were pandered to and allowed to fulminate. They remain angry, just like you, burning with the same crazy rage.

A fury illuminates the eyes of Lolo Sono's mother, Caroline. The same bitterness you hold within you wracks her voice—she almost has no words. Her pain is so grand, so large and frightening, she could almost be you. She is disgusted and outraged and just as articulate in her aggression as you. She too is a mother, and she too has suffered an unbearable loss.

She has no sympathy for your hurts—the torture and detention, the nights you missed Nelson—and you have none for her—the nights she nursed her son as a baby, the days she watched him toddle and grow. You are two black women brutalised by apartheid, victims in your own ways of ancient and modern oppressions. Had things been different, you might have been friends, but you are not and never will be.

This charade is not about love or forgiveness. It is about what some people think those things are. It is about a kind old man of God who thinks people ought to be better than they are. It is about the indignation of people who think of themselves as decent. It is about legal processes and politics and investor confidence. And so, amid all of this, there is little that can be said. No wonder, then, that when she is asked, Caroline Sono, who has called you a murderer, says,

'I think nothing about the TRC session. Nothing has been done. There's no justice in this land.'

She is right. As family after family comes forward to ask where their loved ones may be, and as perpetrator after perpetrator denies knowledge of the facts, or refuses to participate, the commission is held hostage by its terms of reference. White men with meaty fists and red faces look down and profess not to remember. Over and over again, they say they do not know what happened. The TRC wants to be a place of reconciliation, but sometimes the parties are not ready to reconcile. You are not alone in this regard.

When this is the case, the commissioners seem stuck, trapped in the facts and the dates and the details. They want reconciliation so badly that sometimes it is easy to forget that at the heart of all of these words and tears lies the question of justice. But justice is not the same for everyone.

The justice you seek looks like vindication. You want the TRC to tell you it was all for a good cause and you are a hero. Caroline Sono wants the TRC to tell her where her son's body lies, and she wants it to say you are a murderer, and in this way to say his life meant something. Neither of you wins.

And in the end, nothing is resolved and nothing is settled.

Ubuntu

I am not prepared to apologise for anything we did whilst we were fighting ... I will continue being the white man's enemy for as long as I am alive.

—Winnie Mandela

There is no more football club and there is no more struggle.

The residents of Diepkloof do not burn down your house. They let you stay.

The leaders of the movement take positions in government. They become ministers and deputy ministers and assistant chief directors and advisers on this and that. Many of them move to the suburbs.

Nelson appoints you as a cabinet minister, responsible for arts and culture, but this does not work out. Charges of fraud trail you. People say you overspend your travel allowances and don't account for your spending. On top of this, you only go the functions and meetings that appeal to you, attending only the events that suit you. You are an activist and a fighter. This job, this role, is just not who you are.

But the fire is no longer burning, and the people of Diepkloof let you stay.

Nelson is now Madiba, and in time you learn to look at him without that mixture of love and pain that previously defined your gaze. You see him with the girls and with the grandchildren, all of whom look so much like him, and there are long periods in which you manage to let go of the rancour.

You hold on to your secrets, though. You cling to them because they are all you have left for yourself that the movement cannot take away, and that the whites who will be your enemies until you die cannot take away. You hold on to the knowledge that men once shouted from the rooftops and issued statements from Lusaka and waged intellectual battles from the distance of Robben Island while you shot your fist in the air and led the troops on the ground. Amandla! Power to the people!

You hold on to this knowledge because it is what you have left of the struggle. You were the one who was strong.

You grow frail. And then one day you die.

When you die, the people come to your house to mourn. They weep and they wail and they shake their heads.

They let you stay.

There is a word—ubuntu—that is more than just a word; it is a philosophy. It is untranslatable. It loses its power in English. Its synonyms in this language are humanity and interconnectedness, but they are insufficient. Ubuntu is a concept that exists in every language spoken across the length and the breadth of the African continent.

It is the only word I know that explains what it means that they let you stay.

Conclusion
A Woman in Full

'Unhappy the land that has no heroes.'
'No, unhappy the land that needs heroes.'

—Bertolt Brecht

In one of my favourite images, Winnie Mandela stands in front of the tiny house in Brandfort to which she was banished. She is still relatively young—perhaps in her mid-thirties. She leans against a wire fence wearing a dark headscarf and a t-shirt emblazoned with her prisoner number. Just below her breasts, like a chunky band around her waist, are the words 'government property'. The photo is rich with irony. Winnie was nobody's property.

Even as she kept her husband's name alive, Winnie also carved out a space for herself. She believed she was important—so important that she wrote herself into history.

She risked her life to record her thoughts and ideas and to share her story. She published two books—*Part of My Soul Went with Him*, and *491 Days: Prisoner 1323/69*. Her words are well worth reading, but they can only make a difference if people read them. They will not matter if nobody knows where to find them.

In the end—despite her own fame, and due in large part to her tireless efforts—Winnie Mandela's husband overshadowed her. His place was sealed in history because he was a man, and could therefore be elevated to the rank of great man, of statesman. It is impossible to imagine how their story would have played out if the roles were reversed. Had a great woman been imprisoned, would her loyal husband have campaigned for her so tirelessly? Would the world have cared as much about the life of a black woman?

It cannot be denied that Winnie Mandela's public persona was defined as much by her sex as it was by her actions. She was cast as wife and mother—wife to a great man, mother to a nation—and then found wanting, reproached for the very qualities that made her such a formidable activist. Many men—black and white, within her movement and among her opponents—found Winnie insufferable. She was too loud, too wilful, too angry, too outspoken. She was an early and public victim of slut-shaming. Her interrogators accused her of sleeping with various white men. Her comrades gossiped about her and intimated that she was sexually promiscuous. Winnie fought back. She challenged her detractors openly in the press, demonstrating a fearlessness that could not have come easily, but which served to give courage to others. Winnie knew how to make her notoriety work for her, even as it worked against her.

Some people called Winnie Mandela arrogant. She could be. Her arrogance protected her from the racists and the sexists who sought to stand in judgement of her. Yet it also wounded her, and caused her to wound others. In the years after her detention and banishment, Winnie could not admit that she had lost her way and was in need of help. She was under immense emotional and psychological pressure—anyone would have struggled. Still, the particular ways in which she cracked and the response of the society in which she lived are both heartbreaking and fascinating.

Winnie became dangerous—a soldier who refused to take orders. Even the violence she did in the name of the struggle took on criminal dimensions. The political party for which she had fought so bravely responded by disavowing her. Male leaders who exhibited similar violence in the face of racist oppression were protected. Winnie suffered the indignity of repeated public admonitions.

Looking across the span of her life it is obvious that Winnie was neither 'good' nor 'bad' (whatever those terms even mean). She could be cruel and reckless, but she had great strength and courage too. It is easy to discount the pain of those who ran afoul of her, calling them informers or spies, but I don't want to fall into that trap. I don't want to see the pain of Stompie Seipei or Lolo Sono or their grieving mothers erased, any more than I want to see Winnie Mandela erased from history. I want to find a way to herald her while also honouring the memories of those who were victims of the Mandela United Football Club.

There is little appetite in today's world for stories that aren't straightforward, especially when those stories are about women. We like our heroines to be courageous, but we don't want them to be messy. We want them to confront patriarchy, but we don't want them to have lovers half their age. We praise women for surviving abuse and torture, but when the resultant trauma and suffering make them angry and volatile, we fear and deride them.

There aren't enough stories shared of real-life women who are both courageous and messy. There aren't enough stories about women prepared to use violence. Whether or not you endorse that violence, the point is that such women challenge every stereotype there is about women and their 'nature'. Winnie Mandela's story is crucial in this regard—it follows an unconventional path. She was her husband's voice throughout those long years he spent in prison, but she was so much more than that. Winnie was her own person. She fought for others, and when you read her words and reflect on her life, you can see that she fought for herself too.

Restoring Winnie Mandela to her rightful place in history in spite of her contradictions is only just. The larger-than-life figures who populate our history books capture our imagination because they have lived their lives in ways that give us deeper insight into what it means to be human. They allow us to glimpse what is possible. Even when they fall short, their attempts to fly are inspiring. Men are given this latitude all the time. In seeing Winnie more fully than she might ever have thought possible—affirming her existence, recognising and remembering and critically appraising her life in all its complexity and drama—we reward her sacrifices without exonerating her sins.

But when we shine the spotlight on Winnie we shine it on her country. The world sees South Africa as the place where black and white came together to end apartheid. United by the saintly figure of Nelson Mandela, they negotiated a settlement in a peaceful manner and walked hand in hand towards a new future. Winnie Mandela reminds us that this is only partially true. Her saintly husband was a guerrilla fighter, imprisoned for openly and unapologetically embracing violence as a means to end apartheid. Peace was hard-fought and therefore hard-won. Acknowledging Winnie makes it very hard to diminish the horror of apartheid, because her treatment at the hands of the regime was shocking. She was walking testament to the truism that brutalised people become brutal themselves.

Glossing over the difficulties by erasing this inconvenient woman is tempting—yet it comes at a cost. If we erase Winnie, then we must also erase those she fought against:

the terrifying police with their vicious dogs; the prison guards who tortured her; the authorities who banished her from her home. We must erase her horror and that of her comrades when yet another dead activist was found in a crumpled heap after an 'interrogation'. She reminds us that the structural violence of racism, poverty and oppression didn't end when apartheid was dismantled. Winnie Mandela was a fighter, and her legacy is precisely this—to remind us to keep fighting. For this we owe her—and all the unruly women like her—an everlasting debt.

Acknowledgements

Many thanks to my close readers—Simon, Genevieve, Mavuso and Eusebius in particular.

A special note of gratitude to Shireen Hassim for her writing, thinking and intellectual mentorship. Her work on women and nationalism has been invaluable not just to me but to South Africans.

I'd also like to thank the Wits Institute for Social and Economic Research (WISER) and the Governing Intimacies Project for facilitating my attendance at the 'Telling Lives: Truth Lies History' workshop in Johannesburg on 6 August 2018.

As ever, many thanks to the team at Jonathan Ball, and to Ester and Jeremy in particular for your chutzpah, and thanks, Nkanyezi, for your quiet strength. This has been a labour of love and grit.

Lastly, many thanks to the team at Text, and to Elizabeth Cowell in particular. You edit with both grace and authority, walking that fine line with elegance.

Sources

Throughout this work, I have frequently drawn on the words of Winnie Madikizela-Mandela as recorded in her memoirs: *Part of My Soul Went With Him* (WW Norton & Co, 1984) and *491 Days: Prisoner Number 1323/69* (Ohio University Press, 2014).

Shireen Hassim's work on Winnie Mandela and the complexity with which she has thought about her life and politics have been especially helpful; and while I have not quoted from either directly, Njabulo Ndebele's *The Cry of Winnie Mandela* (David Phillip, 2003) and Antjie Krog's *Country of My Skull* (Random House, 1998) were both important in my background reading for this book.

Additional sources for each chapter are listed below.

MBIZANA

Alan Cobley, 'Literacy, Libraries, and Consciousness: The Provision of Library Services for Blacks in South Africa in the Pre-Apartheid Era', *Information & Culture*, vol. 32, no. 1, 1997, pp. 57–80.

Timothy Johns, 'The 1820 Settlement Scheme to South Africa', in Dino Franco Felluga (ed.), *BRANCH: Britain, Representation and Nineteenth Century History*, 2013, available at: www.branchcollective. org/?ps_articles=timothy-johns-the-1820-settlement-scheme-to-south-africa.

Justus, 'The Murder of Hintza, King of the Amakhosae', in *The Wrongs of the Caffre Nation: A Narrative*, James Duncan, London, 1837, pp. 210–28.

Terrence Ranger, '"Great Spaces Washed with Sun": The Matapos and Uluru Compared', in Kate Darian-Smith, Liz Gunner and Sarah Nuttall (eds), *Text, Theory, Space: Land, Literature and History in South Africa and Australia*, Routledge, London, 1996.

Timothy J. Stapleton, 'The Memory of Maqoma: An Assessment of Jingqi Oral Tradition in Ciskei and Transkei', *History in Africa*, vol. 20, 1993, pp. 321–35.

Jacobus Vorster, 'Is the Private Ownership of Land a Fundamental Human Right?', in E. van der Borhat (ed.), *The God-Given Land: Religious Perspectives on Land Reform in South Africa*, Rozenberg Publishers, Amsterdam, 2009.

JOHANNESBURG

Meghan Healy-Clancy, 'Women and Apartheid', *Oxford Research Encyclopedia of African History*, June 2017, Oxford University Press, New York, available at: africanhistory.oxfordre.com/view/10.1093/acrefore/9780190277734.001.0001/acrefore-9780190277734-e-184.

Deborah Posel, 'What's in a Name? Racial Categorisations Under Apartheid and Their Afterlife', *Transformation*, vol. 47, 2001, pp. 50–74.

Jonathan Stadler & Charles Dugmore, '"Honey, Milk and Bile": A Social History of Hillbrow, 1894–2016', *BMC Public Health*, vol. 17, suppl. 3, 2017, p. 444.

NELSON

Elleke Boehmer, *Nelson Mandela: A Very Short Introduction*, Oxford University Press, Oxford, 2015.

Nelson Mandela's statement from the dock at the opening of the defence case in the Rivonia Trial, 20 April 1964, available at www.anc.org.za/content/nelson-mandelas-statement-dock-rivoniatrial.

Mercury Correspondent, 'The Day Mandela Got Arrested', *The Mercury*, 5 August 2013, available at: www.iol.co.za/news/south-africa/kwazulu-natal/the-day-mandela-got-arrested-1557672.

David James Smith, *Young Mandela*, Weidenfeld & Nicolson, London, 2010.

PRISON

Anne Marie du Preez Bezdrob, *Winnie Mandela: A Life*, Zebra Press, Cape Town, 2003.

BANISHED

Alan Cowell, 'Winnie Mandela Held for Second Time', *New York Times*, 31 December 1985, available at: www.nytimes. com/1985/12/31/world/winnie-mandela-held-for-second-time.html.

Kevin Harris, 'The Banishment of Winnie Mandela', video in *No Middle Road to Freedom*, Kevin Harris Productions, 1984/5, available at: www.kevinharris.co.za/category/filmography-apartheid.

Rea Khoabane, 'Exile in Dust: Madikizela-Mandela Left Her Mark on Brandfort', *Sunday Times*, 8 April 2018, available at: www. timeslive.co.za/sunday-times/news/2018-04-07-exile-in-dust-madikizela-mandela-left-her-mark-on-brandfort.

UNGOVERNABLE

ANC, 'The Future Is Within Our Grasp', pamphlet quoted in Martin Legassick, *Armed Struggle and Democracy: The Case of South Africa*, Stylus Pub, University of Michigan, 2002.

Riedwaan Moosage, 'A Prose of Ambivalence: Liberation Struggle Discourse on Necklacing', *Kronos*, vol. 36, no. 1, 2010.

Sello Motseta, 'The Political Significance of Winnie Mandela's Position in the African National Congress', MA thesis, Rhodes University, March 1999, available at: https://core.ac.uk/download/pdf/11983823.pdf.

James Myburgh, 'How the Necklace Was Hung Around Winnie's Neck', *PoliticsWeb*, 17 April 2018.

Monica Eileen Patterson, 'Constructions of Childhood in Apartheid's Last Decades', PhD dissertation, University of Michigan, 2009, available at: http://citeseerx.ist.psu.edu/viewdoc/download?doi=10.1.1.901.1137&rep=rep1&type=pdf.

Oliver Tambo, 'Render South Africa Ungovernable: President OR Tambo's Message Delivered at Lusaka on January 8, 1985', available at: www.historicalpapers.wits.ac.za/inventories/inv_pdfo/AK2145/AK2145-B2-1-4-001-jpeg.pdf.

TRIALS AND TRIBULATIONS

George Bizos, *Odyssey to Freedom*, Penguin Random House, Cape Town, 2009.

Rebecca Davis, 'Winnie, the Missing Soweto Youths and the NPA', *Daily Maverick*, 19 December 2012.

Nelson Mandela, 'Statement by Nelson Mandela on Separation from His Wife, Winnie Mandela', 13 April 1992, available at: www. mandela.gov.za/mandela_speeches/1992/920413_winnie.htm.

Mass Democratic Movement, 'Statement by Mass Democratic Movement on Winnie Mandela', 16 February 1989, available at: www.sahistory.org.za/sites/default/files/DC/sta19890216.043.027/ sta19890216.043.027.pdf.

Jerry Richardson, 'Winnie Mandela, These Murders and Me – Jerry Richardson', *PoliticsWeb*, 5 April 2018.

Paul Trewhela, 'The Trial of Winnie Mandela', *Searchlight South Africa*, vol. 2, no. 3, 1991.

Juan Williams, 'Daddy Stayed in Jail. That Was His Job', *Washington Post*, 8 November 1987.

Christopher S. Wren, 'South Africans Bury Slain Youth', *New York Times*, 26 February 1989.

Christopher S. Wren, 'Judge Convicts Winnie Mandela as Accessory in Assault on Youths', *New York Times*, 14 May 1991.

TRUTH AND RECONCILIATION

Pascale Lamche (director), *Winnie*, Pumpernickel Films/Submarine/ Big World Cinema/IV Films, 2017.

Wally Mbhele, 'Winnie Accuses Mandela at TRC', *Mail & Guardian*, 23 October 1997.

South African Parliament, *Promotion of National Unity and Reconciliation Act 1995* (Act 95-34, 26 July 1995), available at: https:// fas.org/irp/world/rsa/act95_034.htm.

South African Press Association, 'TRC Labels Winnie's Testimony "Painful"', 4 December 1997, available at: www.justice.gov.za/trc/ media%5C1997%5C9712/s971204q.htm.

South African Press Association, 'Winnie Complies with Tutu's Appeal for Her to Say Sorry', 4 December 1997, available at: www. justice.gov.za/trc/media%5C1997%5C9712/s971204v.htm.

UBUNTU

Malou von Sivers, *Interview with Winnie Madikizela-Mandela*, Channel 4 (Sweden), 4 November 1991, available at: www.youtube. com/watch?v=FglyANfd1s4.